Praise for the Fourth Edition of
Parenting the Strong-Willed Child

This classic book gets better with each iteration! In this fourth edition, Forehand, Jones, and Long offer enriched and updated guidance for parents, expanding their coverage of family diversity, dealing with family stressors like COVID-19, managing children's screen time, and fitting parenting skills to each unique child. The extensive practical guidance conveyed in a beautifully accessible style makes this book an essential resource for parents of young children.

> —**JOHN R. WEISZ, PHD**, ABPP, Henry Ford II Professor of the Social Sciences, Harvard University, Cambridge, MA, and coauthor of *Principle-Guided Psychotherapy for Children and Adolescents: The FIRST Program for Behavioral and Emotional Problems*

This new edition of a classic keeps getting better by providing parents a highly interactive and accessible read with even more examples of how to use the skills in a wide variety of day-to-day scenarios and simultaneously care for themselves. As both a parent of a young child and provider working with parents of strong-willed youth, I am particularly impressed by how compassionately and brilliantly Forehand, Jones, and Long address the huge range of challenges today's caregivers are facing and provide actionable steps toward change.

> —**CHLOE ZACHARY, PHD**, Licensed Clinical Psychologist, The Triangle Area Psychology Clinic, Durham, NC

Parenting! The most rewarding and most challenging job ever! The fourth edition of *Parenting the Strong-Willed Child* describes the very latest in scientifically based positive parenting skills. From "catching your child being good" to handling tantrums in the grocery store to managing screen time, this book gives you skills for maximizing harmony in your household and setting your child up for good behavior and relationships at school. There will always be challenging days and situations, but this book will give you the confidence that you are doing the best for your child that can be done. This is a must-read for all parents, especially those of us with strong-willed children!

—**AMANDA M. THOMAS, PHD,** Professor of Psychology and
     Past Provost, Loyola University Maryland, Baltimore

This brilliant fourth edition, written by foremost experts in the field, is a must-read for any parent raising a strong-willed child! Written in a conversational manner, this step-by-step guide teaches parents evidence-based tools and gives them space to practice and reflect; a bonus is the increased emphasis on parents' own mental health!

—**ANDREA CHRONIS-TUSCANO, PHD,** Director, Maryland
     ADHD Program and Joel and Kim Feller Professor
     of Psychology, University of Maryland, College Park;
     President of the American Psychological Association's
     Society of Clinical Child and Adolescent Psychology;
     and coauthor of *Supporting Caregivers of Children with
     ADHD*

The timely release of the fourth edition of *Parenting the Strong-Willed Child* contains a wealth of information for parents and clinicians alike. This newest version expertly weaves together the foundational teachings of behavioral parent training with valuable additions that help parents navigate modern challenges, such as screen time. As a clinical psychologist working in private practice and as a parent myself, this wonderful resource will remain a staple in my reading rotation!

> —**CARLYE KINCAID, PHD**, Licensed Clinical Psychologist,
> Silber Psychological Associates, Cary and Raleigh, NC

This book is one of the originals *and* is one of the best. Supported by decades of evidence and experience, *Parenting the Strong-Willed Child* is a wealth of information for parents who are struggling with child behavior issues, or simply want to make sure their kids get the best start in life. Highly recommended!

> —**MARK DADDS, PHD**, Professor of Psychology, University
> of Sydney, Sydney, Australia, and coauthor of *Integrated Family Intervention for Child Conduct Problems*

This is an excellent guide for parents of any young child, particularly those children who are strong-willed! The book provides concise and clear solutions to everyday practical problems. I especially liked the "Time to Reflect" throughout the book. This provides parents with the opportunity to think through ways to respond to their child.

> —**GENE BRODY, PHD**, Regents Professor and Director,
> Center for Family Research, University of Georgia,
> Athens

This book is an essential resource for parents of young children. It impressively distills decades of research evidence and clinical experience into science-based practical strategies that will help families thrive. As a researcher and clinician, I've seen the power of this program to transform parents' relationships with their children—and as a parent myself, I'm thrilled that this book makes the program accessible to parents everywhere!

—**JACQUELINE NESI, PHD**, Assistant Professor, Alpert Medical School of Brown University, Providence, RI, and author of *Techno Sapiens*, a Substack featured publication, 2023

This classic, written by nationally recognized authorities, gives parents everything they need to help their strong-willed children excel and behave well.

—**ROBERT E. EMERY, PHD**, Professor of Psychology and Director of the Center for Children, Families, and The Law, University of Virginia, Charlottesville, and author of *Two Homes, One Childhood*

The fourth edition of *Parenting the Strong-Willed Child* is an invaluable resource for parents and professionals alike who are looking for empirically supported strategies to reduce challenging behaviors among children. The authors have packaged decades of research and clinical experiences into a relatable, accessible, and informative book that provides individuals with a wealth of knowledge that can improve not only child behavior, but also parent-child interactions more broadly.

—**DONTE BERNARD, PHD**, Assistant Professor, Department of Psychological Sciences, University of Missouri, Columbia

This is an excellent guide for the many parents who have a strong-willed child! By following the five-week program laid out by the authors, parents can eliminate or reduce many of the problems associated with strong-willed behavior. In addition, this substantially revised version of *Parenting the Strong-Willed Child* presents solutions to current-day problems, like children's screen time. I highly recommend this book to parents of young children!

—**LISA ARMISTEAD, PHD**, Professor of Psychology, Dean, Graduate School, Georgia State University, Atlanta

The fourth edition of *Parenting the Strong-Willed Child* is a timely, fully updated, user-friendly, authoritative guide written by three internationally renowned experts on the important subject of parenting. It will serve as an indispensable resource for caregivers who seek to understand their strong-willed child, to constructively navigate common parenting challenges (such as responding appropriately to intense emotions, tantrums, arguments, and aggression), to help them appreciate their strong-willed child's strengths, to manage their own stress, to enhance positive parent-child interactions, and to promote better outcomes for their children.

—**BRADLEY WHITE, PHD**, Associate Professor of Psychology, Center for Youth Development and Intervention, University of Alabama, Tuscaloosa, and coeditor of the *Oxford Handbook of Child and Adolescent Clinical Psychology*

The newest edition of *Parenting the Strong-Willed Child* provides a step-by-step, illustrative approach to parenting strong-willed children that is thoughtful, inclusive, and effective. Forehand, Jones, and Long masterfully place child development and caregiver experiences in context, allowing for deepened understanding of the caregiver-child relationship and empowering caregivers to navigate everyday challenges with more confidence. A go-to approach for producing lasting positive changes within any family in a short period of time!

> —**JESSICA CUELLAR, PHD**, Licensed Clinical Psychologist, Co-Director of the Family Therapy Training Program, VA Palo Alto Health Care System, Palo Alto, CA

PARENTING THE
STRONG-
WILLED
CHILD

PARENTING THE STRONG-WILLED CHILD

EXPANDED 4TH EDITION

THE CLINICALLY PROVEN FIVE-WEEK PROGRAM FOR PARENTS OF TWO- TO SIX-YEAR-OLDS

REX FOREHAND, PhD
DEBORAH J. JONES, PhD
NICHOLAS LONG, PhD

Mc
Graw
Hill

NEW YORK   CHICAGO   SAN FRANCISCO   ATHENS   LONDON
MADRID   MEXICO CITY   MILAN   NEW DELHI
SINGAPORE   SYDNEY   TORONTO

1 2 3 4 5 6 7 8 9   LCR   28 27 26 25 24 23

ISBN   978-1-265-00228-2
MHID   1-265-00228-2

e-ISBN   978-1-265-00525-2
e-MHID   1-265-00525-7

McGraw Hill books are available at special quantity discounts to use as premiums and sales promotions or for usc in corporate training programs. To contact a representative, please visit the Contact Us pages at www.mhprofessional.com.

McGraw Hill is committed to making our products accessible to all learners. To learn more about the available support and accommodations we offer, please contact us at accessibility@mheducation.com. We also participate in the Access Text Network (www.accesstext.org), and ATN members may submit requests through ATN.

*This book is dedicated
to the many parents
of strong-willed children.*

The challenges of parenthood are daunting, but its rewards go to the core of what it means to be human—intimacy, growth, learning, and love.

—Carnegie Corporation

CONTENTS

PART III
USING YOUR NEW SKILLS EARLY, OFTEN, AND CONSISTENTLY!

PART IV
(DE-)STRESSING YOUR PARENTING

PREFACE

Parenting is one of the most difficult tasks that we, as adults, face. While most of us receive training for our occupations, we enter the world of parenting with little instruction or guidance. As a result, we either model (or try to do the opposite of) what our own parents did or rely largely on trial and error in our attempts to be effective parents. Unfortunately, with a strong-willed child, there is little time for trial and error. You need effective parenting skills, and you need them now! The first three editions of this book were well received by parents with strong-willed children and by the professionals with whom those families worked. Based on the feedback from parents and advances in research, we decided an updated and expanded version of *Parenting the Strong-Willed Child* was due.

In this edition, we also make a number of additions, including the following:

The first and most important update was that Deborah J. Jones, PhD, was added as a coauthor. She has extensive clinical and research experience with families with strong-willed children. In addition, her research focuses on implementing and evaluating the program on which *Parenting the Strong-Willed Child* is based. These experiences shaped the writing of this edition in important ways.

Other revisions include:

- More attention is given to the diversity among families of young children.
- A "Time to Reflect" on the presented material was introduced in most chapters.
- Updated research is included that demonstrates the effectiveness of this book and related programs.
- There is expanded information about how to apply the program skills to a range of problem behaviors.
- More specific guidance is provided on how to use the program skills in a child's daily activities such as dressing, meals, bedtime, and chores, as well as a new chapter by two experts on screen time.
- There are opportunities to apply the program skills to positive youth development, including self-esteem.
- Updated information is provided on topics such as ADHD.
- Greater attention is given to the link between stress (including recent stressors such as COVID) and parenting, as well as tips to manage stress.
- Tips are offered that will help you change the way you, as a parent, think about your child's behavior
- There is an additional helpful guidance section for parents and for professionals using our program.

Perhaps almost as difficult as parenting a strong-willed child is writing a book about how to parent such a child. You have to believe that you know something that can help parents through the difficult times. Fortunately, among the three of us, we have spent many decades developing, evaluating, and delivering programs for parents of strong-willed children, as well as training generations of therapists to do the same. From the research data that we have systematically collected and the reports of the many parents with whom we have worked, we know that the skills we have taught parents have helped them improve their relationships with their children. The skills also have helped these parents decrease their children's problem behaviors associated with being strong-willed and enabled the children to capitalize on the positive aspects of their strong wills.

Beyond our research and clinical work with parents and their strong-willed children, we bring to this book the collective experience of being parents of four grown children and grandparents of five children ranging in age from 1 to 22. We have seen and experienced it all (we hope!). This personal experience is no small part of what informs this book. We know that parenting is not easy under the best of conditions. We know the difficulties of applying the parenting skills taught in this book. We know the highs and lows of parenting. We have experienced it all on a personal level, and this has helped us be realistic in our advice about parenting.

ACKNOWLEDGMENTS

This edition of the book could not have been written without the diligent work of many people. Several people in particular stand out. First, Robert J. McMahon has served as a guiding light and a wonderful colleague in much of our efforts to understand, implement, and disseminate our parenting program. He is the senior author of the clinical program *Helping the Noncompliant Child: Family-Based Treatment of Oppositional Behavior* (Guilford Press), on which this book is based. Second, with patience and constant encouragement, Irene Knight typed and retyped numerous versions of the manuscript. Without her, there would not be a revised and updated edition!

We also want to express our appreciation to Donya Dickerson at McGraw Hill for the support, encouragement, and feedback she provided. Her skills go far beyond those typically associated with being an editor. We also want to thank the other staff members at McGraw Hill for their valuable contributions.

As you will read throughout this book, the support, love, and learning that come from a family should never be underestimated. This is certainly the case for the authors. As our children have grown and become parents themselves, we have learned more from them, as well as from our spouses and parents, about parenting; however, we believe our comments of thanks from the first edition still apply for two of the authors (RF and NL). Thus, we are pleased to repeat them here and, in addition, add those of our new coauthor (DJJ).

The first author (RF) has been fortunate to have received support, love, and numerous invaluable learning experiences from his now deceased parents (Rex and Sara Forehand), his children (Laura Forehand Wright and Greg Forehand), and their children. Thank you! There may be only one person who fell in love in the first grade, never loved anyone else, had the fortune to marry that person, and has been happily married for 58 years. I am that person. Lell, thank you for your support, excitement about life, strength to fight difficulties we have faced together, ability to laugh at the darkest moment, and through your need for change, the introduction of new and higher experiences into our lives. But most important, thank you for your love and for being!

The second author (DJJ) would also like to thank her grandparents (Gladys and Robert Mattiko) and parents (Jeanie and Gene Jones). Together they worked incredibly hard to ensure that I (and my younger siblings, Michael Jones and Michelle Cheberenchick) had opportunities that they did not—including going to college. Even when I was a very little girl, my grandmother would tell me variations of, "You should write this down . . . you will use it in your book one day." I do not know if this is the type of book she was envisioning, but I am quite sure she would be proud. I would also like to thank Lawrence Sizemore, who is a lovely example of how one puts much of what we talk about in this book into day-to-day life with his daughter, Annalee, which isn't always easy when you have a psychologist watching your every move! And speaking of being a psychologist, I must thank the many graduate students whom I have trained in our university clinic over the years and the families with whom they work. I often say that I learn as much from them as (if not more than) they learn from me. Finally, I would like to thank Rex and Nick for giving me the opportunity to join them in the writing of the fourth edition. This is a book that I recommend often in both my professional and personal life to parents who are looking for support, guidance, and hands-on strategies. It is an honor to be a part of something that I have seen work and work so well for so many families.

The third author (NL) also has been blessed with a loving and supportive family. I would like to thank my now deceased parents, John and Jean Long, for providing wonderful examples of what it means to be loving and caring parents. My brother, Adam Long, who was born when I was 15 years old, helped me realize how wonderful children are and greatly influenced my decision to pursue a career working with children. I want to thank my adult sons and their wives, Justin (Erin) and Alex (Sharonda) Long, and their children for their continued love and support. I am extremely fortunate to have such wonderful sons and grandchildren, Trennon, Addison, and Jack. Finally, I want to thank my wife, Sharon, for being whom I consider the best mother in the world. You have taught me so much through your absolute love of being a parent and grandparent!

The three authors have a friendship that has spanned over 30 years. The writing of this book, as well as the many other professional and personal interactions we have, has deepened this friendship. We have provided each other inspiration, support, and positive reinforcement. Indeed, we are fortunate to have each other as friends and to have had the opportunity to share this writing experience.

INTRODUCTION

Parenting is incredibly rewarding—children do things every day that make us think, smile, and laugh. Parenting, of course, can also be challenging—and sometimes this can be harder for parents to admit to themselves, let alone to others. That said, it can in fact be and most often is true for *all* parents— the dialectic of parenting—it is both at once! Parenting can be even more challenging for parents of strong-willed children; we will talk more about what we mean by this, but chances are if you are a parent of a strong-willed child, you know it already and may be picking up this book because you are finding it challenging and even frustrating. It may be even more frustrating to not feel comfortable talking about these challenges with others or to know whom to turn to for guidance and resources. Importantly, if you are one of these parents, you are definitely not alone. Equally or more importantly, there are strategies or skills for dealing with the aspects of your child's strong-willed behavior that you are not yet sure how best to manage (while preserving the parts that you like, enjoy, and want to nurture!).

We have spent years developing, evaluating, and using a clinical treatment program that addresses the behavior problems often seen in young children who are very strong-willed, especially problems of not obeying their parents. We know that on one hand you may want to nurture your child's independence and assertiveness (these are good skills to have!), but at the same time you know that there are times when your child needs to listen to and comply with what you (or other adults like teachers) are asking of them. These may include day-to-day things like the steps that need to happen to get them out the door in the morning for daycare or school or even more significant safety-related moments like holding your hand or staying by your side while walking down a busy sidewalk. We developed our clinical program to help parents of these children in these and other situations, focusing on teaching parents skills that they can use to acknowledge and celebrate their child's strong-willed spirit while also helping them to harness and channel that spirit into behaviors that will serve them well now and in the future.

Over the past 50 years, we and many other researchers around the country have studied our clinical program, and the research has shown that if parents can learn and consistently use the skills, it works! Typical results for families who complete the program include improved relationships between parents and their children, children who mind their parents more, and fewer child problem behaviors at home and, sometimes, in other settings such as preschool. Researchers who followed children for up to 15 years after completion of the program have found these benefits to be lasting. We have described these studies in professional journals and books (see the Appendix) and also provided training for psychologists and other professionals at our own universities and around the country so that they can use it in their own clinical work with families.

That said, we realize that not all children necessarily require clinical treatment and that some parents may want to try using the program at home before deciding whether to consult a professional. That is why we decided to initially write and again revise this book that is written for you—parents! *Parenting the Strong-Willed Child* covers most of what is taught in our clinical program, but tailored in a way that provides opportunities for parents to understand the rationale behind our program and skills and lots of opportunities to practice those skills at home. If you use these parenting skills consistently, they have the potential to improve your relationship with your child and reduce many of the problems and frustrations that can be associated with your child's strong-willed behavior.

In fact, two published studies provide support for our conclusion that reading this book can change your child's strong-willed behaviors. In an independent research study, Dr. Nicola Conners at the University of Arkansas for Medical Sciences and her collaborators found that participation in a parenting group that used *Parenting the Strong-Willed Child* as the curriculum was associated with less parenting stress, use of more effective parenting behaviors, and fewer child behavior problems. And more directly related to you reading this book, two of the authors and two of our colleagues, Mary Jane Merchant and Emily Garai, found that parents who read *Parenting the Strong-Willed Child* reported significant decreases in their child's behavior problems. For specific strong-willed behaviors, these parents reported significantly greater decreases than did parents who read a more general parenting book on understanding three- to six-year-old children and their development. However, *Parenting the Strong-Willed Child* was more effective *only* if parents reported reading most or all of the chapters on implementing our five-week program (Chapters 5 through 11). Not surprisingly, this means you must actually read this book if you expect to change your strong-willed child's behavior. (The complete citation for each of the two studies is in the Appendix under the "References for Professionals" section.)

It is findings such as these that led to an earlier edition of *Parenting the Strong-Willed Child* being selected for the Book of Merit Award presented by the Association for Behavioral and Cognitive Therapies (ABCT), an organization devoted to the advancement of evidence-based science and practice in mental health. This award is given for educating the general public about the benefits of psychological treatments that have been proved to work, highlighting the ABCT's confidence in the potential for our five-week program to improve your child's behavior!

While this book is based on our clinical program, it is not a substitute for individual professional help if your child has severe behavior problems or might be experiencing types or levels of problem behaviors that may require professional attention to have the best effects, such as attention deficit/hyperactivity disorder (ADHD). (See Chapter 4, "Does My Child Have ADHD?".) If you are a parent who suspects or has been told by a teacher or professional in your child's life that your child's behaviors may be more significant, we present steps you can take to contact a professional (see "Seeking Professional Help" in the Appendix). There are a number of websites of professional organizations (e.g., Association for Behavioral and Cognitive Therapies) listed in the Appendix that can be helpful in finding the appropriate professional help. However, even for many of the families that may need more one-on-one professional guidance, we believe that the skills presented in this book can likely complement that work as well.

OVERVIEW OF THE BOOK

Our strategy for addressing strong-willed behavior has four dimensions. The first dimension involves helping you understand your child's strong-willed behavior and how various factors influence such behavior. The second uses specific parenting skills for addressing the behavior problems most commonly exhibited by strong-willed children who are two to six years old. The third involves using these skills to address a variety of problem behaviors you may be encountering with your child. Included in these behaviors are ones that occur regularly during daily routines (e.g., mealtime behavior, chores, dressing, bedtime) as well as an issue for many parents: screen time. As part of the third dimension, we review several ways you can promote positive youth development such as self-esteem and positive social skills. After all, these should be our ultimate goals as parents. The fourth dimension involves a focus on *you*! Believe it or not (and we are sure you do), how you handle the stresses in your life affect how you parent. We present some ways to handle these stresses, including how you think about your child and how you communicate with others with whom you interact, particularly those with whom you might co-parent. When combined, these four dimensions form a holistic strategy you can use to understand your child's behavior, learn how to change it, and promote positive growth, reduce your life stresses, and simultaneously enjoy your child (and life) more.

The book is divided into four parts that map onto the four dimensions just delineated. Part I explains the factors that cause or contribute to your child's strong-willed behavior. We start by examining the role of temperament in setting the stage for strong-willed behavior. We then address how your reactions to your child's behavior can affect and sometimes actually increase this behavior. We then go on to consider how factors such as financial hardship, family conflict, changes in your relationships, parental depression, and traumatic stress can affect your parenting and your child's behavior. Finally, as parents often have difficulty differentiating strong-willed behavior from attention deficit/hyperactivity disorder, we end this part with a chapter addressing this issue.

The parenting skills in Part II take the form of a five-week program for dealing with the behavior problems associated with a child being strong-willed. You will learn and practice a new skill every week. By the end of the five weeks, you should notice a significant improvement in your relationship with your child and in your child's behavior if you are consistently using the skills as we recommend.

In Part III, we focus on using the skills to help you address a variety of problems your child may display, to help you get through the daily routines (e.g., bedtime, mealtime) when having a young strong-willed child, and, importantly, to promote positive development in several areas (e.g., self-esteem).

Part IV offers strategies for you to manage the many stresses in your life. Handling these stressors in adaptive ways will not only make being an effective parent more enjoyable for you but also promote your child's "okay" behavior (a term you will read throughout this book).

As we have noted already, in this edition, we include an Appendix listing a number of websites where you can obtain further information on parenting. We also include a list of books parents may find beneficial and a brief list of references to some of the research on our program that professionals may find helpful.

Since *Parenting the Strong-Willed Child* was first published, we have had the opportunity to continue to think more richly and deeply about the diversity of families we have the honor of studying and seeing in our clinical practice. This diversity includes but is not limited to race and ethnicity, socioeconomic status, and family structure, including single-parent families and families with two moms or two dads. Although we can't say that our five-week program (or related programs) has been tested with families that necessarily perfectly reflect your own, we do know that strong-willed child behavior and parenting difficulties appear to exist in families of all identities and that skills like those in our program and shared in this book can be helpful. Of course, this presumes parents can learn the skills and use them consistently—that is the key! That said, if you read something in these pages that feels inconsistent or uncomfortable with any aspect of your identity (or your child's) or your family's lived experience, we encourage you not to stop reading. Instead, we hope you will try to think about the rationale for what we are suggesting and come up with responses to your child's behavior that are still in line with the principles we discuss but may feel more consistent with your own views as a parent based on your culture, experience, and identities.

In a similar way, while it is true that the vast majority of research on parenting has long focused on mothers and female caregivers, research on the father's role in the family has increased in recent years. Our research and that of others shows that in some families fathers may use parenting skills at different levels or intensities than mothers; however, what is most important is for fathers to be actively involved in parenting and, to the extent possible, for mothers' and fathers' parenting to be consistent. When possible, all caregivers should read this book and work together to change their strong-willed child's behavior. If this is not possible, this approach can still be helpful when used by a single parent.

We hope that this book will help you understand your strong-willed child's behavior, learn effective parenting skills, and learn how to enhance and maintain these parenting skills. We hope that learning how to use these skills, along with other recommendations that we offer to effectively address your major concerns regarding your child's behavior, will, in turn, increase your sense of competence as a parent.

Authors' Note: We thought a lot about the role of gendered language in writing this book. Initially, especially in our vignettes, we attempted to avoid gendered language such as "he" and "she" in favor of "they" for example. However, we realized in reading the vignettes that included at least a parent and a child and sometimes multiple parents and children, such language while ideal could be quite confusing. As a result, we refer more clearly to the gender of parents in our discussion of example families and vignettes, including such identifiers as "Ms.," "she," and "mother" for parents. In referring to children in these examples and vignettes, however, we tried to rely on non-gendered language to the extent possible.

UNDERSTANDING STRONG-WILLED BEHAVIOR

For parents picking up this book for the first time, you may be wondering, "Is my child strong-willed?" If you have used "strong-willed" to describe your child (whether you said it out loud or not!), you may then wonder, "Is being strong-willed good or bad?" The answer, like much of life, is that "it depends." In Part I of this book, we consider what being strong-willed tends to look like in young children and how it develops (Chapter 1). In particular, we consider the role temperament plays in your child's strong-willed behavior and introduce the role of parenting. We then consider in more depth how parenting (Chapter 2) can shape strong-willed behavior in young children, as well as how the stressors that parents like you can face affect parenting. Finally, we turn to how you can tell the difference between typical strong-willed behavior and a disorder many parents think about when their child's behavior is difficult: ADHD (Chapter 4). As we emphasize throughout this and subsequent parts of this book, parents have a critical role to play in understanding what strong-willed behavior is, where it comes from, and how to increase the likelihood that it is one of your child's strengths rather than something that gets in the way of them being their best self now and in the years to come.

CHAPTER 1

WHAT IS STRONG-WILLED BEHAVIOR

(AND IS IT OKAY IF MY CHILD IS STRONG-WILLED)?

Parents picking up this book for the first time may have these very questions: "What does it mean to be 'strong-willed'?" and "Is it okay if my child is strong-willed?" In this chapter and those that follow, we will do our best to answer both of these questions for you. Before we try to do that, let us introduce you to three children:

First, meet Ethan, who is two years old. Ethan's mother, Avery, says Ethan was "born with a strong will!" Avery says it started while still in the delivery room when the nurses described Ethan as "fussy." Ethan's father, Reese, said Ethan continued to be "difficult" after coming home from hospital, including that Ethan "cried and cried" and "could not be soothed." Avery and Reese thought that it was colic and that Ethan would cry less with time,, but the "crying" and "fussing" continued. Ethan's parents say that by 18 months, it seemed Ethan was "crying and fussing" purposefully to avoid taking a bath, getting dressed, and getting ready for bed. Avery and Reese worry Ethan's behavior just isn't improving and feel guilty that they are frustrated, exhausted, and not finding being parents very rewarding (e.g., "If only Ethan smiled at us more!").

Now let us introduce you to four-year-old Jacob, whose mother, Ms. Williams, describes Jacob as very "outgoing" and "independent," which Ms. Williams wants to encourage. Yet Jacob's mother also finds Jacob to be "demanding" and "never satisfied" with the amount of time, energy, or attention at home or at preschool. Ms. Williams and the preschool teacher also say Jacob is "as stubborn as they come" and quickly becomes "upset" (e.g., "whining" and "tantruming"). When asked what the tantrums looked like, Jacob's mother and teacher describe crying, yelling, clenched fists, stomping feet, and even throwing things. They also describe Jacob as very "active," "on the go," and "filled with boundless energy," which results in bumping into walls, knocking things over (accidentally!), and falling often. Although rarely appearing to be physically hurt (i.e., no bumps, bruises, or broken bones), Jacob is at times inconsolable. Ms. Williams wants to help Jacob, but is "at a loss," as nothing seems to be working.

Finally, meet Emily, who is a six-year-old first-grader. Testing at school indicated that Emily has above-average intelligence and academic skills. Emily's teacher also describes a child who is "very confident" and one who "perseveres in challenging activities long after most other children give up." Emily's father, Mr. Gonzalez, admits that Emily has never been great at listening or following directions. Although things seem better at school than at home, Emily still often ignores teacher's instructions or says things like, "No, I will not do it!" Mr. Gonzalez worries that the teacher's investment in Emily will be affected by this behavior and that it will begin to affect schoolwork as well if they don't "nip it in the bud."

TIME TO REFLECT

- Do any of these situations remind you of the reasons you chose this book?
- Do any of these children remind you of your child?
- Do any of these children's behaviors remind you of your child's behavior?
- Do any of these parents' feelings, worries, or concerns about their child's behavior and the impact of their child's behavior remind you of your own?

If you see yourself or your child in any of these examples, you are not alone! In a group to help parents manage the behavior of two- to six-year-old children, we asked whether they thought their child was strong-willed and what they believed were the characteristics of being strong-willed. Nearly half (48 percent) of the parents reported that their young child was "strong-willed," and as you will see, they described their strong-willed children in a variety of ways. These included characteristics that many parents will find positive and want to see and nurture in their young children, such as "assertive," "confident," and "persistent." Yet parents in our parenting group also identified aspects of their strong-willed child's behavior that felt more frustrating to navigate, including characteristics like "argumentative," "headstrong," "stubborn," "temperamental," and "unpredictable." Still other characteristics were things that could be seen as positive but at times frustrating (see inside the parentheses), including "determined" (versus "cries to get own way"), "independent" (versus "everything is a fight or struggle"), "outgoing" (versus "demands constant attention"), "has own ideas" (versus "talks back a lot"), and spirited (versus "always on the go").

In light of these very mixed descriptions, we need to consider the possibility that having a strong-willed child can be both a strength and challenge for parents! Indeed, if we turn to the *Merriam-Webster Dictionary*, "strong-willed" is defined as "very determined to do something even if other people say it should not be done." It is perhaps the two distinct parts of this definition —"very determined to do something" and "even if other people say it should not be done"—that may explain some of the tensions parents in our group were feeling and you may be feeling as well. That is, being "determined" in and of itself can be positive and a characteristic that parents likely want to nurture. For example, one need only see the joy on parents' faces when it is clear that their baby is trying to roll over or crawl or stand for the first time to realize the value parents (and society more generally!) places on stick-to-itiveness! And such determination can serve young children incredibly well as they encounter new milestones (e.g., tying their shoes, starting school, going to their first sleepover, trying a new sport) or face any challenges (e.g., learning struggles, developmental issues, peer conflict).

Yet any parent who has navigated their child stalling when told to put on their shoes or tantruming when told to share a toy or adamantly refusing to go to bed ("No!") recognizes the flip side of determination (or assertiveness, confidence, persistence) in a young child as well. That is, we hear things like "My child is very determined to do (or not do) something even when I (or someone else) tell them otherwise!" Even if parents do want to nurture determination in the long term in their children, stalling, tantruming, and "No!" can be extremely frustrating in the short term, leading to parents being more likely to use more negative terms (e.g., "argumentative," "headstrong," "stubborn") rather than positive terms (e.g., "assertive," "confident," "persistent") to describe the very same behavior when it happens over and over and over again. So how do parents help their two- to six-year-old children harness and channel their strong-willed nature more effectively now and in the future? To answer this question, we first must talk a little bit about your child's temperament.

TIME TO REFLECT

List your strong-willed child's strengths and challenges.

Strengths   **Challenges**

_____   _____

_____   _____

_____   _____

TEMPERAMENT (NOT TEMPER TANTRUM)

How does a child become strong-willed? Many of the positive *and* potentially frustrating characteristics associated with being strong-willed have their roots in temperament. You may or may not have heard the word "temperament" before, but we tend to describe it to parents as your child's innate or biological predisposition for navigating the world—or the sort of hardware (to borrow a computer analogy!) that provides the basis for how your child thinks, feels, and behaves. This is probably not a surprise to you if you are a parent to more than one child and have noticed that your children have some similarities, but also lots and lots of differences that emerged fairly early on when they were babies (e.g., "easy" versus "fussy") and have continued as your children get older (e.g., "agreeable" versus "argumentative").

Or you may see it when you compare your child with another child at the daycare, preschool, or playground. In fact, you may have seen something like the following at some point: There are two 15-month-old children who fall down while running in a carpeted room. Neither child is injured, but one child is seemingly inconsolable after the fall—screaming, crying, and refusing to get up and play. The other child experiences the very same fall, but rolls around in fits of giggles before getting up and taking off across the room again. The different ways these children handle the very same experience, in this case a fall while playing, in part, illustrates their different temperaments.

After reading those examples, one child's reaction to falling may remind you more of your own child. Certainly, one is easier for you as a parent, but you may be wondering, "Is one temperament better than another?" That is a good question, but like much of human behavior, there is not an easy answer. Moreover, just like you have a temperament you were born into the world with, so too does your child, and for better or worse, we are likely not going to be effective at changing that—rather, we want to nurture the more positive or adaptive aspects of your child's temperament and channel or harness the aspects that may be less helpful now and in the long run.

So is there a strong-willed temperament? The short answer is "not really," but we do see several consistencies in temperament traits across children who tend to be described as strong-willed. These traits include:

- **Reactivity**, or how intensely a child reacts either positively or negatively across situations
- **Emotionality**, or the balance of the positive and negative aspects of a child's mood or emotions
- **Adaptability**, or how well a child adapts to changes in situations and events
- **Persistence**, or how long a child sticks with an activity

Building upon our earlier list of words that parents in our group used to describe their children, we can say that strong-willed children are more likely than other children to react intensely (e.g., "big emotions"), to have a difficult time adapting to transitions (e.g., bargaining for more time to play before bedtime), to persist when they want to have their own way (e.g., pretending not to hear parents saying no to a request), and to have inconsistent or sometimes more negative or irritable moods (e.g., pouting, sulking, tantrums).

If these characteristics remind you of your child, you may now be wondering if these early strong-willed traits are linked with later behavior problems. Again, there is not necessarily an easy answer, and one answer may not be the right answer for every child. But in this book, we are going to turn to research and our clinical experience to tell you about the average or typical strong-willed child, and it is up to you to decide if what we are talking about sounds familiar (and, in turn, if we are likely to be helpful to you!). To this end, research to date does suggest that a child's early temperament is related to later behavior. For example, infants and toddlers who are more irritable, are restless, and have trouble adapting to new situations do, on average, have more behavior problems as they get older. In addition, a more difficult temperament in toddlers is strongly related to behaviors like aggression, noncompliance, and oppositionality in adolescence. A child's early temperament has also been linked to more difficulties in peer relationships, preschool adjustment, and even academic achievement. However, all is not lost—as we will show you, there are ways that you can help your strong-willed child!

TEMPERAMENT, PARENTING, AND BEHAVIOR

As parents, it would be normal here to start to feel uneasy—either you are bristling at the suggestion that there is perhaps something wrong with your strong-willed child, or alternatively, you now fear that your strong-willed child is doomed for life-long problems! Based on those very normal feelings, you may even be considering closing this book and finding another that offers what you hope is a more positive or hopeful message. That makes total sense because as a parent it is hard to hear that there may be something about your child that could be a sign of difficulties to come. We hear you, and we encourage you to keep reading because there is indeed good news—parenting matters!

Many parents ask us whether it is their child's temperament or their parenting that has "caused" their child's strong-willed behavior. Such a question is like the often-debated question of whether nature or nurture is most important in determining our personality. Since temperament and parenting continually interact to shape each other, we seldom can know which is more important in determining a child's strong-willed behavior. What is clear is that temperament *and* parenting are both important and clearly linked.

Research suggests that many of the temperament traits we have been discussing can change as a child develops. That is, many of these temperament traits are not biologically fixed but rather are tendencies that can be modified by parenting style and other environmental factors. Herein lies the good news—you can influence your child's behavior, and our five-week program (Part II of this book) lays out specific skills that will allow you to increase the behaviors you want to see or see more (i.e., "okay" behaviors) and decrease the behaviors that are causing problems now or may increase the likelihood of problems for your child and others later (i.e., "not-okay" behaviors). In fact, the data work in your favor here, as several research studies have found that children with difficult temperaments are more affected by parenting practices than children with average or easy temperaments. So before we turn to Chapter 2 and more discussion of the important role that parents can play, we want you to take a minute to think about the okay behaviors that your strong-willed child displays that you want to see or see more. We also want you to think about the not-okay behaviors, or the behaviors you want to see less or not at all. We are not necessarily going to start working directly on these behaviors until Part II, but keeping them at the forefront of your mind as you read (and revising them as you think of new or different things!) will help this material feel more personal and useful to you.

TIME TO REFLECT

Take a minute to reflect on your child's behavior—including what you are seeing now, as well as what you would like to see one month from now, six months from now, and one year from now.

- What are the *top three* behaviors you want to see or see more (i.e., okay behaviors)?

  _____

  _____

  _____

- What are the *top three* behaviors you want to see less or not at all (i.e., not-okay behaviors)?

  _____

  _____

  _____

Note: You can refine and change these as you continue to read. This will get you started!

CHAPTER 2

STRONG-WILLED TEMPERAMENT AND BEHAVIOR

CHICKEN OR EGG?

As we discussed in Chapter 1, children are born into the world with a temperament or disposition for feeling, thinking and, in turn, behaving in particular ways. Temperaments are not "good" or "bad." Temperaments just are—much like the color of your child's skin, hair, or eyes. That said, if you are a parent of a child with a temperament characterized by more of the strong-willed traits described in Chapter 1 (e.g., more reactive, less adaptable, more emotional), you may find yourself dealing with more not-okay behaviors (see your list in Chapter 1) such as whining or tantrums or even more aggressive behavior (e.g., hitting or throwing toys). While you, of course, love your child dearly and it may be hard to admit it, these types of behaviors can be incredibly frustrating to manage. After all, you are a human being with thoughts and feelings of your own! Yet it can also feel awful to have negative thoughts (e.g., "My child is annoying me," "My child is trying to push my buttons") and feelings (e.g., anger, frustration) about your child and how you handle your child's behavior (e.g., yelling sometimes and doing nothing at other times).

We know how frustrated and ineffective parents can feel, which is one of our motivations for writing this book—because we are here to tell you that it can be different. The key as parents is to realize how to harness your love for and attention to your child in order to increase behaviors you want to see and see more (e.g., your child's determination!) and decrease or eliminate those behaviors that are likely to serve your child less well now and in the future (e.g., tantrums). To do this, we turn now to a discussion of how temperament is only one piece of the puzzle. That is, your child is born into the world with a predisposition to think, feel, and behave in certain ways, but whether those behaviors occur, occur more often, or occur not at all can be shaped by their environment.

CHILDREN ARE SOCIAL CREATURES!

We mentioned in Chapter 1 that your child's temperament is sort of hardwired. To continue with this example, we want you to think about your desktop computer (or tablet or smartphone). Your computer's hardware, for example, includes everything from the casing, operating system, and monitor to the mouse.

The hardware is for the most part fixed or rigid—what you see is what you get (e.g., your desktop computer cannot be turned into a smartphone . . . at least not with today's technology!). But you have much more flexibility about what software to load and run on your computer, including choices about word processing programs, email, calendars, and games. Similarly, your child does have a hardwired temperament (i.e., their hardware), but how that temperament and the traits associated with it function day-to-day, month-to-month, and year-to-year depends on the input from others and the ways they interact with them (i.e., their software). Indeed, children are social creatures, and much of how a child behaves is learned from interactions with others, which has been termed "social learning." Temperament and other factors lay the groundwork, but it is through social learning that children are more (or less) likely to behave in specific ways. Social learning occurs in a variety of ways, including modeling and consequences.

MODELING

This aspect of social learning is basically learning by example. *Modeling* occurs when a child learns how to behave a certain way by seeing or hearing others behaving that same way. Your child may see another child having a tantrum because that other child wants a cookie. If the other child gets the cookie after the tantrum, your child learns, by observation or example, that a tantrum may be an effective way to get something. The next time you say no to your child's request for a cookie, there may be an unexpected tantrum—your child learned this *should* work!

Observing someone behave in a certain way does not mean your child will automatically behave that way, but it does increase the chances. Whether your child will imitate someone depends on many things, including whether your child wants to be like that other person (e.g., another child at daycare), how many times your child has the opportunity to observe the behavior (e.g., five days a week while you are at work), and whether the behavior had a positive outcome (e.g., the daycare provider gives the tantruming child the cookie).

Children also watch, listen to, and learn from (i.e., model) their parents. Since children love and look up to their parents and typically see them most every day, the opportunities for modeling are plentiful. Such opportunities allow parents to model more adaptive behaviors (e.g., deep breathing when frustrated or angry) as well as less adaptive behaviors (e.g., yelling). Indeed, children often look to their parents for examples of how to behave in difficult situations. Unfortunately, the oft-cited "Do as I say, not as I do" does not work as well in practice as in theory, given that modeling is more powerful than words in teaching children how to behave.

TIME TO REFLECT

- Is there something you do that you would *not* want your child to model?
- How can you do a better job of catching yourself in the moment before you do that?
- What can you do instead to provide the type of example you want your child to model?

For example, you may answer the first question by saying "I tend to yell when I am angry." If this is the case, try to do a better job of catching yourself before you yell by noticing that you are angry, or start keeping track of situations in which you are likely to get angry (e.g., someone cutting in front of you in the grocery store checkout). Once you realize that in this situation you are likely to get angry and yell, you instead take a deep breath (i.e., self-soothing) and say, "Excuse me. Perhaps you did not see us here." Or alternatively, if you choose not to be assertive in this situation (because being assertive can be very hard at the end of a long day!), you play a fun "I spy" game with your child that might distract you in the moment and also show your child a way to cope with frustration and anger.

To sum up, your child learns by observing you and other adults and children in their life. You can control some of what they observe, but not everything since your child is not with you all the time. Further, you, like all other parents, are not perfect and will sometimes behave in ways in front of your child that you may not even realize they are paying attention to (e.g., rolling your eyes when someone you are talking to on the phone is annoying you). This unfortunately happens to the best of us! We encourage you to make adjustments to your behavior to try to be the best example you can be for your child.

CONSEQUENCES

Beyond modeling behavior, there are other ways your child is learning as well—and that includes consequences. There are two types of consequences: reinforcement and punishment.

REINFORCEMENT

When most people think of *reinforcement*, they tend to think of giving children things like candy or money for good behavior (i.e., bribery). This notion of reinforcement is actually quite inaccurate, immensely oversimplified, and just not helpful, as reinforcement can be much more and play a critical role in your child's behavior. Instead, a more accurate and helpful way to think about reinforcement is that if a behavior is followed by something positive, the behavior is more likely to occur in the future.

The misconception regarding bribery comes from the notion that reinforcers are necessarily "things." For example, "If you put away your toys, you can have a piece of candy." There is nothing necessarily wrong with using things like candy as a reinforcer, but material things are not necessary or even the best reinforcer for a young child. That is, most reinforcers are social in nature. These *social reinforcers*—words of praise, laughter, and so on—are immediately and easily accessible and thus have the potential to have the greatest impact on behavior.

For this point to hit home, think about a situation like work. When you first think of reinforcers at work, you may think about your paycheck; and of course, adults, like children, are motivated by material things like a paycheck. That said, we typically are paid once a week or every two weeks or once a month, and while this is important, there are usually lots of social reinforcers at play that keep you getting up, going to work, and doing the same thing day after day. For example, you are more likely to talk to someone at work who is smiling at you than someone who scowls or walks away. In part this is because you have learned from your past experiences that smiles tend to precede pleasant interactions. Similarly, you probably spend more time talking to someone at work about your ideas if they pay attention to what you are saying and seem interested (e.g., leaning in, eye contact, head nods). And even more so if the person to whom you are talking is someone more senior to you (e.g., a supervisor, boss, or even another employee you admire), and they say, "Wow! That was a great point you made in the meeting earlier today!"

In the same way, your child is reinforced more effectively by small (but frequently occurring) social responses, including those that are both verbal (e.g., "Wow!" or "Nice job stacking the blocks") and nonverbal (e.g., a high five or a pat on the back) than by material rewards such as toys, candy, or money. And you might even find that if you give a lot of social reinforcement to your children, they will use more social reinforcement in return. As one mother told us, "When I started smiling more at my child, my child started to smile more at me. It made me feel so good."

TIME TO REFLECT

- Can you think of a time when you used positive reinforcement to shape your child's behavior?
- What was the behavior you were trying to increase?
- What was the positive reinforcer you used (i.e., what did you do or give?) in order to increase that behavior?

Another kind of reinforcement is *negative reinforcement*, which can be a little less intuitive than positive reinforcement. Many people confuse negative reinforcement with punishment, but they are not the same. Negative reinforcement, like positive reinforcement, strengthens behavior. However, with negative reinforcement, a behavior is reinforced not because it results in something positive (e.g., "Great job," high five, pat on the back) but because it results in the removal or end of something negative. Suppose your child is playing in a sandbox. Another child begins throwing sand, which blows into your child's face. Your child goes over to the other child and, like a true strong-willed child, assertively says, "Stop throwing the sand." If the other child stops throwing the sand, your child's assertiveness will have been negatively reinforced. That is, your child's assertiveness was followed by the end of something negative (blowing sand), increasing the likelihood your child will be assertive in the future! To liken this again to our experience as adults, parallel examples would be asking a significant other, friend, or colleague to please stop interrupting us when we are talking. If the other person stops interrupting us, we will be negatively reinforced for our willingness to speak up and ask for what we need from them.

TIME TO REFLECT

- Can you think of a time when you used negative reinforcement to shape your child's behavior?
- What was the behavior you were trying to decrease?
- What was the negative reinforcer you used (i.e., what did you take away?) in order to decrease that behavior?

PUNISHMENT

Whereas reinforcement increases the likelihood that a behavior will occur again, *punishment* decreases the likelihood of a behavior (or stops it altogether). In the minds of some parents, punishment may be synonymous with spanking. For example, parents who experienced spanking as a punishment when they were children may think, "I was spanked and I turned out okay." Other parents who were spanked as children may decide not to spank their own children, but have less experience with alternative forms of punishment. Still other parents may have no family history of spanking, but still have little understanding of what consequences they can use to effectively decrease (or stop) their child's not-okay behavior (e.g., noncompliance, hitting, rule breaking). Spanking is certainly one type of punishment, but one that often leaves both parents and children feeling bad. Moreover, spanking may actually be less effective than other types of consequences at decreasing or eliminating children's not-okay behavior and may actually increase (rather than decrease) problems in the long term.

The good news is that there are more effective alternatives that change child behavior in the short *and* long term, including *combining* positive and negative reinforcement with punishment for not-okay behavior. Indeed, anything that follows a behavior and *decreases* the likelihood it happens again is punishment (e.g., reprimands, removal of privilege), but any single punishment when used alone is unlikely to lead to long-term behavior change. In part, this is because punishment alone tells children what not to do (e.g., "Stop playing with your toys") and not what you want them to do instead (e.g., "Come to dinner"). We will talk much more in a later chapter about specific forms of the punishment that we recommend and why, but general rules of thumb for more effective use of any punishment include focusing on a specific not-okay behavior, using a calm voice, and using it consistently every time the behavior occurs. Importantly, punishment of any kind should be used in *combination* with other parenting skills (e.g., reinforcement).

TIME TO REFLECT

- What behaviors have you tried to address using punishment?
- What types of punishment or consequences have you tried with your child?
- Have any of those punishments led to short-term (or long-term) improvement in behavior?
- Have any of those punishments led to no change in (or even worsening) behavior?

PARENTING TRAPS!

Parenting a strong-willed child can be tricky. As we talked about in Chapter 1, there may be certain traits of your child that you want to maintain and nurture (e.g., determination). And these traits can be adaptive as your child manages new situations as described in the sandbox example presented earlier in this chapter. That said, you are probably reading this book because there are other aspects of your strong-willed child's behavior that you want to help channel or decrease (e.g., negative reactions in new situations). Given that these traits are in part a function of your child's temperament and quite literally a reflection of who they are and how they navigate the world, it can be easy to inadvertently increase (rather than decrease) not-okay behaviors that result in part from these traits.

Take this example: You are shopping with your child who asks you to buy a toy to which you respond "No, you have enough toys." Your child starts to whine, saying things like "*But I really want this one!*" You again say no but also try to comfort your child by saying, "Well, we can play with your other great toys when we get home." Your child is hearing none of this—and instead of calming down now starts to cry and continues to ask for the toy through tears. You hate to see your child upset, or maybe you are just embarrassed by what now feels like a bit of a spectacle. So to end this as quickly as possible, you agree to buy the toy. In the short term, you feel relieved (i.e., you are not disappointing your child or drawing attention from onlookers). But no battle is so easily won! In fact, you just inadvertently reinforced your child for crying, whining, and testing limits by giving attention, comfort, and a new toy! What has your child learned? Yes, your child just learned that one path to a desired outcome (e.g., a toy) is crying and whining. The next time your child wants something, what is likely to happen? Right again! Your child is more likely to cry and whine because this worked well before! We call this the "positive reinforcement trap"— we as parents reinforce and increase the likelihood of the very behavior we want to decrease.

TIME TO REFLECT

Do any of these sound familiar?

- Comforting your child during a tantrum
- Responding to "Mom," "Mom," "*Mom!*" while you are on the phone with a friend
- Smiling or laughing at (or video-recording) your child's not-okay behavior (because it can be funny!)
- Giving your child candy in the grocery store in an effort to stop the "Please, please, *please!*"

Note: If your answer is yes to any of these questions, you have fallen into the positive reinforcement trap. You are increasing the likelihood of not-okay behavior by giving your child attention, comfort, or candy, or something else your child desires.

A similar chain of events may occur when you tell your child to do something (e.g., "Pick up your toys"). Your child may whine or cry or ignore you. You try once more . . . twice more . . . but there is no move to pick up the toys. Instead, your child starts to cry, calls you "mean," and slams the bedroom door. You decide that it's just not worth the frustration, so you pick up the toys. What happened in this situation? Well, your child just learned that by crying, calling you a name, and slamming the door, the toys would get picked up by someone else (you)! This is an example of what we call the "negative reinforcement trap." As with the positive reinforcement trap, this trap reinforces and increases the likelihood of the very behavior a parent wants to decrease.

TIME TO REFLECT

Do any of these sound familiar?

- Letting your child skip their bath because they cry when you say "Bathtime"
- Letting your tantruming child leave an event
- Canceling the babysitter because your child cries while you are getting ready to go out
- Letting your child leave the dinner table during a tantrum
- Taking your crying child out of the car seat

Note: If your answer is yes to any of these questions, you have fallen into the negative reinforcement trap. You are increasing the likelihood the not-okay behavior occurs again by ending or removing something unpleasant.

One thing to clarify here: Sometimes parents who are caught in the positive or negative reinforcement trap will tell us that they think their child is "trying to manipulate them." We see how it can feel this way, as your child's behavior is indeed pushing your buttons and leading you to potentially feel more and more ineffective as a parent. That said, it is important to point out that your child is learning how to shape their interactions with you through experience, but in this age range (two-to-six years old) they likely do not have the cognitive ability to think thoughts like "I am going to try to get on Mom's nerves!" or "Let's see how mad Dad gets when I do this!" Rather, they are just learning "what works" through experience, and when these sorts of examples happen over and over and over again, the behaviors are likely to worsen rather than improve. The positive thing for you to pay attention to is that if these sorts of behaviors can be learned, then they can also be unlearned, and that is where we are here to help!

Importantly, a single incident of the positive or negative reinforcement trap will not permanently affect your child's behavior. However, when these types of interactions occur repeatedly, it can increase the likelihood of a specific pattern of interaction between you and your child and, in turn, increase, rather than decrease, not-okay behavior (the familiar downward spiral!).

THE DOWNWARD SPIRAL

In the earlier example with the toy where the parent gave in to the child, everyone felt better in the short term (i.e., parent could shop; child got the toy!), but in the long term the parent has inadvertently increased the likelihood of a similar (or worse) situation in the future. So let's fast-forward, say, two weeks later, same parent and child, same store, and the child is eyeing another toy. The parent wants to stay firm (no toy), but the child learned that whining and crying last time worked. So the child whines longer, cries louder. When that is still met with "No toy" from the parent, the child may even stomp around the aisle or lie down on the floor and refuse to move. If your child has not done this in public, you have probably seen another child do it at some point. The parent is embarrassed, frustrated, and stressed and yells *"Get off the floor* or you will *never get another toy again!"* The child is stunned, gets up, and leaves the toy aisle— the parent is negatively reinforced (the tantrum ended!) by yelling at the child. But at the same time, this will increase the chances that the parent will yell at the child again—it worked, at least in the short term. But the child probably does not feel good, and the parent likely doesn't either (nothing like every- one in the store watching your parenting meltdown!). For some parents, these scenarios can get worse with more and more dif- ficult child behavior to manage (e.g., more and louder whining, protesting, flailing), and the parent's response to that behavior becomes increasingly inconsistent (e.g., you can have the toy; you can't have the toy) or harsh (e.g., "You will *never get another toy again!"*). This downward spiral will unfortunately continue as both the parent and the child are reinforced for their not-okay behavior. Another example of the downward spiral process is provided in Figure 2-1.

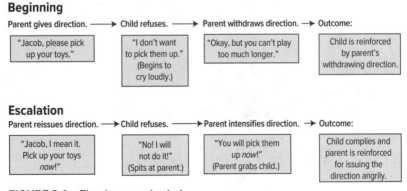

Beginning

Parent gives direction. ⟶ Child refuses. ⟶ Parent withdraws direction. → Outcome:

| "Jacob, please pick up your toys." | "I don't want to pick them up." (Begins to cry loudly.) | "Okay, but you can't play too much longer." | Child is reinforced by parent's withdrawing direction. |

Escalation

Parent reissues direction. ⟶ Child refuses. ⟶ Parent intensifies direction. → Outcome:

| "Jacob, I mean it. Pick up your toys *now!*" | "No! I will not do it!" (Spits at parent.) | "You will pick them up *now!*" (Parent grabs child.) | Child complies and parent is reinforced for issuing the direction angrily. |

FIGURE 2-1 The downward spiral

TIME TO REFLECT

- Do downward spiral examples sound familiar to you?
- When was the last time you and your child experienced a downward spiral?
- In hindsight, are there moments when you had a choice in terms of how you responded to your child and a different option may have led to a different outcome?

WHAT OTHER FACTORS SHAPE MY STRONG-WILLED CHILD'S BEHAVIOR?

Besides the positive and negative reinforcement traps (both of which increase the likelihood of downward spirals in your interactions with your strong-willed child), several other factors can shape whether your strong-willed child's behavior is a strength or more likely to be a problem. For one, parents who have children with behavior problems tend to pay less attention to their child's positive behaviors. This makes sense for a lot of reasons! You may feel sometimes like you are putting out so many fires with your child's not-okay behavior (e.g., *"No!"* to this; *"Stop!"* doing that) that you have little time, energy, or attention left over to realize that your child is likely also doing a lot of okay things as well. So think about this: Instead of focusing all your time and attention on the not-okay behaviors (e.g., "Stop yelling!"), "catching" your child doing behaviors you want to see or see more (e.g., talking in an inside voice) will actually save you time and energy in the long run. Why is that? Well, your child will begin to learn what to do instead and learn that those okay behaviors will get the most prized reward (your attention!).

It is also natural for parents of strong-willed children to start to lose confidence in the best way to manage child problem behavior. You may be worried that you will inadvertently squash the characteristics of your child that you like and that are likely quite adaptive (e.g., determination) when trying to address more problematic aspects of strong-willed behavior (e.g., noncompliance). You also may begin to lose confidence in the "right" thing to do because nothing seems to be working. In fact, a common refrain of the parents with whom we work is "[Fill in the blank] worked with my older child, but it is just not working with [child's name]." We can hear the frustration and confusion in these parents' voices. In turn, feeling like you are not managing your child's behavior well (or at all) can lead to a full spectrum of feelings in parents ranging from sadness (e.g., hopeless, helplessness) to anxiety (e.g., "Am I a bad parent?," "What if my child does this at school?") to anger (e.g., "I am the parent here!"). This lack of confidence, resulting uncertainty, and range of emotions can then lead to responding to your child's behavior in increasingly inconsistent ways. For example, parents who feel overwhelmed and question their ability to manage problem behavior may give up and do nothing. At other times the same parents may become frustrated with their child and themselves and, in turn, lose their temper, yell, or spank. If this is happening once or twice, it is not going to permanently affect a child. After all, we are all human! However, your behavior and emotions may not feel good to you and likely are not helpful to your child's behavior in the long run either.

If your child is increasingly engaging in behaviors that you think reflect less positively on their strong-willed nature,

Table 2-1 may help. It summarizes reasons that children may demonstrate increasingly more problematic aspects of their strong-willed nature.

TABLE 2-1 Some Reasons Children Become Increasingly Strong-Willed

Peers model not-okay behavior.
Parents model not-okay behavior.
Parent falls into the positive reinforcement trap.
Parent falls into the negative reinforcement trap.
Child receives little attention for okay behavior.
Parent is inconsistent in response to not-okay behavior.

Do any of the reasons in the table apply to your child? If so, which ones? Presuming you said yes to at least one of these, you are in the right place! This book has many ideas to prevent the downward spiral that we discussed and you may be experiencing with your strong-willed child. Our goal is to help you strengthen the positive aspects of your strong-willed child's behavior (the behaviors you want to nurture and maintain) while decreasing or eliminating behaviors that are problematic at home.

CHAPTER 3

PARENTS ARE STRESSED!

So far we have talked about how your child is born into the world with a predisposition to think, feel, and behave in certain ways. The good news, as we talked about in the last chapter, is that your child also has the equivalent of computer software that is receptive and malleable in response to the inputs of lots of things—including parents! Indeed, you as a parent have the power (e.g., attention, reinforcement, punishment) to nurture the aspects of your strong-willed child's temperament that you want to see or see more (e.g., determination) and decrease the likelihood of other less adaptive characteristics (e.g., noncompliance). While we talked about some general principles in the last chapter and will talk about specific skills later in the book, we also want to acknowledge here that we realize that parenting in the way that is ideally tailored to your child's temperament is easier said than done. It is hard work!

There are things that happen every single day that can make it hard to be our best selves as parents. You did not sleep well the night before and find yourself yelling "What!" when your child says "Mom" for the twentieth time in a row with seemingly no breaths in between. You have a big project due at work, find yourself distracted, and miss an opportunity to say "Good job!" when your child uses an inside voice to ask if it is okay to play outside (instead of shouting!). After saying, "No, you have not had your dinner" to your child's request for a candy bar in the grocery store checkout, you find yourself taking off the wrapper and handing over the candy because you do not have enough patience for your child to have a meltdown today. These moments may not feel like your best and brightest as a parent, but we are here to tell you that bad days here and there are not going to affect your strong-willed child's behavior permanently or detrimentally (or your relationship with your child). So cut yourself some slack and read on!

That said, there are a number of stressors you may experience that can have an impact on your parenting and, in turn, on whether you are more likely to see adaptive (e.g., determination) or maladaptive (e.g., noncompliance) aspects of your child's strong-willed nature. We would, of course, be remiss if we did not start this discussion with acknowledgment of the COVID-19 pandemic and shutdowns, which was not only a global health crisis, but an unparalleled day-to-day stressor for families at home as well. Some families had members who contracted COVID, which was a stressor in and of itself in terms of quarantining and trying to prevent spread both within and outside the home. Some of you may have had family members who were hospitalized or even died at a time when both hospital visitation and funeral arrangements were complicated by social distancing and stay-at-home orders. To have dealt with the grief of hospitalization or death under these conditions is challenging to say the least.

On top of the health aspects of COVID, some of you may have owned businesses or worked in settings that were greatly affected by the economic fallout of the pandemic (e.g., travel, hotel, restaurants). Still other parents were and may still be trying to balance work and their child's daycare or school lessons and assignments, often with the entire family at home and on screens, or trying to balance in-person work at the office or other settings with a child's schoolwork at home. To say the least, COVID likely increased your exhaustion as a parent while potentially increasing your and your child's mental health issues. It was not an easy time to be a parent!

We all hope that anything similar to the COVID pandemic will not occur at that same level or intensity again in the future, but as various surveys revealed, it did highlight and really increase stress for many parents and their young children. COVID spotlighted stressors that many parents have been dealing with for a long time and also reminds us that these stressors will impact families in different ways in the years to come.

How you handle the stresses you face is important—for both you and the parenting of your child. As a result, we devote Part IV to how you can improve your own self-care. In order to help you begin thinking about the stressors you may face, we highlight some of them that your family may (or, we hope, may not) confront (see Figure 3-1). For our purposes, we focus on how these examples of stressors can affect your parenting.

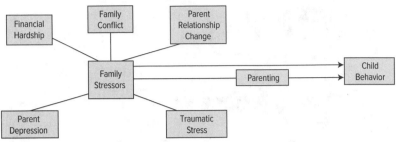

FIGURE 3-1   Family stress, parenting, and your child's behavior

FINANCIAL HARDSHIP

Many parents face financial hardship at some point. For some parents, this may be more temporary, such as unexpectedly losing a job or coping with a rise in inflation and increased costs for everything from gas to groceries. For other parents, financial hardship may be a longer-term stressor. Whether short or long term, financial hardship can impact parenting for a variety of reasons. First, parents who are having difficulties paying their bills are more likely to have jobs with shifts or irregular hours. Parents facing financial stressors may also work multiple jobs in order to pay the bills. Multiple jobs and/or shiftwork may decrease the likelihood that parents have predictable and consistent time to spend with their young children.

Parents experiencing financial strain are also more likely to feel stressed. Financial strain is a stress in and of itself, but it also compounds other stressors like finding quality childcare when you are looking for or at work, finding or maintaining reliable transportation, and making decisions about healthcare. The stress associated with finances can increase the likelihood that parents respond to their young children in a variety of ways including being more lax (e.g., "Sure, sure, have the cookie"), inconsistent (e.g., saying yes to the cookie one day and no the next for reasons that are unclear to your child), harsh (e.g., *"No! You cannot have the cookie, and if you ask again . . ."*), or even more distracted and withdrawn (e.g., not even realizing the cookies are gone until your child asks you to buy more).

FAMILY CONFLICT

Financial hardship is a common cause of arguments in families, and adults who are co-parenting (whether married or not) are no exception. There are, of course, other causes of conflict in relationships as well, including arguments about parenting and children! Children, whether adopted or biological, do not come with a rule book, and parents often do not know what kind of parents they are going to be until they are in the thick of doing it! On one hand, parents have to parent in a way that best "fits" their child's temperament (the point of this book!). On the other hand, adults who are parenting together need to find a good "fit" with each other as well, and sometimes this is hard to do. You will, of course, have at least some disagreements with the other adults in your child's life (e.g., co-parent, grandparents). The good news is that resolving disagreements in a constructive way may actually serve as an example to your strong-willed child of how to deal with conflict with other siblings, at daycare or school, or on the playground.

So what are some rules of thumb that can reduce the effects of family conflict? Try to limit disagreements in front of children, but when they do happen, try to talk in a normal tone of voice, be as respectful as possible with each other, and try to listen and understand as much as you talk and ask that your point of view be heard. If it is clear that one or more of these guidelines will be difficult (or impossible) depending on what is happening that day, or how you are feeling, or what other stressors are on your plate, try to schedule a later time and place to talk in more detail. If possible, some parents even schedule a daily or weekly check-in that is set aside for any issues that need to be discussed about parenting or other matters. One couple we know does this Fridays at 5 p.m., and they call it "Happy Hour" (to try to diffuse some of the anticipated stress a bit). They get their favorite snacks and appetizers, and they bring their lists of items to discuss. Strategies like this can prevent the stress from building up and spilling over into your relationship with your child as well.

While healthy disagreements handled appropriately can be an example for strong-willed children, day-to-day, week-to-week, and month-to-month arguing in front of your child can be harmful. First, if you are doing things like yelling, pounding your fists on the table, or stomping out of the room, you are likely modeling what you don't want your child to do when they experience conflict. You are also not teaching your child what to do instead, such as take deep breaths, listen, and reflect what you heard to make sure you understand before you give your opinion or point of view. Lots of arguing also just makes it harder to parent in a way that you feel good about because your mind is elsewhere and you are feeling angry, sad, or resentful. Perhaps it is not surprising then that high levels of conflict between parents are associated with more conflict between those parents and their children as well. Finally, if your child is watching the adults in their life argue more and get along less, they may start to feel sad and anxious, worrying about things like divorce if their parents are married.

CHANGES IN PARENTS' RELATIONSHIP STATUS

Of course, not all conflict in couples leads to separation or divorce, but relationships between parents can and do end, and many children must navigate this reality in their families. As child psychologists, we have had many parents ask us if such transitions are harmful for children. The answer—again, like so much else in life and parenting—is that it depends. That is, there is research, for example, that shows that divorce can have a negative impact on the behavior of children; however, this impact is not nearly as great as the public media often report and likely not for the reasons you may expect.

First, there is some evidence that suggests that the behavior of preschool children actually improves (rather than declines!) over the two years following divorce. How can this be true? Well, it is key to note that many of the problems children have following parental divorce are not simply a result of the separation of their parents. Instead, children's adjustment following divorce depends in large part on the situation existing after the divorce. Building upon the section above ("Family Conflict"), we can say that if parents make the decision to end their relationship because they are fighting too much but they continue to fight during and after the divorce, their child is more likely to adjust poorly. If instead co-parenting, while no longer being a couple, allows two adults to navigate conflict in general and conflict about parenting in particular more effectively, then chances are that children may do just fine. After such transitions, chances are that parents will find new partners who also are now a part of the child's life as well. As with relationships ending, the start of new relationships itself is often less important to the child than how the parents handle those new relationship with each other and with the child. Rules of thumb include trying to be clear with each other and the child about the roles that each person will play, making sure that the rules between houses are consistent (or as consistent as possible), and ensuring that regardless of how the adults are feeling, they behave respectfully to each other. And of course, reassuring children that they are loved and will be taken care of!

DEPRESSION

Although there are many causes of depression, one well-established factor that can cause depression, maintain it, or make it worse is relationship conflict. Parents who are experiencing conflict in their relationships, whether with a spouse, partner, or child, may find themselves feeling sad, irritable, withdrawn, and/or tired—all of which can be symptoms of feeling depressed.

Depression can be a clinical term or diagnosis, and some parents may see a therapist or take medication for clinical depression. Other parents may find themselves feeling sadder, feeling irritable, or just having less energy for or interest in the things they used to enjoy (including spending time with their children). Feeling depressed can be a by-product of conflict in families, but as you likely know, it can also affect other family members including children.

Let's look at some ways being depressed can affect your strong-willed child through your parenting. Parents who are feeling more down, sad, or blue are more likely to parent inconsistently or harshly. When you feel down, you may be less understanding and tolerant of your child. As a result, sometimes you may have a more extreme reaction to problem behaviors and be more negative, harsh, and critical. At other times you may withdraw and not react at all to your child's behavior. And at other times you may use guilt to deal with your strong-willed child's behavior (for example, "You make me feel so bad when you act that way!"). Once your mood improves, you may be more consistent, effectively enforcing rules and even having lots of positive interactions, but this can be confusing to your child. And as a consequence of that confusion, your strong-willed child's behavior may take a turn toward the not-okay behaviors you don't want to see (e.g., noncompliance) rather than the okay behaviors you want to nurture (e.g., compliance).

TRAUMATIC STRESS

Similar to the term "depression," the term "trauma" often is used in a clinical sense such as the diagnosis of post-traumatic stress disorder commonly given to people who have served in the military or experienced interpersonal violence. "Trauma" and "traumatic stress" can also be used more generally to refer to a very normal response to experiencing or even witnessing an abnormal or shocking event. We started this chapter talking about COVID-19, and we will circle back to it here because so many experienced (and may still be experiencing) traumatic stress as a result of it. In addition, we will touch on two other events (racial violence and mass shootings) as examples facing families today.

Many family members witnessed unprecedented levels of illness and death during a time when social distancing did not permit visiting with sick relatives or even attending or having funeral services. Healthcare providers were called to treat a highly contagious illness and early on had few effective tools at their disposal, meaning that they faced daily loss of their patients. Even for those not directly affected by a COVID diagnosis, the constant media images broadcast from inside and sometimes outside hospitals were distressing, to say the least. During the same period, the Black Lives Matter movement highlighted ongoing racial, ethnic, and economic disparities in the United States. Media coverage allows adults, as well as children, opportunities to not only hear about but see sometimes in graphic detail incidents of racially motivated violence against people who are Black or Asian, for example. Breaking news about mass shootings in schools, churches, and businesses have also become far too familiar.

As parents, it can be challenging to process our thoughts and feelings about these events, and our anxiety can spill over into how we parent and, in turn, how we help our children to navigate their own thoughts and feelings. Similar to depression, traumatic stress and anxiety can lead to more withdrawn, inconsistent, or even harsh parenting. In addition, parents may think, "I don't know how I feel, so how am I going to help my child?" Other parents may think, "Maybe talking to my child about it will *cause* more worry," so they don't say anything at all. Chances are that your child is picking up on your stress and anxiety, and their uncertainty can indeed increase their strong-willed behavior.

TIME TO REFLECT

Parents deal with many stressors. You may have experienced one or more of the stressors that we mention here. You may have experienced others as well.

- What is a stressor that you have been dealing with recently?
- How do you think that stressor may affect the way that you parent your child?
- How do you think your stress and the possible effect on your parenting may shape the way your child is behaving?

COPING WITH FAMILY STRESSORS

We have talked about multiple stressors that many parents face and the ways in which these stressors may affect parenting and in turn your child's strong-willed behavior. You may also have thought of other stressors you are experiencing now or have experienced in the past. Identifying these stressors and how they may be influencing your parenting is an important first step, and we hope that the information we present here helps you do that. That said, recognizing the problem does not necessarily mean it is easy to change it. If you are looking at our list (or your own) and thinking, "Where do I start?," take a deep breath and try to prioritize. There is a parallel that debt managers will suggest and that we have found useful—pay the smallest balance first! If you have or have ever had debt (e.g., college loan, car or house loan, credit cards) like each of us has, you may know that feeling of being similarly overwhelmed. And the tendency can be to focus on the biggest debt and try to pay that down. While not necessarily wrong, paying off big debts may mean multiple small payments and very little noticeable change in your balance, which can lead to frustration and even hopelessness ("I will never be out of debt!"). So a common suggestion is to pay the smallest debt off first, get a chance to experience that success and check it off the list, and then move on to the next smallest debt, and so on.

While not a perfect analogy (i.e., family stressors are not necessarily big or small), the idea of picking a place to start where you are most likely to make a helpful change makes sense. That is, if working two jobs with erratic shifts is leading you to feel tired, irritable, and less positive about your parenting, investing time now in finding a new job with better hours (or hours that match better with your child's or your co-parent's schedule) may pay off in more quality time with your child in the long term.

You also may need or want help dealing with family stressors. That is okay, and we encourage it. We list resources in the Appendix, including those available online and for free. Still other parents may seek the help of a professional whether that be a member of the clergy, a counselor, a psychologist, or a psychiatrist, especially if you are dealing with high levels of family conflict and/or feelings of depression or anxiety. Remember this analogy (to which we return in Part IV): When in a plane, the flight attendant tells you that in the event of a drop in air pressure, you should put your oxygen mask on first before helping your child. Similarly, you are more likely to parent effectively if you are taking good care of yourself and your relationships. Of course, we must acknowledge that there are some stressors that mental health and other professionals cannot necessarily fix (e.g., financial hardship, race-related stress). But mental health and other professionals can help you cope with those chronic stressors more effectively, which, in turn, helps you to be a better parent for your child and, in addition, model self-care skills.

TIME TO REFLECT

We have talked about many stressors facing parents. You may have thought of some of your own that we did not mention.

- What resources do you have in place to help you cope with stressors that you are facing and that may in turn affect your parenting and your child's behavior?
- What friends or family members are in place who are a dependable and helpful source of support?
- What resources in the Appendix may be useful to follow up on?
- What stressors do you think may be best helped by someone outside of your family, such as a member of the clergy or a mental health or other professional?

CHAPTER 4

DOES MY CHILD HAVE ADHD?

In Chapter 3 we talked about issues and stressors like depression and trauma facing many parents and how those can affect parenting. Parents are also likely to hear various labels for a child's behavior and wonder if they apply to their strong-willed child, including the label "attention deficit/hyperactivity disorder" (ADHD). Indeed, one of the most common questions that parents ask us is, "Does my child have ADHD?" There is certainly overlap, as many children with ADHD would also be described by their parents, teachers, and other adults as strong-willed. But many, in fact most, strong-willed children do not have ADHD.

Since early diagnosis and treatment are important for the long-term social, academic, and mental health functioning of children, this chapter aims to help parents like you to have the information you need to determine whether your child would benefit from an ADHD evaluation. You will also find resources in the Appendix at the back of the book that provide much more detailed information as well. We start with a brief history of ADHD, its potential causes and symptoms, and, most relevant to this book, the importance of early diagnosis and treatment.

While we tried to refer to children in gender-neutral language in our vignettes in particular, we do use "boy" and "girl" in this chapter. Specifically, we use these terms when talking about potential sex differences in patterns of ADHD diagnosis and symptoms. Since this research has historically relied on what is now commonly referred to as "sex assigned at birth," we do not yet necessarily know if and how it applies to gender diverse children.

IS ADHD NEW?

The increased attention to ADHD in the media may make parents think it is a new disorder. Indeed, many famous athletes, comedians, actors and musicians, journalists, and even astronauts reportedly have ADHD. While it may seem as though we hear about ADHD more today, the constellation of symptoms have been recognized in some form for over a hundred years. Historians have observed that many famous and accomplished people, including Benjamin Franklin, Thomas Edison, and Albert Einstein, had behaviors consistent with what we now call ADHD. Part of the confusion about when we began talking about ADHD may stem from the fact that it has had different labels over the years, ranging from "hyperkinesis," to "hyperactive child syndrome," to "attention deficit disorder," to "attention deficit/hyperactivity disorder" as we call it today. In part these changing labels reflect our evolving understanding of the symptoms and likely underlying causes of the disorder.

WHAT IS ADHD?

Today ADHD is considered one of the most common neurodevelopmental disorders, meaning that the symptoms are likely a function of the way a child's brain grows and develops. Like many other physical and mental conditions, ADHD and its subtypes (i.e., inattentive, hyperactive/impulsive, combined) are probably caused by multiple factors interacting with one another. One factor is likely genetics: various adoption, twin, and family studies indicate that variants in genes or regions of genes are probably a primary factor underlying a diagnosis of ADHD. This does not necessarily mean that if a parent has ADHD, a child will have ADHD as well, but it does increase the odds of a diagnosis.

Further, it is likely not just one gene that "causes" ADHD because genes can interact with one another, as well as with the environment, changing the actual odds of ADHD in any given child. Factors occurring in utero or after birth that may increase the risk of ADHD include any of the following: injury to the child's brain (e.g., lack of oxygen during delivery); maternal tobacco or alcohol use during pregnancy; exposure to toxins, such as lead, during pregnancy, infancy, or childhood; premature delivery; and/or low birthweight. Similarly, while things like too much sugar, family stress, or parenting style have not been shown to *cause* ADHD, these factors can interact with a child's genetics or other risk factors to literally affect the way a child's brain works.

What we know about ADHD is constantly evolving. For example, there is increased discussion about the link between ADHD and higher-level cognitive processes (i.e., executive functioning) that affect how well children can think ahead about, weigh the pros and cons of, and control which behavior they do (versus or do). These types of processes include working memory, or how children retain and manipulate information in their short-term memory. As an illustration of trouble with executive functioning, one parent described a bedtime routine in which telling a child to "go upstairs, brush your teeth, and get in bed" resulted in the child in bed (fully clothed!), holding a toothbrush—the child remembered the steps, but not the order!

Another executive function is inhibitory control, or how children override urges and ignore distractions. As an example of this, you may have seen videos on YouTube or TikTok of children doing the "marshmallow test" or any version of a child sitting at a table and told to wait to have the treat. Some young children can wait . . . other young children have much more difficulty waiting and may just eat the marshmallow!

Another executive function is set-shifting, or cognitive flexibility—how children update mental information to meet the demands of new or challenging tasks. For example, your child may want to wear the red shirt to school but finds out that shirt is dirty, so it cannot be worn. Some children may be able to easily move on from the red shirt and wear the blue (or yellow or striped!) shirt, whereas other children may get really stuck on the red shirt, at best feel sad or frustrated the red shirt isn't an option, and at worst refuse to wear any shirt at all!

As reflected in these examples, these executive functions, or cognitive processes, can, in turn, affect how a child feels or how they regulate emotions. As in the example above with the red shirt, one child may be able to adjust and move on, whereas another child may feel very sad or frustrated that the red shirt is not available and also have more difficulty regulating those feelings, resulting in crying or a tantrum. How children handle these cognitive processes obviously impacts how they behave. Cognitive processing is complex and difficult to grasp for many of us. However, it is an important step in helping us understand what goes on with a child who has ADHD. With this in mind, let's turn to the criteria for ADHD.

WHAT ARE THE SYMPTOMS OF ADHD?

As currently defined, ADHD is characterized by symptoms of inattention, impulsivity, and/or hyperactivity, although children do not have to have all these symptoms to be diagnosed with the disorder. That is, a child may have an ADHD subtype—primarily inattentive type, primarily hyperactive/impulsive type, or a combination, which means inattention and hyperactivity/impulsivity are both present and problematic. In order to give you a better sense of what each of these categories of symptoms—inattention, hyperactivity, and impulsivity—is referring to, we give you a snapshot of them in Table 4-1 and define and give examples of them below.

TABLE 4-1   Symptoms of ADHD

SYMPTOMS OF INATTENTION
Displays poor listening skills
Loses and/or misplaces items needed to complete activities or tasks
Is sidetracked by external or unimportant stimuli
Forgets daily activities
Has diminished attention span
Lacks ability to complete schoolwork and other assignments or to follow instructions
Avoids or is disinclined to begin homework or activities requiring concentration
Fails to focus on details and/or makes thoughtless mistakes in schoolwork or assignments
SYMPTOMS OF HYPERACTIVITY
Squirms when seated or fidgets with feet/hands
Exhibits a marked restlessness that is difficult to control
Appears to be driven by "a motor" or is often "on the go"
Lacks ability to play and engage in leisure activities in a quiet manner
Is incapable of staying seated in class
Is overly talkative
SYMPTOMS OF IMPULSIVITY
Has difficulty waiting turn
Interrupts or intrudes into conversations and activities of others
Impulsively blurts out answers before questions are completed

Adapted from *Diagnostic and Statistical Manual of Mental Disorders*, 5th edition, Text Revision (DSM-5-TR) (Washington, DC: American Psychiatric Association, 2022).

INATTENTION

Problems with inattention are sometimes difficult for parents to recognize because inattention can be most obvious in situations that occur outside the home—ones that require continued attention to activities or tasks that are at best unexciting and at worst boring. In contrast, most children, even those with ADHD, can focus or pay attention when watching television or playing computer games that are novel, intentionally engaging and, in turn, literally capture their attention! This hyperfocus or tendency for children with ADHD to focus in on a fun or interesting activity for hours on end if allowed to do so can be especially confusing and even frustrating for parents, given the disconnect with their child's seeming inability to focus on chores or schoolwork or other less interesting tasks.

Problems with inattention are often more noticeable to teachers (and sometimes coaches!) because children have to focus and maintain their attention for longer than usual on something that may not be immediately rewarding. Here you may imagine the child with pencil in hand but looking out the window instead of working on an assigned activity. Interestingly, these are precisely the types of behaviors that teachers may not easily or immediately recognize as ADHD because they do not necessarily disrupt the class. Other examples may include not paying attention to details, not being able to sustain attention long enough to complete tasks, making what seem like "careless mistakes" in their work, and being disorganized. Your child's teachers (or you!) may describe these behaviors as "absent-minded," distracted," or even "flaky." Teachers may also say things like your child "seems off track," "daydreams," or "zones out." Girls with ADHD may be more likely to present with this inattention as their primary issue and, therefore, may be more likely to be overlooked by teachers and other adults in their lives as potentially benefiting from an evaluation.

HYPERACTIVITY

Children with ADHD (hyperactive subtypes) are more active, fidgety, and restless than children of the same age and sex who do not have ADHD. Parents often report that their child with ADHD (who has a hyperactive subtype) is "always on the go," is "on fast-forward," "talks nonstop," or "just can't sit still." These children have a hard time staying in their seats, especially at places like school or home at the dinner table. When they are sitting, parents and teachers may observe that they move around in their seat, rock (tip!) their chair back and forth, kick their feet (or kick the backs of other chairs), or twirl their pencil (pen, hair, or paper) like a windmill. Although controversial (and even banned in some schools), "fidget spinners" and other variations of these toys evolved in part from marketing claims to help children with ADHD and other issues by giving them a potential outlet for their increased activity and restlessness.

Similar to impulsivity, hyperactivity can lead to children being (or being perceived to be) noncompliant (i.e., not following instructions or rules), and parents and teachers feeling as though they have to constantly repeat things such as "Stop interrupting!," "Sit still!," or "Keep your hands and feet to yourself!" As you probably noticed, some of these behaviors are the same ones displayed by strong-willed children.

IMPULSIVITY

Most children who are impulsive often do not wait for instructions to be finished before they start an activity. They tend to act before they think and, as a result, frequently do not understand what is required in a particular situation. This can lead to a child with ADHD not following rules or instructions, as well as to a number of other difficulties. In school, these children may not do well on tests, partly because they may start answering questions before they fully read the test instructions or understand the question. Children with ADHD also may blurt out answers to questions before a teacher or another person has finished asking the question. Unfortunately, because they do not wait for the entire question to be asked, their answers are more likely to be wrong.

Impulsivity can also lead to other problems. Waiting in line at school and waiting for their turn in games can be very difficult. In these and other social situations, impulsive children tend to have poor physical boundaries and may be seen as intrusive or bothersome by other children or adults. They also sometimes respond impulsively when they feel they have been treated unfairly, even when the other person did not intend any harm (for example, when someone accidentally steps on the child's foot or bumps the child in line). Finally, acting before thinking can lead them into dangerous situations (for example, running into the street to retrieve a ball or diving into shallow water).

TIME TO REFLECT

- Based on our definitions, would you describe your child as (circle all that apply):

  Inattentive   **Impulsive**   **Hyperactive**

- If yes, what are examples of each one that applies? (For example, if you circled "inattentive," you may say "always seems to be daydreaming.")

  _____

  _____

  _____

AREN'T ALL YOUNG CHILDREN INATTENTIVE, HYPERACTIVE, AND IMPULSIVE?

The answer is yes. Indeed, most young children have some level of inattention, impulsivity, and hyperactivity. That is a characteristic of a young child, so perhaps it is not surprising that approximately half of preschool-aged children are considered at some time by their parents to be inattentive or overactive! Yet most young children *do not* have ADHD. Estimates vary, given the evolution of how we think about the disorder and how it is measured, but current estimates suggest that ADHD affects approximately 5 percent of children worldwide. This is common enough that you probably know a child with ADHD—one of your friend's children, a child in your child's class, or perhaps your child has been diagnosed—but this still means that most (95 percent) young children do not have ADHD.

Boys are more likely to be diagnosed with ADHD than girls. Girls' symptoms often look different than our stereotyped sense of the hyperactive child with ADHD. Notably, girls seem more likely than boys to present with inattention (more than impulsivity or hyperactivity), and even when they are also impulsive or hyperactive, it tends to be less severe than boys. In turn, ADHD has been called a "hidden disorder" among girls, too often going unnoticed or misdiagnosed, leading to frustration among parents and teachers when girls with ADHD seemingly fail to meet their potential. Such frustration and criticism can affect the self-esteem of girls, who may begin to think that their difficulties are reflective of their intelligence or ability rather than a function of ADHD.

There are also mixed data on whether the likelihood of an ADHD diagnosis varies by the race or ethnicity of a child, but one thing is clear: Children from communities of color tend to be diagnosed with or treated for ADHD later (or not at all) compared with white children. There are a number of potential explanations for this, including systematic inequalities that increase the likelihood that communities of color experience socioeconomic disadvantage. In turn, these children are likely to have fewer resources, such as psychologists in the schools and communities, to lead to an evaluation and treatment. There is some research on bias as well suggesting that teachers (and other professionals, including those in mental health) may be more likely to perceive or interpret a Black or Hispanic child's inattention, impulsivity, or hyperactivity as willful, oppositional, or defiant rather than a symptom of an underlying disorder like ADHD. In turn, children of color may be more likely to be disciplined rather than referred for treatment or recommended for educational services, which is an issue, given the importance of early diagnosis and treatment for long-term educational outcomes and overall health and well-being.

With this information about symptoms, sex, and race/ethnicity in mind, you may be wondering, how do you know whether your child has ADHD or not? This is a good question, and there are a few things that set children with ADHD apart from other children. For one, many children have only one or two of the behaviors associated with ADHD, rather than a persistent pattern of numerous behaviors that is necessary for diagnosis. When there are only one or two behaviors of concern, preschool-aged children often will grow out of them. That is, we know that as most children get older, their attention span improves, they become less impulsive, and they show less overactivity. For example, research studies indicate that the vast majority of concerns about the inattentiveness or overactivity of three- to four-year-olds decreases over the course of six months without professional help.

On the other hand, some young children do have the persistent pattern of behaviors required for the diagnosis of ADHD. In fact, many parents of children diagnosed with ADHD later in childhood state that they first became concerned about their child's behavior when the child was three or four years old. In addition, lots of young children have symptoms of inattention, impulsivity, or hyperactivity in just one setting (e.g., home), but children diagnosed with ADHD have those symptoms in at least two settings (e.g., home and school). Finally, the behaviors must occur frequently, be clearly outside the typical range for children at a particular developmental level, *and* be severe enough to cause impairments in areas such as social interactions (e.g., difficulties making or keeping friends) or school (e.g., difficulty focusing, problem behavior, underachievement) functioning. Given that it can be hard for parents to be objective about how "typical" a child's behavior may be, as well as whether or not it is causing problems for them, a professional evaluation is critical if you have suspicions that your child may have ADHD.

TIME TO REFLECT

If your child is displaying inattention, impulsivity, or hyperactivity:

- Does it seem to be more frequent or severe compared with other children their age?
- Is it happening in more than one setting (e.g., home, daycare, school)?
- Is it causing problems (e.g., with peers, siblings, teachers)?

HOW IS ADHD DIAGNOSED AND TREATED?

Severe cases of ADHD are relatively easy to diagnose, especially with older children. Most cases in preschool-aged children, however, as well as mild cases in older children, are much more difficult to assess accurately. The line between a diagnosable disorder and the upper limit of typical behavior can be quite murky in this age range for all the reasons we talked about earlier. Moreover, we used to believe that most children outgrew ADHD, and some do, but many young children with ADHD will continue to have symptoms in adolescence and adulthood. As children with ADHD age, they are less likely to have some symptoms like hyperactivity, but other symptoms such as inattention are more likely to persist with age. Even when symptoms do improve with age, those with ADHD can still have significant academic and social problems into adolescence, and many can have continued symptoms and associated occupational and social difficulties in adulthood. If you have a child with ADHD or suspect your child has ADHD, we understand that these statistics may be difficult to read—we are not trying to alarm you! Rather, as we said earlier and will say again here—early diagnosis and treatment are key!

If you decide to pursue a professional evaluation, it is important to know that there is no definitive test for ADHD. Also, professionals vary widely in how comprehensively they assess a child. Your first step should be to have your child examined by a pediatrician to rule out other problems, such as visual or hearing difficulties that may be leading to inattention or other problem behavior. In addition, although very rare, symptoms of chronic physical problems, such as thyroid difficulties, can sometimes mimic the symptoms of ADHD. Once such problems have been ruled out, the next step is to have a professional with expertise in assessing children with ADHD evaluate your child. This might be a psychologist, psychiatrist, pediatrician, or other professional who is trained in the diagnosis and treatment of ADHD in particular.

A comprehensive ADHD evaluation typically involves the trained professional collecting information from you (and any other parents or caregivers), teachers, and, depending on age, your child. Tools that are typically used to assess for ADHD include questions about the onset, frequency, and severity of symptoms, as well as paper-and-pencil (or electronic) surveys about the child's behavior and other aspects of your child's day-to-day functioning (e.g., peers, school performance), physical activities (e.g., ballet, soccer), and even more mundane everyday happenings (e.g., riding in the car, behaving in a preschool setting). Often an evaluator will want to observe your child not only at their office but in settings in which your child is engaging in one or more of the daily activities just delineated (e.g., at preschool). A comprehensive evaluation such as this, in contrast to a brief screening, is important to definitively rule a diagnosis of ADHD in or out.

If your child receives (or already has received) a diagnosis of ADHD, there is unlikely to be a "cure"—meaning that if before treatment your child meets criteria for an ADHD diagnosis, then after treatment they will likely still meet criteria. Given the strong genetic component, as well as the likely interaction between genes and other experiential and environmental factors, a true "cure" for ADHD is challenging and unlikely with our current treatment options. That said, we do have treatments at our disposal that can help to reduce ADHD symptoms and help parents to help young children effectively manage the disorder until they are old enough to begin to manage it more effectively themselves.

The good news is that this book will begin to teach you skills that professionals also use to help families of children with ADHD. That is, current recommendations suggest that a course of Behavioral Parent Training (also called "Behavioral Parenting Interventions," "Parent Management Training") should be tried with young children before medication management is considered or in combination with medication management. While medication is often the treatment used with many children with ADHD, we highly recommend it follow or be used in combination with you changing your behavior with your child—the very thing the principles in this book can help you do.

We will not go into too much detail here, as Part II of this book will focus on the types of skills that parents of young children learn in programs for families of children with ADHD and related problem behavior. Essentially, parents are taught some of the principles you learned in Chapters 1, 2, and 3 regarding how to increase attention to behaviors they want to see or see more (okay behaviors) and decrease attention to or use other effective consequences in response to behaviors they want to see less or not at all (not-okay behaviors). They are also taught how to use the skills to target symptoms of ADHD in particular. As we talk about in Part II, these skills work best when parents use them consistently, but also when all adult caregivers in the child's life use them as well. So programs for young children with ADHD also typically try to include other adults like teachers who can use the skills in the other settings and encourage communication and consistency between the adults in those settings. As children age, these types of treatments can increasingly focus on them learning skills to manage their own behavior as well, but continued parent and teacher involvement and support remain critical as well. Beyond skill use, your child's ADHD diagnosis may also mean that they have the opportunity to receive accommodations at school (e.g., extra time for assignments, tailored instructions, breaks to move around) through an *individualized education plan* (IEP) to optimize their ability to focus, regulate their behavior, and learn.

WHAT ARE MY NEXT STEPS?

If after reading this chapter you are feeling fairly confident that you have a strong-willed child, but your child is unlikely to have ADHD, then continue to Part II, where you will begin to learn specific skills to manage your child's strong-willed behavior. If this chapter sparked or increased your suspicions that your child may have ADHD, we recommend that you schedule an assessment with a trained professional. In the meantime, you should also continue with this book, as the skills can be helpful. In addition, see the resources, particularly the various websites and Russell Barkley's book for parents of children with ADHD, included at the end of this book in the Appendix. (For professionals, we recommend the book by Andrea Chronis-Tuscano, Kelly O'Brien, and Christina Danko, *Supporting Caregivers of Children with ADHD*.)

One caveat before you continue. If you are a parent of a child with ADHD or you suspect your child's has ADHD, you may also have ADHD yourself. As we noted earlier, the odds are not perfect, but there is a genetic link, and ADHD can persist into adulthood. This means that as a parent, you may be dealing with some of the same symptoms we discuss in this chapter—for example, higher levels of inattention. You may also be navigating some of the cognitive characteristics underlying ADHD (i.e., compromised or delayed executive functioning) that we talked about above that can make the day-to-day tasks of being a parent (e.g., planning, organizing) more challenging. If you also have a child whose behaviors can be challenging, as a function of being strong-willed and/or having ADHD, these tasks can even be more difficult, and the challenges may make you feel more emotional yourself (e.g., quick temper). On one hand, having ADHD yourself may give you more empathy and understanding for your child's experience. On the other hand, if you are also managing the stressors we discussed in Chapter 3, parenting can be stressful, and any additional stressors can make it even more so. We will do our best throughout Part II to be mindful of these realities that parents face and help you to use the skills in a way that honors your strengths and challenges as a parent and helps you find a way to use the skills with your child in the most effective way possible.

ADDRESSING STRONG-WILLED BEHAVIOR

A Five-Week Program

At this point, you should better understand the various factors that contribute to your strong-willed child's behavior. This understanding can help you appreciate the next step in our strategy discussed in Part II: learning parenting techniques to address problems associated with your child's strong-willed behavior. In Chapter 5 we help you to further crystallize which behaviors you consider okay behaviors or behaviors you want to see or see more and which behaviors you consider not-okay or behaviors you want to see less or not at all. Then in the subsequent chapters, we detail our five-week program that teaches parents the skills they need to achieve those goals.

Each chapter discusses a specific skill, which you will practice for one week before progressing to the next skill. As the skills build upon one another, we want you to understand the rationale for the skill and practice it before learning and practicing a new skill. The skills you will be learning are Attending (Chapter 6), Rewarding (Chapter 7), "Effortful" Ignoring (Chapter 8), Giving Clear Instructions (Chapter 9), and Using Time-Outs for Noncompliance (Chapter 10). Each of these skills has been shown in our research and research conducted by others to be important for improving the behavior of strong-willed children. However, as we discuss in Chapter 11, it is the integration of these skills that leads to maximum effectiveness in changing your child's behavior.

CHAPTER 5

WHAT BEHAVIORS DO I WANT TO INCREASE (AND DECREASE)?

If you are still reading this book, then chances are you have decided that at least some aspects of your child's behavior need to change. On one hand, you want to honor their temperament or hardwiring and allow them to be who they are meant to be in this world. As we have said before, being strong-willed may mean that they are also *assertive, confident,* and/or *persistent.* Such characteristics may result in lots of okay behaviors you want to reinforce in your child, including being brave in new situations, social on the playground, and willing to raise their hand in class. These are all things that will likely serve your child well now and in the future! Yet having a strong-willed child may also mean that they have other characteristics like those we have mentioned earlier, including being *argumentative*, *headstrong*, *stubborn*, *temperamental*, or *unpredictable*. In turn, your child may be more reactive, less adaptable, and more emotional, resulting in at least some not-okay behaviors you want to see less or not at all. Common not-okay behaviors that lead parents to pick up this book are listed below. Feel free to put a check next to any behaviors that describe your child.

Common Not-Okay Behaviors Identified by Parents of Strong-Willed Children

- ❏ Is aggressive
- ❏ Argues
- ❏ Seeks attention
- ❏ Blames others
- ❏ Breaks rules
- ❏ Curses
- ❏ Is demanding
- ❏ Disobeys
- ❏ Is destructive
- ❏ Is emotional
- ❏ Fights
- ❏ Is irritable
- ❏ Lies
- ❏ Is oppositional
- ❏ Provokes or threatens others
- ❏ Is sassy
- ❏ Screams
- ❏ Is stubborn
- ❏ Has tantrums
- ❏ Tests limits

These are just some examples, and you also may be thinking of others. That is fine, as we will ask you to get much more specific in the sections that follow.

WHAT ARE YOUR CHILD'S NOT-OKAY BEHAVIORS?

The key as you launch into Part II and the new skills that you will learn is to begin to decide a bit more clearly which behaviors you consider to be okay and those that are not okay. Let's start with the not-okay behaviors, because depending on how frustrated you are with your child's behavior, these can sometimes be easier for parents of strong-willed children to enumerate, especially at the start of this program. Indeed, some parents reading this book may already have a list of the behaviors they consider to be not okay. In this case, we believe it would be helpful at this stage of the book to pick just two or three behaviors with which to start (e.g., not doing what you say the first time, having tantrums, whining). As with anything else you do, tackling your child's not-okay behaviors in small steps is important—we are not going to reduce all the not-okay behaviors at once! In addition to our list above, one way to generate (or narrow) your list is to consider, "Do I think my child is doing [insert behavior] more than other children?" A classic example is biting. It is not unusual for very young children to bite—they are trying out their new teeth, may be playing, or just may not have a lot of other coping strategies to deal with anger or frustration. That said, if an older child is still using biting as their "go-to" when unhappy or frustrated, then their behavior likely looks different than that of other children their age.

TIME TO REFLECT

List three not-okay behaviors that your child does more than other children the same age:

- _____

- _____

- _____

In addition to comparing your child's behavior with other children's to determine what may or may not be typical, another way to identify the not-okay behavior you want to work on initially in this program is to consider, "Is [insert behavior] causing a problem?" A problem could mean, for example, that the behavior is getting in the way of learning at preschool/school, or it could be causing stress and frustration to other adults (e.g., caregivers, teachers) around your child, or it could be affecting your child's peer relationships.

TIME TO REFLECT

Are any of the not-okay behaviors you listed above (or other not-okay behaviors you are thinking about now) a problem for your child, you, or others in your child's life? List these behaviors:

- _____

- _____

- _____

For some parents, a child's not-okay behavior may feel like it is a problem more often than not. In these cases, parents may say, "Every time I ask my child to do something, it feels like a struggle that ends with my child crying and me giving in and just doing it myself." In other cases, parents may notice that the not-okay behaviors occur in some situations more (or much more) than others. For example, many parents talk about transitions (e.g., from the house to the car, between home and school) being a particularly challenging time when the child is more likely to whine, protest, or disobey entirely. Other parents may notice the not-okay behavior is worse at particular times of day (e.g., "telling my child to get dressed before school") or under particular circumstances (e.g., child is tired or hungry).

TIME TO REFLECT

How often do the not-okay behaviors you listed above (or other not-okay behaviors you are thinking about now) happen, and are they more likely in certain situations or certain times of day?

Not-Okay Behavior	How Often?	Situation or Times of Day
_____	_____	_____
_____	_____	_____

Now one caveat to the question about whether the behavior is a "problem" sometimes or all the time is that some parents will tell us about a behavior (e.g., tantrums, noncompliance), but then tell us the behavior is not a problem. This is interesting, and what we have learned when we dig a little bit deeper is that the behavior is not a problem because the parents have likely made significant changes to their lives to manage or avoid the behavior altogether. So, for example, a parent may tell us that tantrums and noncompliance are no longer a problem because they don't tell the child to do things that they know are going to be upsetting. Some parents even change their own day-to-day lives and routines. For example, they may change their work schedules, if and when they go to the grocery store or run other errands, and if and how much they see their own friends and extended family as they try to accommodate their child's not-okay behavior. So the question here is if the behavior is not causing a problem, is that because you made adjustments to manage or avoid the behavior?

TIME TO REFLECT

Are there any other not-okay behaviors that used to be a problem but you avoid or manage by significantly changing your family's day-to-day routine and schedule? If so, list them:

- _____

- _____

- _____

At this point you have a list (or lists!) of not-okay behaviors. Are there one or more behaviors that are showing up on multiple lists? For example, are there behaviors that you suspect are atypical for your child's age and are causing problems either throughout the day or in some situations more than others? For now, let's put those behaviors at the top of your list for this next exercise. That is, in this exercise we want you to be as specific as possible about a not-okay behavior by defining it in very concrete terms so you know it when you see it (and can explain it to your child when you start responding to it differently!). So, for example, if one of the items on your list is "emotional," there is likely nothing necessarily problematic about your child having emotions. In fact, we want children to have and increasingly be able to recognize and identify their own emotions. What is likely more of a problem for you or the child's teachers, siblings, or playmates is how your child displays those emotions. So here you may say instead something like "My child is quick-tempered. When they don't get their way, my child starts yelling, stomping, and kicking, and refusing to do what I have asked." Okay, this is great because now we have some specific behaviors that include yelling, kicking, and noncompliance. With this in mind, let's revisit your top three not-okay behaviors you listed above to see if you can make them more specific.

TIME TO REFLECT

Revisit and refine your top three not-okay behaviors to make them as specific as possible:

- _____
- _____
- _____

Now that you have a working list of the not-okay behaviors you are concerned about, let's think about your child's okay behaviors or behaviors you want to see or see more.

WHAT ARE YOUR CHILD'S OKAY BEHAVIORS?

Starting with not-okay behaviors as we did in this chapter is helpful, because as we say above, these behaviors are often the ones at the front of parents' minds—this is why you are likely reading the book! But starting with not-okay behaviors is also helpful in another way, as it allows you to think about what you want to see instead—i.e., okay behaviors! (See Table 5-1.) As you will learn soon in Chapter 6, one way to decrease not-okay behaviors, which usually get lots of your attention, is to give attention to the opposite, or okay, behaviors you want to see instead! Let's see how we would do this with our list from the example above that included yelling, kicking, and noncompliance.

For example, the opposite of yelling is talking in an inside voice. So you may start Chapter 6 thinking, "I want to decrease how much my child is yelling, and I want to increase how much my child is talking in an inside voice." Similarly, the opposite of kicking may be "keeping feet to yourself," or "keeping feet on the floor," or "gentle feet." Finally, the opposite of noncompliance may be "doing what I ask the first time."

TABLE 5-1   Not-Okay Behaviors and Their Opposite Okay Behaviors

NOT-OKAY BEHAVIOR	OKAY BEHAVIOR
Yelling	Talking in an inside voice
Kicking	Keeping feet to yourself
Noncompliance	Doing what you say the first time
Hitting or pinching	Using your gentle hands
Knocking toys off the table	Keeping toys on the table
Grabbing blocks from sibling	Sharing blocks with siblings

Perhaps it is becoming clear to you: One way to decrease behavior of your child you think is not okay or problematic is to increase a behavior you wish to see more (an okay behavior). In other words, rather than thinking about your child's problematic behavior, begin thinking about their positive behavior that does not occur often enough.

Your turn! What are the opposites of the not-okay behaviors that you have on your list above (i.e., your okay behaviors)?

TIME TO REFLECT

List each of your not-okay behaviors from above. Then try to find the opposite of those behaviors or what you want to see instead.

Not-Okay Behavior   **Okay Behavior**

_____   _____

_____   _____

_____   _____

DECREASING NONCOMPLIANCE (AND INCREASING COMPLIANCE!)

As reflected in our example above, one common not-okay behavior that parents identify is noncompliance. Strong-willed children often want to do things their own way and in their own time, which is not necessarily correlated with following their parents' directions immediately or the first time. That said, it is sometimes hard for parents to know whether their child is more noncompliant than other children their age because again some degree of noncompliance is normal in young children—testing limits is a part of their growth and development.

So if you want a more definitive answer regarding whether your child's noncompliance may be a "problem," we encourage you to set aside some time, gather a few toys, and spend some time alone playing with your child. We are borrowing this activity from Mark Roberts, professor emeritus at Idaho State University, who has developed a standard set of 30 instructions, called the "Compliance Test," that parents can use to examine how compliant their child is. We will only ask you to do 10 of those instructions, because having children do more without a professional on hand to assist you can lead to your child (and you!) feeling distressed. Moreover, the first 10, described in Table 5-2, should be sufficient for our purposes. You will tell your child that you want them to do some things for you. Lay out the toys (or a similar range of toys) described in Table 5-2; then issue the instructions exactly as they are presented. Do not say or do anything else! This may be difficult and feel uncomfortable, as you probably are used to giving your child reasons for why you are telling them to do things. However, by only giving instructions, you will have a clear picture of how your child responds to your directions.

TABLE 5-2 Compliance Test Instructions

Toys needed (or a similar variation based on what your child has at home): cat, bear, dog, frog, box, two cars, dump truck, rabbit, person, two blocks
1. Put the cat in the box.
2. Put the bear in the box.
3. Put the frog in the box.
4. Put the dog in the box.
5. Put the rabbit in the box.
6. Put this block in the truck.
7. Put this car in the truck.
8. Put the person in the truck.
9. Put this block in the truck.
10. Put this cat in the truck.

Source: Adapted Mark W. Roberts, professor of psychology emeritus, Idaho State University. Reprinted with permission.

For each instruction, record whether or not your child complies within five seconds; then issue the next instruction. Continue until you have issued all 10 instructions. You probably will observe several things as you issue the instructions. First, your child may comply less often as you issue more instructions. This is common, so don't be surprised. Second, very few children comply with all the instructions. Therefore, you should not expect perfect compliance; it is neither realistic nor desirable.

How do you know if your child has a problem with compliance? If your child complies less than 60 percent of the time (six of the ten instructions), you have some evidence that the level of noncompliance is atypical or potentially problematic. However, you should consider other factors as well. For example, does your child talk back to you ("You can't make me do it"), become aggressive (e.g., throw the toys), or sulk (e.g., cross arms and pout)? All these behaviors, as well as your child's actual compliance, should provide you with valuable information about your child's behavior and the extent to which your child is strong-willed. Not surprisingly, parents whose children score low on the Compliance Test have reports such as the following about their child's routine behavior. For this example, we circle back to Ms. Williams and Mr. Gonzalez, whom you met in Chapter 1:

"It's so frustrating!" Ms. Williams says. "I can't get Jacob to bed at night, and then it is challenging in the morning. I tell Jacob to get up, I pull back the covers, I keep going back into the bedroom, but nothing seems to work. I finally sit Jacob up in bed and put clothes on through lots of screaming and pouting. By then we are both in a bad mood, and it is so late that breakfast is equally frustrating and rushed. Who would have ever thought that we would start out almost every day this way!"

And Mr. Gonzalez says: "Emily never wants to take a bath, but won't get out once in! As soon as I say that it's time for a bath, Emily screams and runs. If I can get Emily in the water, there is lots of laughter and playing with toys. But then as soon as I tell Emily bathtime is over, it starts all over again! Sometimes I actually have to take Emily out of the tub while being kicked and hit—try to dry off and dress an irritable and crying child!"

So why is noncompliance such a common not-okay behavior identified by parents of strong-willed children? Well, several clinical researchers have suggested that noncompliance is actually a cornerstone of behavior problems for young children.

What does this mean? First, noncompliance is the most frequently occurring behavior problem among young children. Second, and perhaps even more important, noncompliance is the problem behavior that sets the stage for other problem behaviors. That is, if noncompliance is not a problem early on, a child is unlikely to engage in behaviors that may be problems in the preschool years or even later on. These other problem behaviors, which may include things like aggression, lying, and rule breaking, build upon the original behavior of noncompliance. Thus, it is important to determine if noncompliance is a primary not-okay behavior of your child—which is likely among strong-willed children whose parent(s) purchased this book.

Let's return to the situations you listed above in which you are more likely to see not-okay behavior. Is your child noncompliant in some or most of these situations? For example, does your child fail to comply when you say "Go to bed," "Come to the dinner table," or "Get out of the bathtub"? Each of these situations represents a time when you are trying to have your child comply with instructions. In addition, how did your child do on the Compliance Test (Table 5-2). For example, was your child compliant less than 60 percent of the time? Or did your child comply but do it while arguing, screaming, or even becoming aggressive? As you probably are beginning to see, all the information about your child's behavior that you've gathered from the observations and exercises in this chapter fits together to suggest that your child may indeed be strong-willed and that is why you are here. In the next section, we introduce you to the five-week program that will help you start to turn not-okay behaviors like noncompliance into okay behaviors that you want to see or see more (compliance!).

INTRODUCTION TO OUR FIVE-WEEK PROGRAM

Our five-week program for addressing strong-willed behavior consists of five parenting skills to be learned, one skill at a time. The skills build on one another, so it is important to master the first skill before moving to the next. Mastering a skill involves more than simply understanding the skill and knowing what to do; you must actually use the skill on a daily basis with your child. That is why you learn only one skill per week. Believe it or not, it takes at least a week to master a new parenting skill and make it part of your daily routine!

Thus, in each week of our five-week program, you will be introduced to a skill and then practice that skill daily over the course of a week. Once you have mastered the skill, which should require a week but could well take longer (so don't get discouraged!), you move on to the next skill. However, you do *not* move on until you have mastered the skill. This is the strength of the program—it involves actual behavior change on the part of you and your child. So you should practice each skill repeatedly until it is part of your everyday routine with your child.

It is far more effective if all the adults involved in daily child-rearing undertake our five-week program. This may involve biological or adoptive parents in two-parent homes or extended family (e.g., stepparents, grandparents) and other caregivers (e.g., babysitters) depending on family structures and routines. By doing this program together, you can expect greater improvement in your child's behavior as well as improved relationships among all family members. Furthermore, if more than one adult participates in families where multiple adults are involved in daily child-rearing, you can practice skills privately with each other before you try them with your child. One parent or another caregiver can play the role of the child, and the other parent can play the role of the parent. One adult practices the skills, and then the roles are reversed. This might be uncomfortable at first, but it can help you learn the skill so that you use it consistently and effectively with your child. Okay, let's get started!

CHAPTER 6

WEEK 1: ATTENDING

The first skill in our five-week parenting program is *Attending,* which is an ongoing running commentary of your child's behavior during playtime, as well as intermittently throughout the day. An example we often give parents is to think about a play-by-play sportscaster telling you what is happening during a sporting event or match. Even if you are listening to the game on the radio or doing other things while the game is on the screen in the background, you can likely imagine what is happening based on what is being said. Let's use football as an example. During a game you may hear something like this: "[Your favorite player's name] intercepted the ball . . . he made a break . . . he is at the 30-yard line . . . the 20-yard line . . . [your favorite player's name] scored . . . touchdown!" Even with this minimal description, you can likely see in your mind's eye what is happening on our imaginary field. Now for those who don't follow sports, you can also think of a narrator of a book who is describing to you what each character is doing. So what does this look like when parents do a running commentary of their child's play? That is a good question, and here are some examples of parents using Attending during play:

- "You are putting the red block on the blue block!"
- "You are turning the truck around in a circle!"
- "You are coloring the sky in your picture blue!"

In those examples, Attending is being used to simply describe the child's play. Attending can also be used during playtime to give positive attention to those okay behaviors you listed in the last chapter (or other behaviors that you have thought about since then) that you want to see or see more. By giving positive attention to behaviors you want to increase (okay behaviors), you automatically decrease behaviors that are not okay. For example, if aggression is a behavior that you are trying to decrease, you can use Attending to give positive attention to all the ways in which your child is doing the *opposite* of being aggressive:

- If your child is likely to throw toys, which is an example of a not-okay behavior, you can find opportunities to say, "You are keeping all the blocks on the table!"
- If your child is prone to playing roughly with or breaking toys, you can seek out opportunities to say, "You are playing gently with the toys!"
- If one of your child's not-okay behaviors is hitting or getting too rough with you, siblings, or peers during play or at other times, you can look for opportunities to say something like "You are using your gentle hands while we are playing!"

Attending can be used *not only* during play *but* throughout the day to give positive attention to those okay behaviors or the behaviors you want to see or see more:

- If "yelling" or "screeching" is on your list of not-okay behaviors, then you can look for opportunities during play and throughout the day to say things like "You are talking in your inside voice!"
- If one of the not-okay behaviors you identified is "impulsive," you can look for opportunities to say things such as "You are waiting patiently!"
- And if noncompliance is an issue like it is for so many parents of strong-willed children, you can look for chances to use Attending when your child does what you asked the first time: "You are brushing your teeth the first time I asked!"

TIME TO REFLECT

Refer to your list of not-okay and okay behaviors in Chapter 5. Also feel free to add any new ones that you have thought about since working on that list. Pick one to practice here. First you will list the not-okay behavior, then the opposite, or what you want to see instead (okay behavior), and then a description of or running commentary on that okay behavior (just like we did above!).

- What is the not-okay behavior?

  _____

- What is the opposite, that is, the okay behavior?

  _____

- What is an Attending statement you could use with that okay behavior?

_____

ATTENDING SEEMS SILLY—SO HOW CAN IT POSSIBLY HELP?

That is a great question and one we often get from parents. As we have talked about in the chapters leading up to this program, young children like your own child are highly motivated by parental attention. So if they do a not-okay behavior and it gets lots of attention from you or other adults (even if it is negative attention like you correcting or yelling at them), they are more likely to do that not-okay behavior again (i.e., they are not trying to upset you; they have simply learned the behavior works to get what they want the most—your attention!).

One way that Attending works is that it gives you a relatively simple tool (a running commentary) to quickly increase the dose of positive attention your child is receiving for okay behavior during play and throughout the day. One thing we remind parents is that there are only 24 hours in the day. So if we can use skills like Attending to increase the likelihood your child is getting positive attention for behaviors you want to see or see more, then there is simply less time in the day for them to do the not-okay behavior!

In addition to that very practical reason, Attending also starts to teach your child through experience what behaviors will earn them positive (rather than negative) attention. So, for example, if your child typically gets lots of negative attention for yelling in the house (e.g., "Stop yelling!") and now they get lots of positive attention for the opposite of yelling (e.g., "You are talking in your inside voice!"), then the scales should start to tip toward more and more okay behavior (e.g., talking in an inside voice).

Starting with Attending also helps more generally with the relationship that you and your child have with each other. That is, often by the time parents pick up a book like this, they are frustrated with their child and their child's behavior. Some parents even tell us that they love their child but are not liking them or enjoying their company very much, which feels awful as a parent. We understand, and as we have said earlier, there are lots of potential advantages of being strong-willed, but these children can also do many things that create challenges for themselves and others, including you!

We recognize that Attending may feel silly at first because it is not the typical way that parents talk to and interact with their young children. But it can help you to "recalculate" a bit (to borrow the commonly used GPS term) by creating opportunities and spaces to give your child positive attention for the behaviors you want to see and see more. In reality, they are likely doing some of those okay behaviors at least some of the time, but we adults are just less likely to notice and give those okay behaviors attention! It is also often not lost on strong willed children that adults can get frustrated with them—this does not feel good to you or them and can even be really confusing to young children. Remember, they are primarily motivated by *your* attention whether it is negative or positive. Focusing on your child's okay behaviors can reduce frustration and help you begin to enjoy your time with your child.

By building upon these even subtle initial changes in your parent-child relationship by using Attending, you can then learn the remaining skills more effectively, and your child's behavior will improve more quickly and to a greater extent. So that is the rationale for Attending, a skill that we hope you will try to learn and use with your child. That said, we understand that it will still feel silly, as many parents tell us Attending is the most difficult skill to learn. Even if they understand why we are asking them to do it, parents tell us that Attending feels "awkward," "unnatural," or "weird," as it is not the way that parents usually talk to their children. We get it—it will be awkward at first because it is new and different—but typically what happens is that parents start to see and feel even small positive changes in their interactions with their children fairly quickly, and they are motivated to keep practicing ("Fake it till you make it" applies here!). And research summarized across many studies on teaching effective parenting skills indicates that positive attention skills like Attending are critical ones for increasing okay behavior in all children, which is why you picked up this book!

TRY TO AVOID SO MANY QUESTIONS AND INSTRUCTIONS

Okay, you are still reading, which means you are willing to trust us that even though Attending may feel silly at first, it is important! Now how do you do it well? In our examples above, you will notice that the parents are simply describing the child's behavior—they are not asking questions or giving instructions. There is nothing inherently wrong with asking your child questions or giving them instructions. In fact, there are lots of scenarios in which doing so is quite appropriate. That said, parents of strong-willed children are more likely to use a lot of questions and instructions (e.g., "Why don't you do it this way?," "Do this!," "Don't do that!," "Are you sure that is a good idea?"). In turn, strong-willed children hear a lot of questions and corrective feedback from parents and other adults in their lives and can actually start to tune it out. At times, it can be hard to tell whether a strong-willed child is being noncompliant or has just zoned out and hasn't even heard the instruction or question! The instructions and questions can literally become background noise to them, but instead of backing off, parents of strong-willed children tend to respond by asking even more questions and giving even more instructions. It is almost as if parents of these children think, "If I ask my child to do something five times, maybe they will eventually do it." Moreover, as the parents get more and more frustrated, they give the child less and less time to respond, further increasing (rather than decreasing) the likelihood their child will be noncompliant. And so a vicious pattern is created and maintained. (Does this sound to you like the downward spiral in Chapter 2? It should!) Let's look at this example:

> As we have shared, Ms. Williams is frustrated by her four-year-old Jacob's behavior. She feels like she is constantly redirecting Jacob who rarely seems to pay attention or follow through. Let's see how this translates to the way they are spending time together during play:
>
> **MS. WILLIAMS:** Are you ready to play? (Question)
>
> **JACOB:** Yes!
>
> **MS. WILLIAMS:** What do you want to play? (Question)
>
> **JACOB:** Hmmmm. I could get my blocks. Or the puzzle! Or . . .
>
> **MS. WILLIAMS:** Well, we don't have long. You'd better decide quickly. (Instruction)

JACOB: Let's play blocks!

MS. WILLIAMS: Are you sure you want to play with the blocks? (Question) The last time we did that I ended up having to pick them all up. Remember (Instruction), you got mad because what you were building didn't look the way you wanted it to look.

JACOB: I will pick them up this time.

MS. WILLIAMS: Okay, what are you going to make? (Question)

JACOB: I am going to make a castle and a moat! I will use the brown blocks for the moat. I will build the moat first.

MS. WILLIAMS: That is what you did the last time, and it didn't work the way you wanted. Shouldn't you build the castle first, then the moat around it? (Question)

JACOB: No! I want to build the moat first!

MS. WILLIAMS: I think you should build the castle first. (Instruction)

JACOB: I want to do the moat first! [Bangs the blocks on the table]

MS. WILLIAMS: Stop banging your blocks on the table. (Instruction)

JACOB: I don't want to play with you! [Stomps away]

As a parent of a strong-willed child, you may be on the edge of your seat knowing where this interaction is headed. You have seen it hundreds of times before. You sit down to do something as simple as play with your child, and it ends up not feeling fun to either of you.

And perhaps you can start to see in this example how some of the ways that you may have learned to try to manage your child's strong-willed behavior (by questions and instructions) are no longer working the way you want them to (and perhaps even making things worse).

So let's look at an alternative scenario. Same parent, Ms. Williams, and her child, Jacob, but in this case what is different?

MS. WILLIAMS: You are ready to play! (Attending)

JACOB: Yes!

MS. WILLIAMS: You are bringing your blocks and a puzzle to the table to play with me! (Attending)

JACOB: Let's start with the blocks!

MS. WILLIAMS: You picked the blocks to start with today! (Attending)

JACOB: I am going to make a castle and a moat! I will use the brown blocks for the moat. I will build the moat first.

MS. WILLIAMS: You are lining up the brown blocks in a row one by one! (Attending)

JACOB: Now the blue blocks can be the water.

MS. WILLIAMS: You are playing really gently with the blocks! (Attending)

JACOB: Oh no, Mommy, I knocked over part of the moat making the water. I have to set it all back up again.

MS. WILLIAMS: You are frustrated the moat fell over! (Attending) But you are getting right back in there and setting the moat up again! (Attending)

JACOB: I did it!

MS. WILLIAMS: You rebuilt the moat and are starting back on the water! (Attending)

JACOB: Okay, now the castle!

Do you see the difference? We bet you do! In this case Ms. Williams tried really hard to forgo so many questions and instructions (even though there were lots of opportunities for both!) and practiced her Attending skill. As you can see during Ms. Williams and Jacob's playtime, Attending short-circuited a negative pattern that is likely entrenched in their interactions with each other at this point. Ms. Williams had something else to use (Attending!) instead of relying so heavily on questions and instructions, and Jacob had a chance to instead get positive attention.

OTHER ATTENDING RULES OF THUMB

In addition to reducing the number of questions and instructions, another thing you may notice in our examples is that we put an exclamation point after each Attending statement. This is because simply doing a play-by-play account or narrating your child's play or behavior in and of itself may not be terribly rewarding to them. Imagine if the sportscaster sort of droned on and on without excitement in their voice when describing the plays—you likely would not listen for very long even if it was a favorite team of yours playing! Instead, you want your child to hear in your voice, even if they are not yet paying precise attention to your words, that you are interested in and excited by what they are doing. Think about the cartoons your child likes to watch or the video games they like to play, for example. They are loud and colorful and quite literally animated. So lean in, smile, and use the intonation in your voice to say, "I am paying attention to you!"

Second, whether using this parenting skill during play or throughout the day when your child is doing okay behaviors (i.e., you catch your child being "good"), Attending also gives you another trick up your sleeve. That is, you can use your "I am paying attention to you" powers to anticipate problem situations and see if you can prevent or at least manage them a little better. So imagine you tell your child to put on their shoes and your child sits down beside the shoes, but there is a clear choice point where compliance may (or may not) occur. You could wait to see what happens, which may include whining (e.g., "I don't want to put on my shoes") or noncompliance (i.e., not putting on their shoes at all or getting distracted and doing something else altogether). Or you could use your Attending skill to see if you can increase the likelihood that your child starts putting on their shoes: "You are looking at your shoe! You are picking up your shoe! You are putting your shoe on your foot!" This absolutely will feel like it is taking more time in the short term than you may have to devote to your child putting on shoes. But as you are likely already spending a lot of time on your child's not-okay behaviors like noncompliance, it can save you time in the long run.

Third, you do not want to use Attending with not-okay behaviors—that is, behaviors you want to see less or not at all. For now, we ask you to handle those as you usually would until you progress in the program. But at this point you may want to experiment a bit with just pausing your Attending when your child does a not-okay behavior. Then start Attending as soon as they start doing something else. So, for example, if you are playing blocks and your child pushes some blocks off the table in frustration, stop Attending and say nothing. As soon as your child starts playing again more gently with the blocks, you could say, "You are playing gently with the blocks" or "You are keeping the blocks on the table." You are flipping the script and teaching them with your attention what you want to see or see more (rather than focusing only on what you want to see less or not at all!).

SETTING ASIDE PLAYTIME

Now it is your turn! As a first step in your practice, we ask that you try to set aside some time each day. We recommend two 10-minute periods per day, but we also know that this may not always be possible. If you have 5 minutes, then practice for 5 minutes, or perhaps do only one 10-minute period—something is better than nothing. Ideally, these should be times when you and your child can sit down together in a play situation without lots of interruptions from other children, pets, or the phone. Ideally, sit down on the floor, or if for some reason you can't, sit at a table with your child and have a number of toys already picked out for the two of you to play with. Ideally, the toys you pick are those that don't require a lot of skill, don't have lots of rules, and likely will not require lots of corrective feedback (e.g., avoid things like challenging board games, card games, or puzzles). Instead, pick things that your child likes to play with and are fairly simple and easy to use, and it doesn't really matter if they use the toy the "right" or "wrong" way. Some example toys might include stackable, interlocking blocks or tiles, action figures, and dolls.

During the playtime, your job is simply to describe what your child is doing. Again, this could simply be your child's play behavior such as "You are stacking the blue block on the red block!" Or it could be okay behaviors you want to see or see more (e.g., "You are talking in your inside voice!"). If your child does a relatively minor not-okay behavior during the play (e.g., whines, yells), first just try pausing your Attending (say nothing). Then as soon as your child starts doing something else that is an okay behavior, start Attending again! If your child asks you to enter into the play or you want to play and can do Attending at the same time, that is great. Just be sure to do parallel play where you follow or imitate what your child is doing. This says, "I am interested in you and what *you* are doing."

And remember, try really hard during these practice sessions to avoid instructions and questions. You may, of course, find yourself doing both, especially at the start—we do it ourselves sometimes too when we are teaching parents! Just catch yourself doing it and adjust! It may also be helpful to record your practice time with your child and listen to it later—count the number of Attends relative to the number of questions and instructions! Or you can have your spouse or someone else keep track for you if that would be easier. Either way, are you surprised by how many questions you ask and instructions you give? As you practice more, are you more comfortable with using fewer and fewer questions and instructions and more and more Attends? If this is more of a challenge than you expected, try to think about each statement you are about to make. For example, if you think about saying, "Are you stacking the blocks?," you can change the question into an Attending statement by simply saying, "Now you're stacking the blocks!" Such a statement demands nothing of your child but lets them know that you are interested in their activities.

Sometimes a child will say something like "Why are you talking funny?" or "Why are you saying those things?" You can say, "I am just interested in how you are playing." Most of the time this will be enough of an explanation. If your child continues to question you, try to refocus the interaction by continuing to Attend to their okay behavior with interest and enthusiasm, which usually will distract them because they will start to relax, settle in, and have fun! Your child may also say, "Play *with* me!" As we have said, that is fine—just be careful that you don't take charge or lead the play. So instead when practicing Attending, you may choose to just watch a bit or do what we previously called "parallel play"—let your child lead the play, and you imitate or follow along beside them.

If the changes in the ways you are playing lead your child to seem frustrated or overstimulated, do not panic. These are big changes, and they may take some time for both of you to get used to—you may just need to ease in a little more slowly. For example, try reducing the frequency of your Attends for a little while and/or change the volume of your voice and your body language. The goal here is for you to communicate that you are interested and engaged, which may look and feel different depending on your child's temperament. We can tell you that most children immediately like (or very quickly get used to and enjoy!) Attending. They look at their parents with curiosity, smiles start to form, and giggles emerge. They know something is different here, and they like it.

To give you an idea of how much a child may like Attending, let's give you an example. We have a friend whose daughter—Beth—is now grown and in college. But at the time she was three or four, her parents were using skills like Attending with her. One night at a particularly animated dinner, Beth wasn't getting enough positive attention. So beneath the hustle-bustle of adults talking, dishes being passed, and glasses being filled, the adults heard something like this: "Beth is picking up her chicken nugget. She is putting it in her mouth. She is chewing."

The banter and action stopped as they realized Beth was using Attending with herself!

In order to make such progress though, you must do your best to practice. Ideally, continue the two 10-minute practice sessions with your child for seven days. (Sorry, but there are no weekends or holidays for parents!) After each practice session, try to listen to the recording or get feedback from the person you asked to watch you and keep track. You want to be giving at least four Attends per minute (forty in a 10-minute practice session!), and no more than four instructions plus questions during the entire 10 minutes of practice. What is particularly important is that you focus on the positive parts of your interaction with your child. Do not be overly critical of yourself; you are learning a new approach to parenting, and it will take time. Reward yourself for taking the time, putting forth the effort, and improving. Pat yourself on the back; take a couple of deep breaths; listen to your favorite podcast (or at least a few minutes of it!). Parenting is hard work, and your efforts should be rewarded! And if you forget, the guidelines for the Attending practice sessions are summarized in Table 6-1. Remember, two 10-minute practice times are ideal, but if not possible, just do your best, but do at least one session daily!

TABLE 6-1 Guidelines for Practice Sessions: Attending

DO NOT	DO
Give any instructions	Attend to (describe) your child's appropriate behavior
Ask any questions	Imitate your child's play behavior
Try to teach	Video or have someone watch the session
	Evaluate your performance
	Reward yourself for your efforts and performance
	Recognize that learning to Attend requires lots of work (be patient with yourself!)

USING ATTENDING THROUGHOUT THE DAY

Take a look at Worksheet 6-1 and note that after Day 3, you will start a second assignment. Find two "natural times" during the day to use Attending with your child for at least 5 minutes each. This might be while your child is riding in the car, taking a bath, or helping you grocery shop. All of these, as well as many other daily interactions with your child, are excellent times to begin incorporating the Attending skill into your daily routine. And unlike the 10-minute practices, these "natural times" do not require an additional time commitment from you. You are already spending this time with your child but likely not Attending. So turn off the car radio, for example, and Attend to what your child is doing or saying. It is only when the Attending skill becomes a natural part of your day-to-day life that your strong-willed child's behavior and the relationship the two of you have will begin to improve.

WORKSHEET 6-1 Daily Assignments for Week 1: Attending

TASKS	DAYS						
	1	2	3	4	5	6	7
1. Two 10-minute practice times	❑	❑	❑	❑	❑	❑	❑
2. Two 5-minute natural times				❑	❑	❑	❑

Keeping track of these assignments can be hard. Therefore, we encourage you to use Worksheet 6-1 to check off when you have completed each day's assignment(s). It can also be challenging to keep track of how many Attends you are doing. Some parents we have worked with use a fairly inexpensive wrist or finger counter more typically used to count laps (if you are runner) or strokes (if you are a golfer), which they find helpful. The wrist or finger counter may also provide a physical reminder to practice (or you could put a rubber band on your wrist!). If you are not a golfer or runner (and that is fine!), you may find one of these useful to purchase for Attending to your child. Oh yes, for those of you who are technologically advanced, there are also touch finger count apps for your smartphone.

LINGERING QUESTIONS AND DISCLAIMERS

You may be thinking, "Should I never give my child another instruction or ask another question?" By no means is this the case! Your child has to do many things every day of the week while you are learning the Attending skill. At those times, you should continue to issue instructions to your child. Furthermore, there are many times you will want to ask your child a question. However, when you do this, be sure to listen to your child's response. Why ask a question if you are not willing to wait for an answer? Whenever you want to ask a question or give an instruction, consider whether it is necessary in this case. Many times Attending is just as appropriate as issuing an instruction or question and far more effective in improving your relationship with your child.

If this seems difficult, don't despair. The five-week program for addressing strong-willed behavior does involve substantial effort on your part. As one of our grandfathers used to say, "There is no substitute for hard work!" Clearly, parenting is hard work, and changing the way you parent is even harder. Try to reward yourself at least every few days for accomplishing the assignments. Treat yourself to a video, a special lunch, or something else you enjoy. You deserve it!

Please focus only on Attending for the next seven days. Resist the temptation to read the next chapter! This program is most effective when you have a chance to really practice and feel comfortable with Attending before you add the next skill. Parents who try to rush through the program and learn all the skills at once are often ineffective in changing the negative aspects of their child's strong-willed behavior. Your child's strong-willed behavior did not develop quickly, and it is not going to be changed quickly. Patience is key!

CHAPTER 7

WEEK 2: REWARDING

When you practice and use the Attending skill, you are simply describing what your child does while playing (e.g., "You are putting the blue block on the red block!") or while engaging in some other activity (e.g., "You are putting on your shoe!"). The next skill you will learn—*Rewarding*—is designed to show your child not only that you are paying full attention (i.e., Attending), but that you really like what you see! Rewarding does not replace Attending, but builds upon and is used in combination with it. In other words, you should still describe your child's okay behavior, but on some occasions move beyond this by also praising, or Rewarding, the behavior you really want to see or see more. Indeed, one therapist we worked with compared Attendings to pennies—they are meaningful, but low cost and fairly easy to give out during a running commentary of your child's play or other okay behavior. That therapist likened Rewards to dollars—they are not so precious that you don't want to give them away, but precious enough that you want to use them more sparingly to really highlight the behaviors you want to see or see more.

Before moving on to the types of Rewards and which are most effective, we want to acknowledge that some parents may be having lots of less-than-positive thoughts and feelings right now about Rewarding, and that is okay. Let's review some of these thoughts and feelings and how we address them. One common issue with Rewarding that we hear from parents at least initially is "I should not have to Reward my child for doing what I asked!" These types of "shoulds" come from lots of experiences, including how parents were themselves parented (e.g., "My parents didn't Reward me for doing what I was supposed to do!"), as well as parents' experiences with their other children (e.g., "[Name] just does what I ask every time"). Our response here refers to our discussion of temperament and your strong-willed child. That is, *all* children (and, indeed, all humans!) are more likely to do things if there is some sort of Reward (research shows that time and again), but your strong-willed child may be especially likely to need a Reward to help them increase the likelihood that they are doing things you want to see and see more!

A related concern we hear from parents is something like "I shouldn't have to bribe my child to do what I ask." We totally agree, and the nuance to remember here is that a bribe is an incentive to do something wrong (i.e., a not-okay behavior)—instead, we are asking you to Reward okay behaviors or behaviors you want to see or see more. So no bribes necessary! Third, some parents ask, "But won't Rewarding decrease the likelihood that my child has any sort of internal drive or motivation?" The answer is no and just the opposite—instead, positive attention like the combination of Attending and Rewarding helps your child internalize what behaviors adults want to see or see more until those behaviors become more natural and internally motivated. Finally, some parents tell us, "I have already tried using Rewards, and my child's behavior is still terrible." Once we talk with these parents, we often realize that they are using Rewarding differently than we recommend and in ways that are less likely to increase okay behavior (and instead more likely to increase not-okay behavior).

With all of our explanations in mind, you may still be suspicious of the value of Rewarding or unsure about your willingness to use Rewards. That is okay—we simply ask that you read on and give Rewarding a try, in the way we describe, so that you can decide for yourself based on the results that you see. Alternatively, you may be a parent who already uses and is comfortable using Rewarding—we ask that you read on as well because we are going to detail the types of Rewards we recommend and how to use those types of Rewards in combination with Attending to be most effective with your strong-willed child's behavior. Table 7-1 summarizes the types of Rewards. The first type we will talk about is *Social Rewards*. These can be *Verbal*, *Physical*, or *Activity Rewards*.

TABLE 7-1 Types of Rewards

SOCIAL REWARDS
Verbal: Rewarding your child's okay behavior with praise
Physical: Providing physical contact (for example, a pat on the back) following your child's okay behavior
Activities: Doing activities selected by your child following their okay behavior
NONSOCIAL REWARDS
Giving toys or treats following your child's okay behavior

SOCIAL: VERBAL REWARDS

Of all the types of Rewards for young children, *Verbal Rewards*, or praise, are the most important. There are two types of Verbal Rewards—*Labeled* and *Unlabeled*. Labeled Verbal Rewards, in which you praise your child's behavior and label exactly what your child did that you liked, are of particular importance. For example, you might say, "Thank you for picking up your toys!" Think about that statement. Not only is your child being praised, but now your child also knows the exact behavior (picking up the toys) that you want to see or see more. Here are some other examples of Labeled Verbal Rewards:

- "Wow, you are doing a great job sharing those toys with your sibling!"
- "I really like how quietly you are playing with your toys!"
- "Thank you for putting all your blocks back in the box!"
- "I am so impressed by how hard you worked on your homework!"
- "Great job staying by my side while we are shopping!"
- "I liked it when you came to the dinner table the very first time I called you!"

In each of those examples, you can see that parents are highlighting the process (e.g., "Wow, you are doing a great job sharing those toys with your sibling!") or an outcome (e.g., "Thank you for putting all your blocks back in the box!"). On other occasions, parents may not have the time or think they necessarily need to be so specific about the child's exact behavior. In these cases, you can use brief comments, or Unlabeled

Verbal Rewards. Examples of these Unlabeled Verbal Rewards include:

- "Good job!"
- "Great!"
- "Thank you!"

Again, each of these statements lets your child know that they did something that you want to see or see more. However, these general statements tend to be less effective because often preschool-age children are doing lots of things at one time, and what they are doing may include a mix of okay and not-okay behavior. So while it may be obvious to you that you are saying "Good job!" in response to your child sharing toys, your child may actually be unsure what behavior earned your praise or even worse think another behavior (potentially a not-okay behavior) is what caught your attention. Let's look at an example of an interaction between a dad, Mr. Gonzalez, and his six-year-old child, Emily—you first met them in Chapter 1. Emily is sitting down at the table to color with a younger sibling Matthew:

EMILY: *Matthew! Matthew! Matthew!* Here! You can use my crayons!

MR. GONZALEZ: Great job, Emily!

If Mr. Gonzalez is hoping to increase Emily's sharing with Matthew but decrease the yelling, this Unlabeled Verbal Reward is likely to be less effective. That is, it is likely less clear to Emily what part of that interaction pleased dad. Sitting at the table? Playing with Matthew? Yelling? Sharing? In turn, the positive attention may feel diffuse and not necessarily function to increase the okay behavior that Mr. Gonzalez is targeting (i.e., the sharing!). If instead in the same scenario Mr. Gonzalez uses a Labeled Verbal Reward, then he is more likely to communicate to Emily exactly what he wants to see or see more:

EMILY: *Matthew! Matthew! Matthew!* Here! You can use my crayons!

MR. GONZALEZ: Great job sharing your crayons with Matthew, Emily!

Now Emily knows exactly what Mr. Gonzalez considers to be the okay behavior (i.e., sharing). As we talked about in the last chapter, in this example Mr. Gonzalez is not Attending or Rewarding the yelling, as it is a not-okay behavior he wants to see less (or not at all). But given that Emily is getting lots of positive attention for sharing (and no attention at all for yelling), Emily should start to learn what Mr. Gonzalez wants to see and do those behaviors more, leaving less time in the day for the not-okay behaviors!

It can be helpful to think in advance about examples of Labeled and Unlabeled Verbal Rewards for the okay behaviors you are working on with your child. First, consult your list of okay behaviors from Chapter 5, or feel free to add any new ones that are at the forefront of your mind based on recent experiences with your child.

Second, if you are finding the Rewards you are going to use hard to remember in the moment, write them down on a notecard, put them in your phone, or post them on the fridge until they start to come more naturally to you! Remember, practice makes perfect—well, in reality none of us will ever be "perfect" parents, but the more we practice, the more we will learn the skills to improve our strong-willed child's behavior.

And as with Attending, Verbal Rewards are not just about what you say but how you say it. "Good job!" will likely feel less of a Reward to your child if delivered in a soft, monotone, and uninterested voice. So give your child lots of verbal and nonverbal cues that you caught them being good and feel great about that—lean in; smile; turn up the pitch in your voice!

Our research indicates that after reading this book, parents view Verbal Rewards as a relatively easy skill to learn and, importantly, as the most useful skill for increasing their child's okay behavior. This is really important information; however, it does not mean that learning to verbally Reward your child's okay behavior will be easy—it will take thoughtfulness, dedication, and effort by you!

SOCIAL: PHYSICAL REWARDS

In addition to Verbal Rewards, *Physical Rewards* can also be an effective behavior change tool for parents of strong-willed children. Physical Rewards may include:

- A pat on your child's back
- An arm around your child's shoulder
- A wink at your child

These and other Physical Rewards let your child know that you like the behavior you are seeing and want to see that behavior more. Hugs and kisses also can be used as Physical Rewards; however, we recommend using these expressions of love unconditionally with your child rather than reserving them for Rewarding only. Similarly, things like a high five or fist bump may also be Physical Rewards—but consider your child's disposition and behavior. That is, if your child's behavior is more oppositional in general or in this moment in particular, you run the risk of them not wanting to give you a high five or fist bump. In this case, look for other types of Physical Rewards, or use a Verbal Reward instead. We want Rewarding to feel positive and reinforcing to you and your child—that is how it works to increase the okay behavior!

As you think about using Physical Rewards, it will be important to consider how much positive physical contact there is in your relationship with your strong-willed child in general. As we said earlier in this book, we have worked with many parents who are very frustrated with their child's behavior and by the time they come to us are not enjoying their time with their child. This sometimes means that there is not a lot of physical contact between the parents and children with whom we work. We understand, and if this describes your relationship with your child at the time you are reading this chapter, we suggest starting slowly by gently touching your child on the shoulder sometimes or patting your child on the back. A simple wink or a playful tap can also be very meaningful to a child. Try to use these and other Physical Rewards not only in practice sessions but throughout the day. You will be surprised how effective this can be.

SOCIAL: ACTIVITY REWARDS

In addition to Verbal and Physical Rewards, parents of strong-willed children can also think about *Activity Rewards*. As we talked about here and in earlier chapters, the relationship between parents and their strong-willed children can sometimes start to feel stressful and task-focused (e.g., "Do this," "Don't do that," "Come here," "Go there"). Not surprisingly, time together can start feeling like it is taken up by the things you must do together like getting ready for daycare or school and mealtime, bathtime, and bedtime. Unfortunately, this decreases the likelihood of less task-focused and more pleasant interactions around some activity you can enjoy doing together. Using an activity your child enjoys can both serve as a Reward and also increase time and space for other types of Rewards like Verbal and Physical Rewards. Activity Rewards can also give you a chance to discover positive things about your child. These Rewards might include things like:

- Playing a game
- Reading a story
- Going on a walk

How do you decide what is a Rewarding activity for your child? One way is to recall the things your child has asked you to do. Another is to simply ask your child, "What are the things you like to do?" You also might generate a list of Activity Rewards and let your child know that these are things the two of you can do together dependent upon specific okay behaviors. For example, "After you put your toys in the toy box, we can go swing on the playset in the backyard for 15 minutes!"

What types of activities does your child likely find Rewarding? Can you list three or more? We encourage you to do so.

1. _____

2. _____

3. _____

Similar to hugs and kisses, however, don't use these types of activities solely as rewards—the more time you spend with your child, the more opportunity you will have to shape their behavior with skills like Attending and Rewarding and the more you will both begin to enjoy your time together (or enjoy it even more!).

NONSOCIAL REWARDS

In addition to Social Rewards (Verbal, Physical, Activity), there are *Nonsocial Rewards*—desirable objects such as toys or special treats. Often this is the type of Reward that parents are thinking about when they have negative reactions to the idea of incentivizing their child. However, it is important to note that these types of Rewards can be useful, especially when you start teaching a new behavior, because they are immediate, tangible, and desirable! That said, Nonsocial Rewards don't have to be big or expensive. Instead of promising a bag of M&M's for picking up all the toys, think about promising one M&M after picking up each toy! And to be most effective, Nonsocial Rewards should always be combined with Labeled or Unlabeled Verbal Rewards. What is most important to your young child is your attention, so you want to link your positive attention to an immediate, tangible Nonsocial Reward.

Let's look at another example with Mr. Gonzalez and Emily. In addition to increasing the likelihood that Emily is talking in an inside voice and sharing, Mr. Gonzalez wants to increase Emily's compliance to doing things the first time. So let's use the toybox example:

MR. GONZALEZ: Emily, it is time to pick up your toys. I will give you one M&M for every toy you put in the toy box.

EMILY: [Puts doll in the toybox]

MR. GONZALEZ: Great job putting your doll in the toy box the first time I asked! (Labeled Verbal Reward) Gives Emily an M&M. (Nonsocial Reward)

Here you can see Mr. Gonzalez is pairing the Labeled Verbal Reward with the Nonsocial Reward to start making a change in Emily's compliance. Once Emily's compliance starts improving a bit, Mr. Gonzalez may test backing off on the Nonsocial Reward and just start using the Labeled Verbal Rewards. Of course, you can think of other Nonsocial Rewards such as using a brief clip of a favorite show or song. You know your child—pick things they really enjoy.

TIME TO REFLECT

- Are there Nonsocial Rewards that are acceptable to you to reinforce okay behavior?
- If so, consider using one of these Rewards, always pairing it with a Verbal Reward, for an okay behavior you want to see or see more.

REWARDS RULES OF THUMB

As with Attending, there are several rules of thumb to follow in using the types of Rewards we outline above. These include:

- **Use Rewarding with Attending.** Remember that skills in this five-week program build on each other. So each new skill we ask you to do, in this case Rewarding, we will ask you to keep using the prior skill(s) (e.g., Attending). As a reminder, think about Attending as your pennies—you can use those pennies all day every day, just a running commentary of your child's okay behavior. Then save Rewarding as your dollars for those behaviors you really want to work on increasing. Pick one or two!

- **When in doubt, err on the side of Labeled Verbal Rewards alone or in combination with other Rewards.** By using Labeled Verbal Rewards, you are providing your child not only with praise but with information about exactly what you want to see or see more. This is how young children learn best!

- **Use Rewarding immediately after the okay behavior occurs.** You really cannot wait until bedtime to tell your child that you liked behavior that happened earlier that morning. Effective Rewarding occurs immediately (or as soon as possible!) after the okay behavior.

- **Start by Rewarding small improvements in behavior and Rewarding improvement every time it occurs.** We call this "successive approximation," or slowly but surely shaping the behavior or approximations of the behavior you want to see or see more. For example, if you are working on your child being able to dress more independently, then at first you may Reward simply picking out an article of clothing (e.g., "Wow! You picked a great outfit all by yourself!") and work your way up to "Great job getting dressed all by yourself!" over a period of days or weeks.

- **Reward only behaviors you want to see or see more.**
  If you also give lots of attention to not-okay behavior,
  your child will not learn what you are trying to teach.
  Remember, you are flipping the script and teaching
  your child through Attending and Rewarding, and so
  they now are much more likely to receive attention for
  okay rather than not-okay behavior.

NOW IT'S YOUR TURN!

Let's talk about how to begin using Rewarding skills. Review
the guidelines for the Rewarding practice sessions summarized in Table 7-2. First, in the practice session(s) you have each
day, continue Attending and begin Rewarding. Again, Verbal
Rewards do not replace Attends but add to them—you should
be using both skills in your practice sessions. For example, "You
are putting the blue block on the red block!" (Attending), "You
are keeping all the toys on the table!" (Attending), and "You
are doing a great job using your gentle hands with the toys!"
(Rewarding). If you found it useful to record your Attending sessions, continue to do this and pay attention to how you interact
with your child. In particular, keep track of how many Attends
and Verbal Rewards you give. If your spouse or someone else
can watch your play, as you might have done with Attending,
this also would be helpful. Either way, try to find some way to
get feedback to make sure you are practicing this skill correctly
and, in turn, have the greatest chance of achieving the changes
in your child's behavior you want to see.

TABLE 7-2 Guidelines for Practice Sessions: Attending and Rewarding

DO NOT	DO
Give any instructions	Attend to (describe) your child's okay behavior
Ask any questions	Imitate your child's play behavior
Try to teach	Verbally Reward your child's okay behavior by praising and labeling the desired behavior. (For example, say, "Thank you for picking up your toys!")
	Record (audio or video) the session
	Reward yourself for your efforts and performance (be patient with yourself!)

As summarized in Worksheet 7-1 (at the end of this chapter), your goal, during each 10-minute practice session, should be at least two Verbal Rewards and two Attends per minute. (That's a total of 20 Verbal Rewards and 20 Attends!) Also, continue to work on giving no more than four questions plus instructions during the 10-minute practice session. Most important, remember, even if you do not achieve these goals, you should focus on what you did right. Apply your Rewarding skills to yourself—reinforce yourself for small improvements!

Let's revisit Ms. Williams's play session with Jacob from the last chapter to see how she added Rewarding. So, first, here was their play session with Attending:

MS. WILLIAMS: You are ready to play! (Attending)

JACOB: Yes!

MS. WILLIAMS: You are bringing your blocks and a puzzle to the table to play with me! (Attending)

JACOB: Let's start with the blocks!

MS. WILLIAMS: You picked the blocks to start with today! (Attending)

JACOB: I am going to make a castle and a moat! I will use the brown blocks for the moat. I will build the moat first.

MS. WILLIAMS: You are lining up the brown blocks in a row one by one! (Attending)

JACOB: Now the blue blocks can be the water.

MS. WILLIAMS: You are playing really gently with the blocks! (Attending)

JACOB: Oh no, Mommy, I knocked over part of the moat making the water. I have to set it all back up again.

MS. WILLIAMS: You are frustrated the moat fell over! (Attending) But you are getting right back in there and setting the moat up again! (Attending)

JACOB: I did it!

MS. WILLIAMS: You rebuilt the moat and are starting back on the water! (Attending)

JACOB: Okay, now the castle!

Now let's see what their playtime could look like with both Attending and Rewarding:

MS. WILLIAMS: You are ready to play! (Attending)

JACOB: Yes!

MS. WILLIAMS: You did such a great job of bringing your blocks and a puzzle to the table to play with me! (Rewarding)

JACOB: Let's start with the blocks!

MS. WILLIAMS: You picked the blocks to start with today! (Attending)

JACOB: I am going to make a castle and a road! I will use the brown blocks for the moat. I will build the road first.

MS. WILLIAMS: You are lining up the brown blocks in a row one by one! (Attending)

JACOB: Now the blue blocks can be the water.

MS. WILLIAMS: Wow, I really like how gently you are playing with the blocks! (Rewarding)

JACOB: Oh no, Mommy, I knocked over part of the road making the water. I have to set it all back up again!

MS. WILLIAMS: You are frustrated the road fell over! (Attending) But I am so proud of you for getting right back in there and setting the road up again! (Rewarding)

JACOB: I did it!

MS. WILLIAMS: Wow! I love how you stayed so calm and worked really hard to rebuild the road and water! (Rewarding)

JACOB: Okay, now the castle!

As indicated in Worksheet 7-1 later in the chapter, on the third day start using Rewarding with your Attending throughout the day. Pick one behavior to Reward. (Remember, you listed three okay behaviors earlier in this book!) Perhaps pick the least challenging behavior first. You want to start with a success experience. So, for example, if the not-okay behaviors with which you are most concerned include not sharing, noncompliance, and aggression, the okay behaviors you are targeting may be sharing, doing things when asked the first time, and using gentle hands with parents and siblings. If you think sharing is the easiest behavior to change, you could pick it first. So every time your child does something that remotely approximates sharing (remember, this is successive approximation), like bringing toys into a play circle with other children or letting another child touch a favorite toy, jump in with Attending and Rewarding. For example, if we circle back to Mr. Gonzalez and Emily:

- "You are bringing your coloring books and crayons over to Matthew! (Attending)
- "You are sitting down at the table!" (Attending)
- "You offered to share your crayons with Matthew! (Attending)
- "Wow, Emily, I am really impressed that you let Matthew use your crayons!" (Rewarding)

Other examples of behaviors parents often want to increase and the ways they use Rewards to do that are presented in Table 7-3. Reading these might stimulate your thoughts and help you to see various ways to increase your child's okay behavior. It may also help to think about situations in which not-okay behaviors are likely to occur and to start using Attending and Rewarding in those situations in particular to increase okay behavior. These situations may include getting ready for daycare or school, riding in the car, shopping, or mealtime, bathtime, or bedtime.

TABLE 7-3   Desirable Child Behaviors and Ways to Increase Them

BEHAVIOR	SUGGESTED PROCEDURE FOR INCREASING THE FREQUENCY OF BEHAVIOR
Coming when called	1. Tell your child you want to increase the likelihood they will come when called.
	2. Tell your child exactly what you expect. (Say, for example, "When I call you, I expect you to stop what you are doing and come.")
	3. Reward your child as soon as they come in response to your call.
	4. Reward your child every time.
Staying with you in the grocery store	1. Say you want the two of you to work on your child staying with you in the grocery store.
	2. Put your child in a shopping cart so they will stay with you. On the first trip, Reward and Attend to your child every 30 seconds.
	3. On the next few trips, let your child walk beside you as you hold hands. Reward and Attend to your child every 30 seconds.
	4. On the next few trips, lightly rest your hand on your child's shoulder. Reward and Attend to your child every 30 seconds.
	5. On later trips, have your child walk beside you with no physical contact. Reward and Attend to your child every 30 seconds.
	6. Gradually lengthen the time between Rewarding and Attending, but never phase them out completely.
Playing cooperatively with a sibling	1. Explain to both children that you want them to play together sharing the toys without arguing or fighting.
	2. Monitor closely the play between the two children.
	3. Reward okay play behavior.

The more you think about these in advance, the more likely you will be able to respond immediately when you catch your child being good! Once you start to see change in that first behavior, pick a second behavior from your list and start Rewarding that behavior as well. As time moves on, new not-okay behavior may evolve—but the principles and skills are the same. What you as a parent need to do is to be intentional, identify the not-okay behavior you want to decrease, identify its opposite okay behavior, and then use the combination of Attending and Rewarding to make that change happen! Positive attention (Attending and Rewarding) is your parenting superpower with your strong-willed child!

TIME TO REFLECT

- What are some not-okay behaviors you want to decrease?
- What are the opposites of these behaviors—okay behaviors—to increase?
- Which Rewards do you use to increase these okay behaviors?

We have referred to Worksheet 7-1 several times. This worksheet outlines the assignments you need to complete during the second week of the five-week program. (*Remember:* Two 10-minute practice sessions are an ideal. You may not be able to have that much practice time every day.) When you have completed the assignments in Worksheet 7-1, you will be ready to move to the next skill. Note that one assignment in the Worksheet, Task 6, is not undertaken and completed until Week 3.

WORKSHEET 7-1 Daily Assignments for Week 2: Rewards

TASKS	DAYS						
	1	2	3	4	5	6	7
1. Have two 10-minute practices with at least two Verbal Rewards and two Attends per minute.	❏	❏	❏	❏	❏	❏	❏
2. Select three behaviors to increase.			❏				
3. Increase the first of three behaviors.			❏	❏	❏	❏	❏
4. Consider the use of Rewards throughout the day.					❏	❏	❏
5. Increase the second of three behaviors.						❏	❏
6. Increase the third of three behaviors (Week 3)							

CHAPTER 8

WEEK 3: "EFFORTFUL" IGNORING

As you begin Week 3 of our five-week program, continue your practice sessions and work on increasing those okay behaviors that you want to see or see more. In addition, you will be adding a new skill in this chapter—one that will make the Attending and Rewarding skills even more effective. This skill, *"Effortful" Ignoring*, is the first in your series of new skills that you will use to directly decrease not-okay behaviors or behaviors you want to see less often or not at all.

Now at this point you may be asking yourself, "They want me to Ignore my child?," followed quickly by, "That doesn't seem right." To clarify, we are going to ask you to use "Effortful" Ignoring, or to not give any attention to specific not-okay behaviors, which we will talk about more below. The key to highlight here, however, is that we are asking you to practice "Effortful"

Ignoring. This means that you will be thoughtful about which behaviors are going to be the focus of your "Effortful" Ignoring skills, and you are *only* going to use "Effortful" Ignoring in *combination* with Attending and Rewarding. By Attending and Rewarding okay behaviors and Ignoring specific not-okay behaviors, you will increase the likelihood that your strong-willed child has a clearer understanding of what behaviors you want to see or see more (okay behaviors) and what behaviors you want to see less (not-okay behaviors). Notably, while Ignoring was covered in earlier editions of *Parenting the Strong-Willed Child*, as well as the clinical program upon which it is based, the "effortful" aspect of the skill was part of our explanation but not explicit in the name. So we, like others in the field, now make it clearer that Ignoring requires effort, intent, and work on your behalf by calling it "Effortful" Ignoring. Believe us, we know it takes a lot of effort—but it is effective.

HOW TO USE "EFFORTFUL" IGNORING

As you have learned so far, your strong-willed child is very attuned to and motivated by attention in general and your attention in particular. Positive attention (Attending and Rewarding) is your superpower with your strong-willed child. In Chapter 6 on Attending and Chapter 7 on Rewarding, we talked about using those skills to give your positive attention to behaviors you want to see or see more, such as using gentle hands, talking in an inside voice, or doing what you ask the first time. "Effortful" Ignoring is essentially deciding in advance what sorts of not-okay behaviors are not going to get your attention. The ways that you make it clear to your child that you are not giving a behavior attention are:

1. **No look!** If you see a not-okay behavior that is on your list to Ignore, then you will not look at, make eye contact with, or smile at your child when they do that not-okay behavior.
2. **No talk!** Similarly, when that not-okay behavior occurs, you will not talk to or try to reason with your child.
3. **No touch!** Finally, when that not-okay behavior occurs, you will not touch your child, hug your child, or pat your child on the back.

WHAT NOT-OKAY BEHAVIORS SHOULD BE IGNORED?

This is a great question, and the answer is not all of them. In fact, you want to pick what not-okay behaviors will be the focus of your "Effortful" Ignoring carefully. The best way to think about the not-okay behaviors that are best suited for "Effortful" Ignoring is to think about those you would describe as annoying (e.g., whining), bad-mannered (e.g., interrupting while you are talking on the phone), not currently helpful to your child or unlikely to be helpful in the future (e.g., cursing or making obscene gestures), and/or behaviors that are potentially embarrassing to you, others, or even your child in the present or in the future (e.g., throwing a tantrum outside of daycare). These are common behaviors that parents select as a target for "Effortful" Ignoring, and we have seen time and time again that it can work very well. For example, if whining while you are on the phone is being met with consistent "no look, no talk, and no touch" (i.e., no attention), but your child is getting lots of positive attention (Attending and Rewarding) for the opposite behavior (e.g., waiting quietly and patiently while you are on the phone), the whining should decrease.

Some parents may feel torn about using "Effortful" Ignoring with things like obscene gestures or cursing. We get it—it may be funny the first time, but once it starts happening often or in public, it is not so funny. But here is the reason Ignoring could be effective with these sorts of behaviors as well. If your child cursed one time, they likely got lots of attention from adults in the form of either correction (e.g., "Don't ever say that word again!"), education (e.g., "That is a bad word. We don't want you to say that bad word!"), or even laughter (if there is one thing that TikTok has reminded us, it is that kids say really funny things!). All these things can increase (rather than decrease) the likelihood that your child will curse again (and again . . . and again). But based on what you know so far, you also know that if they no longer get attention for cursing (but instead are getting attention for okay words), then cursing should start to decrease (and even disappear). A gesture like giving an adult the middle finger or sticking out their tongue is similar to cursing—it should decrease when parents or other adults respond (or essentially don't respond) by using "Effortful" Ignoring. If your child does these sorts of things and gets your attention when they do them, we can predict that they will likely do them again. If you "don't look, talk, or touch" when the behavior occurs, but Attend to and Reward other behaviors, your child should start to do something else instead.

To summarize, here is a list of not-okay behaviors that are likely to respond to "Effortful" Ignoring:

- Whining
- Interrupting
- Throwing tantrums
- Cursing
- Using obscene or naughty gestures
- Screaming

- Pouting
- Arguing
- "Crying" without tears
- Questioning authority
- Repeating or mocking
- Rolling eyes

Now there are also some not-okay behaviors that you don't want to respond to using "Effortful" Ignoring. Think about this category as any not-okay behavior that has the potential to be dangerous for your child (e.g., running away from you in a store) or to others (e.g., hitting, kicking) or is destructive (e.g., breaking own or others' toys). You also don't want to use "Effortful" Ignoring with your child not doing something when you ask. We will talk about how to deal with these more "urgent" behaviors in Chapter 10, so hang in there, as we know you are anxious to address these behaviors. For now, remember that positive attention is your superpower. You can work on decreasing urgent behaviors by giving lots of positive attention (Attending and Rewarding) to their opposite! If hitting and kicking are problems, Attend and Reward as much as you can every time you see gentle hands and feet! If noncompliance is a problem, give lots of Attending and Rewarding when your child is doing what you ask the first time. The skills you are learning build on one another, and it is important to master one skill before moving on to the next one.

HOW DO I USE "EFFORTFUL" IGNORING?

In order for "Effortful" Ignoring to be effective, you need to remove *all attention* from your child's behavior. This means no look, talk, or touch every time that not-okay behavior occurs. Ideally every adult (e.g., parents, grandparents, daycare providers) is doing the same thing (i.e., no look, talk, or touch) in every context (e.g., home, daycare). We teach parents to be fairly dramatic in these efforts so it is obvious to the child—turn your head away, cross your arms, and seal your lips (no smiling!). You are doing this while keeping track of the child out of the corner of your eye using your peripheral vision, particularly with younger children or if there are any potential safety concerns. We will talk a bit later in this chapter about instances when "Effortful" Ignoring may be more challenging and you may want to step out of the room to take a deep breath, get yourself together, and be sure you are not giving attention to the child.

Now if this doesn't already sound challenging enough, we are going to throw one more thing at you—your child's not-okay behavior may get worse before it gets better. Unfortunately, this is logical. That is, your child is used to a pattern in which they do something (e.g., whining) and eventually you respond (e.g., "Hold on a minute. Daddy is talking on the phone . . . I said Daddy is talking. Please wait . . . just one more minute . . . Okay, okay, what is it?"). As you can see, in an effort to avoid the child's whining, this parent ended up giving it a lot of attention and inadvertently increased the likelihood the child will whine the next time Daddy is on the phone (or listening to the news, or working on the computer, or trying to read a difficult form). So this parent and child are essentially in a rut—the child whines because Daddy will eventually respond. As we have talked about in an earlier chapter, however, new skills like Rewarding and "Effortful" Ignoring allow parents to flip the script and teach children that they are going to get attention for okay behaviors like patience (e.g., "I really liked how you waited patiently for Daddy to get off the phone") and no attention (no look, talk, or touch!) for not-okay behaviors like whining.

It may take several tries for your child to recognize this shift, as they initially may ramp up the not-okay behavior (whine more frequently, more loudly, with more emotion) with the idea that whining has worked before—in other words, your child learned from experience that if I whine, Mom or Dad will give me attention. Now it will likely take a few trials to realize that the attention is coming for the opposite of whining (waiting patiently until Dad is off the phone). So one healthy way to deal with this is to predict for yourself that the whining (or tantrums or yelling or cursing) will temporarily get worse. That way you won't feel disappointed (or quite as disappointed or frustrated) when it happens. Be prepared to take some deep breaths, silently repeat your favorite mantra in your mind ("calm blue lake"), or imagine yourself in your happy place (e.g., beach, mountains, snuggled up reading a book, taking a warm bath) as you ride what may initially feel like a never-ending wave of not-okay behavior. But remember, if the not-okay behavior truly gets no attention (no look, talk, or touch!) *and* other more okay behaviors are getting positive attention (Attending and Rewarding), then the not-okay behavior should begin to fade away! So as soon as your child is doing something that is an okay behavior, perhaps sitting quietly waiting for you to get off the phone or beginning to play with a toy, then Attend to and Reward those okay behaviors as soon as possible. For example, "You are waiting so patiently! Thank you for playing with your toy while I finished my phone conversation!"

Now lest you are starting to feel like this is going to be really challenging, here are some data to give you hope that what we are recommending makes sense and will work. Our research indicates that two months after completing the five-week program, parents see this skill as being as useful as the other skills they learn. What this means is that "Effortful" Ignoring takes time, patience, and consistent use to be effective. However, it works best when combined with Attending and Rewarding for okay behavior: The use of Ignoring for the types of not-okay behavior we talk about in this chapter teaches your child to flip the script and begin to work hard for your positive attention by displaying okay behavior.

To summarize, here are the basic "how-tos" of "Effortful" Ignoring:

- Select a not okay behavior with which you can use "Effortful" Ignoring.
- Remove all your attention from the not-okay behavior when it occurs (no look, no talk, no touch!).
- Once you start using "Effortful" Ignoring with that not-okay behavior, use it consistently (and try to have other adults in the child's life do the same).
- Expect the not-okay behavior to occur more often at first before it starts to occur less often (change will not happen overnight).
- Attend to and Reward okay behavior as soon as it occurs.

TIME TO REFLECT

- What is one of your child's not-okay behaviors that you can "Effortfully" Ignore (start with just one, please)?
- How will you explain to your child that your response to this not-okay behavior will now change (tip: No look! No talk! No touch!)?
- How will you be best prepared to use "Effortful" Ignoring with that not-okay behavior (is it more likely to occur certain times of day, particular locations, or certain situations)?
- What okay behavior will you Attend to and Reward instead?

NOW IT IS YOUR TURN!

During this week, your first assignment, beginning on Day 1 and continuing throughout the week, is to incorporate "Effortful" Ignoring skills into your practice sessions with your child. Combine "Effortful" Ignoring for not-okay behaviors with Rewarding and Attending for okay behaviors. So in your practice sessions, if your strong-willed child does a not-okay behavior such as whining, remove all your attention by turning your back and saying nothing until the whining totally stops. It may seem like it takes forever; however, your goal is to give a clear signal that whining no longer gets attention. Once whining stops, immediately turn back to your child and begin Attending and Rewarding any okay behaviors.

To give you an example, let's pick up where we left off with Ms. Williams's play session with Jacob from the last chapter to see how she can add "Effortful" Ignoring. We will make one change in the second interaction that follows to show how this skill should be used. Here is what it looked like previously when Ms. Williams used Attends and Rewards::

MS. WILLIAMS: You are ready to play! (Attending)

JACOB: Yes!

MS. WILLIAMS: You did such a great job of bringing your blocks and a puzzle to the table to play with me! (Rewarding)

JACOB: Let's start with the blocks!

MS. WILLIAMS: You picked the blocks to start with today! (Attending)

JACOB: I am going to make a castle and a road! I will use the brown blocks for the road. I will build the road first.

MS. WILLIAMS: You are lining up the brown blocks in a row one by one! (Attending)

JACOB: Now the blue blocks can be the water.

MS. WILLIAMS: Wow, I really like how gently you are playing with the blocks! (Rewarding)

JACOB: Oh no, Mommy, I knocked over part of the road making the water. I have to set it all back up again!

MS. WILLIAMS: You are frustrated the road fell over! (Attending) But I am so proud of you for getting right back in there and setting the road up again! (Rewarding)

JACOB: I did it!

MS. WILLIAMS: Wow! I love how you stayed so calm and worked really hard to rebuild the road and water! (Rewarding)

JACOB: Okay, now the castle!

Now "Effortful" Ignoring will be added. In the next vignette Jacob uses a whining voice. Let's see how Ms. Williams adds "Effortful" Ignoring, as well as continues Attending and Rewarding, to address this behavior in their playtime:

MS. WILLIAMS: You are ready to play! (Attending)

JACOB: Yes!

MS. WILLIAMS: You did such a great job of bringing your blocks and a puzzle to the table to play with me! (Rewarding)

JACOB: Let's start with the blocks!

MS. WILLIAMS: You picked the blocks to start with today! (Attending)

JACOB: I am going to make a castle and a road! I will use the brown blocks for the road. I will build the road first.

MS. WILLIAMS: You are lining up the brown blocks in a row one by one! (Attending)

JACOB: Now the blue blocks can be the water.

MS. WILLIAMS: Wow, I really like how gently you are playing with the blocks! (Rewarding)

JACOB: Oh no, Mommy, I knocked over part of the road making the water. I have to set it all back up again! [Whining tone]

MS. WILLIAMS: [Turns her back. No look, no talk, no touch] (Ignoring)

JACOB: [Starts to play quietly with blocks again]

MS. WILLIAMS: You are frustrated the road fell over! (Attending) But I am so proud of you for getting right back in there and setting the road up again! (Rewarding)

JACOB: I did it!

MS. WILLIAMS: Wow! I love how you stayed so calm and worked really hard to rebuild the road and water! (Rewarding)

JACOB: Okay, now the castle!

So instead of Attending to Jacob's whining tone of voice, a not-okay behavior, Ms. Williams used her "Effortful" Ignoring skill to decrease the likelihood she was giving the whining any attention.

Guidelines for practice sessions during Week 3 are presented in Table 8-1.

TABLE 8-1 Guidelines for Practice Sessions: Attending, Rewarding, and "Effortful" Ignoring

DO NOT	DO
Give any instructions	Attend to (describe) your child's okay behavior
Ask any questions	Imitate your child's play behavior
Try to teach	Verbally Reward your child's okay behavior by Rewarding and labeling the okay behavior. (For example, say, "Thank you for picking up your toys!")
	Use "Effortful" Ignoring with the not-okay behavior
	Record (video or audio) the session
	Evaluate your performance
	Reward yourself for your efforts and performance (be patient with yourself!)

ALSO COMBINE "EFFORTFUL" IGNORING WITH ATTENDING AND REWARDING DURING THE DAY!

The second assignment, beginning on Day 2, is to pick out a not-okay behavior that you will respond to now using your "Effortful" Ignoring skill. This should be a behavior that occurs almost daily, such as those we have mentioned earlier in this chapter. When you have selected a behavior, sit down with your strong-willed child and explain: exactly what behavior is not okay; that when the not-okay behavior happens you will use "Effortful" Ignoring, which means "no look, no talk, and no touch" (you should even demonstrate how you will do this); and that you will continue to give attention for okay behavior. Let's look at how Ms. Williams explained this to Jacob:

"Jacob, Mommy has told you many times that I do not like it when you whine. Starting today, when you whine, Mommy is not going to give you any attention. This means that when you whine, I am not going to look at you, talk to you, or touch you. Let me show you how I will do this. [Turns back to Jacob] As soon as you stop whining, I will give you lots of attention!"

Ms. Williams can then ask what she will do when Jacob whines and what she will do when Jacob does not whine. If Jacob does not yet understand, Ms. Williams can repeat what she just said and even role-play with Jacob. She can tell Jacob to pretend to whine. She can then turn her back demonstrating no look, talk, or touch. Then she can tell Jacob to do an okay behavior and demonstrate Attending and Rewarding! This increases the likelihood that Jacob understands the shift that is happening—Ms. Williams (and you!) may still see the not-okay behavior become worse before it gets better. That doesn't mean your child doesn't understand. But try not to explain again. Rather, just do it! Your child will understand best and learn most by you using the skills! So explain only once each not-okay behavior you are going to Ignore—it is easy for a child to trap a parent into continually discussing and arguing about problem behaviors. Also, remember to Attend to and verbally Reward okay behavior; unless this occurs, Ignoring will not work.

Begin Ignoring the selected behavior on Day 2. Work carefully to make sure you totally Ignore this behavior. Then on Day 5 select a second behavior to Ignore. Follow the same procedure as before to explain what you will be Ignoring; then begin Ignoring the behavior.

Using Worksheet 8-1, list the not-okay behaviors you hope to see less of by using the "Effortful" Ignoring skill. Remember, you can find ideas about which behaviors to Ignore earlier in this chapter. You can also turn back to earlier chapters where you listed not-okay behaviors and their opposites that you were going to Attend to and Reward. Then indicate your success in Ignoring not-okay behaviors. If you successfully used "Effortful" Ignoring with a not-okay behavior, place a check in the box for that day. Remember, this process will take time, and it will not be easy! Also, remember to keep using your Attending and Rewarding skills—the skills in this program build upon one another and are most effective when used in sequence and combination!

WORKSHEET 8-1   Charting Your Success in Ignoring Not-Okay Behaviors

BEHAVIORS TO IGNORE	DAYS					
	2	3	4	5	6	7
1.	❏	❏	❏	❏	❏	❏
2.				❏	❏	❏

Worksheet 8-2 outlines the assignments to be completed during the third week of the program. The assignments take time and effort, but you can do it! After you have followed these steps, you will be ready to move to the next skill.

WORKSHEET 8-2 Daily Assignments for Week 3: "Effortful" Ignoring

"EFFORTFUL" IGNORING	DAYS						
Tasks	1	2	3	4	5	6	7
1. Ideally two 10-minute practice times*	❏	❏	❏	❏	❏	❏	❏
2. Use "Effortful" Ignoring with the first not-okay behavior:**							
Select the first behavior.		❏					
Explain to your child.		❏					
Ignore the behavior.	❏	❏	❏	❏	❏	❏	
3. Use "Effortful" Ignoring with the second not-okay behavior:**							
Select the second behavior.					❏		
Explain to your child.					❏		
Ignore the behavior.					❏	❏	❏

*Incorporate "Effortful" Ignoring with Attending and Rewarding.
**Occurs outside of 10 minute practice.

CHAPTER 9

WEEK 4: GIVING CLEAR INSTRUCTIONS

By this time in the program, you may have begun to notice changes in the behavior of your strong-willed child. This is because you have been using your parenting superpower, your positive attention, to increase behaviors you want to see or see more (okay behavior) and trying to not give any attention at all via "Effortful" Ignoring to mild not-okay behaviors that you want to see less or not at all, such as whining, interrupting, and tantrums. Through this combination of skills, you increase the odds that your child will cooperate with you when you give instructions, which you have already found results in you feeling more positive and less stressed when interacting with your child. If you are starting to see these shifts, we know how good this can feel, and we encourage you to keep reading for more skills, including the Clear Instructions skill you will learn in this chapter. It is easy at this stage of the program for parents to say the change is "good enough" and stop here, but with some extra steps, you will get much better results. We know that by continuing with the program you will learn the combination of skills that will lead to the biggest changes in your parenting, the parent-child relationship and, in turn, your child's behavior.

If you are starting this chapter feeling less hopeful because you are not seeing change, we encourage you to consider two things. The first is that the changes may feel small and slow, given the amount of work you are investing. We understand that this can be frustrating, but want to remind you that your child's not-okay behaviors likely did not develop in a matter of weeks. Instead, the not-okay behaviors that led you to pick up this book likely evolved over a period of months and even years, which means that they are not going to be fixed overnight.

The second point is to remind you that reading this book is not enough. You must practice the skills with your child, you must use the skills throughout the day, and you must start using the skills in combination with one another. It is *hard* work, especially for busy parents. We know that, and if we had a simpler, more efficient, and more effective way to change your child's behavior (a magic pill?), we would be the first to tell you. For now, you must take what you are reading in this book and use it in your day-to-day life with your child if you and your child are to make strides! So if you want to go back and reread and apply the skills from Chapter 6, "Attending"; Chapter 7, "Rewarding"; or Chapter 8, "'Effortful' Ignoring," that is fine. Chapter 9 will be here waiting for you when you are ready for this next step, which starts to address not-okay behaviors more directly, including noncompliance.

HOW TO PUT THE "CLEAR" IN CLEAR INSTRUCTIONS

So here we are! You have seen some changes, some increases in okay behavior, and perhaps some decreases in not-okay behavior. Likely some not-okay behaviors continue, because we have not learned skills to address these behaviors directly and more effectively. Let's start by introducing you to ineffective instructions—if positive attention (your Attending and Rewarding skills!) is a parenting superpower, then ineffective instructions are parents' kryptonite! Ineffective instructions include chain instructions, vague instructions, question instructions, "let's" instructions, and instructions followed by a reason. Each of these types of ineffective instructions makes it difficult for your strong-willed child to comply—just the opposite of what you want to happen.

How do you make instructions clear or effective? The main focus should be on eliminating the five types of ineffective or unclear instructions. Many of us frequently use one or more of these types of instructions. Therefore, our first step is to learn more about these ineffective instructions and then to learn to give Clear Instructions. In Table 9-1, we list the five types of ineffective instructions, define each of them, and list some likely consequences of using each of these types of unclear instruction. Also, below we go into more detail.

If you want your child to become more compliant (a reason you are reading this book!), then it is important to make sure they understand what you are asking them to do. Consequently, the importance of recognizing and not using unclear instructions cannot be overstated.

TABLE 9-1 Ineffective Instructions

TYPE OF INSTRUCTION	DEFINITION	LIKELY CONSEQUENCES
Chain instruction	Instruction that involves numerous steps	Your young child may not be able to remember all the things you told them to do. Therefore, your child may not follow such an instruction.
Vague instruction	Instruction that is not clear and may be interpreted by your child in a different way than you intended	Your child may not be able to correctly interpret and follow instruction.
Question instruction	Instruction in the form of a question, which gives your child the option of saying no	Asking your child puts you in a position of having to accept no as an answer.
"Let's" instruction	Instruction that includes the parent in completing the task when the parent intends for the child to complete the task alone	The child feels tricked and increases noncompliance.
Instruction followed by a reason	Instruction after which the parent gives the child a reason for the task	A reason given after an instruction can distract a young child from complying. If you give a reason, keep it short and give it before you issue the instruction.

CHAIN INSTRUCTIONS

If you say, "Get dressed, brush your teeth, comb your hair, and come to the kitchen for breakfast," you are actually telling your child to do four different things. This is an example of a *chain instruction*, which consists of giving several instructions at one time. The problem with a chain instruction is that your young child may not have the cognitive abilities or attention span to process and effectively remember and respond to all parts of the instruction. It is not uncommon in situations such as this for parents to describe a scenario where a child comes to the kitchen still wearing their pajamas holding their toothbrush and comb. Your child tried to follow your instructions, but you made it difficult, if not impossible, for them to do so effectively!

An effective or clear alternative to giving a chain instruction is to break the instruction down into smaller steps and issue each part of it individually. For example, first tell your child to "brush your teeth." Initially you may Attend and Reward while your child is brushing (e.g., "You are picking up your toothbrush, putting toothpaste on the bristles! Great job brushing your teeth up and down!"), but as time goes on and this behavior is more solidly in place, you may Reward the completion (e.g., "You brushed your teeth! Great job!"). Then give the next instruction, such as "Comb your hair" and again use your Attending and Rewarding skills during and upon the completion of the task. You then continue this process for each step in the routine, thereby increasing the likelihood that your child can and will comply.

Now one concern we hear from parents regarding breaking down instructions into smaller parts like this is, "That will take so much time" or "I don't have that much time to follow my child around in the morning." We understand and gently challenge you to think about how much time you are likely already devoting to your child's not-okay behavior. So one way to think about this is that you are investing more time and positive attention up front with the goal of exerting less time, energy, and frustration correcting not-okay behavior in the long run.

VAGUE INSTRUCTIONS

Children have difficulty with *vague instructions* because they are not clear or specific. Examples of the types of vague instructions that parents often use with children include "Behave," "Be good," and "Be nice." The problem with this kind of instruction is that your child may not yet know exactly how this translates into a behavior or behaviors.

It is much more effective to state directly what you want your child to do. Instead of "Play nicely" for example, you may say something like "Please share your toys with your sibling." Your child now knows exactly what behavior you are looking for, and you can use Attends and Rewards to let them know that you see that behavior and like what you are seeing. For example, as Attending and Rewarding, you could say: "You handed the toy car to your sibling! I love how you are sharing your toys!" The more specific you are and the more you Attend and Reward your child's compliance, the more likely your child is to follow your instruction now and in the future.

QUESTION INSTRUCTIONS

Question instructions ask your child to do something, rather than telling them to do so. For example, "Would you like to clean your room now?" is not a Clear Instruction. It creates a problem because your strong-willed child can—and probably will—simply say no. If you are actually intending to give your child an option and you are okay if the answer is no, then this is fine. And it is developmentally appropriate for parents to give young children some choices, but decide in advance what choices you want to offer and what choices you do not want to offer. For example, you may have choices on after-school snacks, such as "Do you want an apple or a banana?" or choices on clothes they wear, such as "Do you want to wear your red pants or blue pants?" In these cases, be intentional with the fact that you are giving your child a choice, and limit the options to just a couple of choices.

But if you are *not* actually intending to offer a choice and you want your child to do the thing you are telling them to do, such as cleaning their room, then you want to rework your questions into specific statements and Attend to and Reward their progress. Here is an example of cleaning a room: "Please put your toys in the toybox. You are putting the blocks in the box! Now you are putting the stuffed animals in the box! Great job cleaning up your toys!" As you can see, a specific request, not a question instruction, was given by this parent, and it was followed by two Attends and a Reward. A similar procedure can be followed with each part of the task of cleaning up your child's room. Again, as you achieve greater compliance, you may be able to offer slightly more general instructions, such as "Clean your room," and wait until the job is finished to Attend (e.g., "You picked up your toys!") and Reward (e.g., "Great job cleaning your room!"). But to start off, it is better to be more specific and Attend and Reward each step until the task is done. And remember, it is important to not phrase instructions as questions unless you mean to give your child a choice.

LET'S INSTRUCTIONS

A *let's instruction* is one stated in a way that includes the parent—for example, "Let's pick up your blocks now." Similar to our point about question instructions, if you actually intend to help your child pick up the blocks, this is an appropriate instruction. However, if your intent is for your child to pick up the blocks with no help from you, then a let's instruction is misleading and increases the chance your child will not comply if you do not help. In that situation, results will likely be unpleasant: You both will be frustrated.

So if your intention is for your child to do the task without your involvement, make this clear. You can say, "Please put your blocks in the toybox." Stated this way, it is clear you will not be assisting in picking up the blocks. As always, use your Attending and Rewarding skills as your child starts putting the blocks in the box, as your child continues putting the blocks in the box, and after your child finishes the task.

INSTRUCTIONS FOLLOWED BY A REASON

The last type of ineffective instruction is one that is *followed by a reason*. An example is "Please pick up your toys because your grandmother is coming over, and you know how she likes a clean house." The problem with this type of instruction is that your child may forget the original instruction or be distracted by the reason that followed it. Remember, a young child's cognitive abilities are not developed well enough to retain the same amount of information that adults can. Giving a reason or rationale after you have issued the instruction may distract your strong-willed child, may cause your child to forget what you originally asked, or may lead to questioning the reason you gave. For example, "Grandma is coming over! When will she be here? Is she bringing me a present?" As a result, your instruction to clean up the room is lost in your child's enthusiasm and questions.

Giving a short reason or an explanation for a particular instruction is certainly appropriate, however. The effective way to do so is to give the reason first. Returning to the previous example, the parent might change the order of the instruction and the reason in the following way: "Grandma is coming over, and she likes a clean house, so please pick up your toys now." In this way, the instruction is the last thing you say and the last thing your child hears. A child is more likely to comply with this instruction than one in which the reason follows the request.

Use Worksheet 9-1 to check whether you can already recognize different types of instructions. Read each instruction and decide whether it is effective or ineffective. Place a check in the box next to each effective instruction. If you believe the instruction is ineffective, indicate whether it is a chain, vague, question, or let's instruction or an instruction followed by a reason. Then compare your answers with the ones at the bottom of the worksheet. If you correctly identified at least nine of the statements, you have a good grasp of what makes instructions effective. Now you can begin to work on not using ineffective instructions.

WORKSHEET 9-1 Identifying Effective and Ineffective Instructions

Place a check next to each statement that is an effective instruction. What makes each of the remaining instructions ineffective?
❏ 1. "Jacob, hand me the red block."
❏ 2. "Why don't you put on your coat now?"
❏ 3. "Please be careful."
❏ 4. "Please sit beside me."
❏ 5. "Put the red block here, and then put the green block over there."
❏ 6. "Emily, you really need to be good when we play together."
❏ 7. "Because I want you to build a high tower, put the red block on top of the blue block."
❏ 8. "Put the red block on top of the blue block because I want you to build a high tower."
❏ 9. "Would you like to go to bed now?"
❏ 10. "Please clean up, put on your coat, and go outside."
❏ 11. "Let's pick up all the toys."
Answers: Numbers 1, 4, and 7 are effective instructions. Numbers 2, 3, 5, 6, 8, 9, 10, and 11 are ineffective. Numbers 2 and 9 are questions. Numbers 3 and 6 are vague. Numbers 5 and 10 are chain instructions. Number 8 is an instruction followed by a reason. Number 11 is a let's instruction.

TIME TO REFLECT

- Which of the ineffective instructions do you use?
- Does your child understand what you are asking them to do when you use this (these) instruction(s)?

THE "HOW-TOS" FOR GIVING CLEAR INSTRUCTIONS

By avoiding the five types of ineffective instructions, our research shows you will enhance the likelihood that your strong-willed child will comply with the request you make. Effective instructions will eliminate confusion for your child and increase the probability of compliance. Making sure you are increasing the likelihood that your child hears and understands what you are asking will also make you feel more comfortable using consequences when your child does not comply, which we will talk about in a subsequent chapter.

So exactly how should you give clear and effective instructions? These are the critical components of that process. First, before giving an instruction, make sure to get your child's attention. Ways to ensure that you have your child's attention are to move close, make eye contact, and say your child's name *before* you actually issue the instruction. Let's circle back to the Williams family to see what this looks like:

MS. WILLIAMS: "Jacob, look at me."

JACOB: [Looks at Ms. Williams]

MS. WILLIAMS: "Thank you for looking at me."

JACOB: [Smiles]

MS. WILLIAMS: "Your grandma is coming over, so I would like you to clean up your toys. Please put the blocks in the toy box."

In addition to getting your child's attention like Ms. Williams does in that example with Jacob, we ask that you use a firm voice. This does not need to be loud or angry or gruff—just firm or no-nonsense. You want your voice to be another source of information to your child that an instruction, a clear one, is being issued. So even if you get their eyes but your child is still distracted, your tone of voice should cue them in that you are giving a Clear Instruction, are serious, and expect compliance. Sometimes we ask parents to practice using this firm or no-nonsense voice with a spouse or partner or in front of a mirror or to record themselves and play it back. If you do this, you may be surprised at how you sound. Many parents are surprised that what they thought was firm or no-nonsense actually sounds like pleading or begging their child to comply, while others, through gritted teeth, sound like a drill sergeant. Neither extreme is necessary or even helpful!

In addition to getting your child's attention before you give the Clear Instruction and using a firm or no-nonsense tone of voice, use gestures to the extent you can. So in Ms. Williams's case above, she may say, "Put your blocks in the toybox" (points to the toybox). Again you want to increase your child's chances of success (compliance!) by using your verbal statements (get their attention, use a firm tone, give Clear Instruction) as well as your nonverbals (gestures) to increase the likelihood that will occur.

In addition to gestures, whenever possible, use positive instructions ("Do this") instead of negative ones ("Don't do this"). For example, let's circle back to Mr. Gonzalez and

Emily, whom we met in an earlier chapter. Let's imagine they are shopping for school supplies at the local mall. Instead of Mr. Gonzalez saying, "Emily, don't run in front of me in the mall," we suggest he say, "Emily, stay by my side in the mall." Mr. Gonzalez is making it very clear to Emily what behavior he wants to see (rather than behavior he does not want to see), which gives Emily a clear direction on how to navigate their shopping together. It also makes it easier for Mr. Gonzalez to Attend to and Reward Emily for following his instructions. For example, he may say, "Nice job holding Daddy's hand, Emily!" or "I really like when you stay by my side in the store, Emily!"

In addition to our suggestions above, the next two suggestions will make more sense after you read the next chapter. That is okay—we ask you to trust us that they will make sense, and a week of practice giving effective instructions under your belt will be helpful. The first of these two is to wait quietly for five seconds after you give a Clear Instruction for your child to begin complying. Count from one to five in your head to allow your child the opportunity to start complying. So let's imagine Emily starts to run ahead in the mall and Mr. Gonzalez says, "Emily, stand by my side." He then counts slowly in his head, "One, two, three, four, five. . .". As soon as Emily is by his side again after five, Mr. Gonzalez says, "You came back to me when I called! Thank you for standing by my side!"

Now remember in Chapter 6 on Attending, we asked you to decrease the number of instructions and questions you used with your child. As you worked on this, you may have realized that you had been in the habit of asking lots of questions and giving lots of instructions: "Do this!" "Don't do that!" "Why did you do that?" This is common among parents of strong-willed children. But it is not necessarily that the instructions are a problem—it is the type and frequency of the instructions. In fact, some situations do require giving instructions; so we now are focusing on making sure that each instruction you give is a clear and effective one. In other words, children need fewer instructions and questions than we usually give them, but when you do tell your child to do something, you should make it an instruction with which they can comply—*and* you should be willing to exert the effort needed to obtain compliance.

The second suggestion, which will take some practice, is to only give instructions that you are prepared to follow through on to gain compliance from your child. If your child does not follow your instruction and you do nothing, what is going to happen? Your child will learn that you do not mean what you say, and the strong-willed behavior will increase. Thus you need to be willing to follow through and use a consequence for non-compliance to your instructions. However, this is what you will learn in Week 5 of our program. For this week, just focus on how to give clear and effective instructions.

NOW IT'S YOUR TURN!

Our research indicates that parents find giving Clear Instructions not only useful but also relatively easy to learn. However, like all the parenting skills in our five-week program, it takes practice.

During the first three weeks of our five-week program, you set aside ideally two 10-minute periods per day (if time allowed) to practice Attending, Rewarding, and "Effortful" Ignoring. It is important that you keep *at least* one 10-minute session (or perhaps two 5-minute sessions) for Attending, Rewarding, and "Effortful" Ignoring. Together these are the core skills you want to continue to practice because they allow you to increase your focus on positive attention to your child's okay behavior *and* your strong-willed child enjoys them (at least Attending and Rewarding!).

On Day 1, pick out a daily activity that usually involves you giving instructions to your child. This may be dressing for preschool or school in the morning, or it may be your evening routine of taking a bath and preparing for bed. In whatever situation you choose, practice using simple, firm Clear Instructions. Give your child time to comply, and Attend to and Reward any movement toward compliance. This is successive approximation (which we discussed earlier in the book). The idea is if you tell your child "Put on your shoes" and you realize your child is looking at the shoes (although not necessarily moving to put them on), you would find opportunities to give at least some positive attention: "You are looking at your shoes!" Then if your child reaches for a shoe, say something like "You are reaching for your shoe!" Then if your child starts putting on a shoe, say, "You are putting on one shoe! Nice job putting on your shoe!" Then repeat for the second shoe. On Day 4, select another situation that involves giving Clear Instructions to your child, and begin focusing on how you give Clear Instructions in that situation. Doing this will help you integrate what you have learned into your daily routine. As we have emphasized repeatedly, slowly integrating what you have learned into your daily interactions with your child will be necessary for your behavior to change and for their behavior to change. Giving Clear Instructions is an excellent way to promote behavior change!

TIME TO REFLECT

- What is a daily activity of your child in which you use unclear instructions?
- What can you say to make the instructions clearer?

Worksheet 9-2 summarizes your assignments for Week 4. When you have followed these steps, you will be ready to move to the final week of the program.

WORKSHEET 9-2   Daily Assignments for Week 4: Clear Instructions

TASKS	DAYS						
	1	2	3	4	5	6	7
1. Set aside at least one 10-minute practice time for Attending, Rewarding, and "Effortful" Ignoring.	❑	❑	❑	❑	❑	❑	❑
2. Select the first daily situation in which to issue effective instructions, and begin issuing instructions.	❑	❑	❑	❑	❑	❑	❑
3. Select the second daily situation in which to issue effective instructions, and begin issuing instructions.				❑	❑	❑	❑

CHAPTER 10

WEEK 5: USING TIME-OUTS FOR NONCOMPLIANCE

By now you have learned a set of skills—Attending, Rewarding, and "Effortful" Ignoring—aimed at improving your relationship with your child and, in turn, increasing the chance that you are seeing behavior that you want to see or see more. You should also be doing a better job of making sure that when you tell your child to do something, your instructions are clear and concise (Clear Instructions) and you are giving lots of Attends and Rewards when your child does comply. These changes are likely helping you to feel better about your relationship with your child, but you probably still see some not-okay behaviors, like noncompliance, even if you are using the skills exactly as we have suggested. This highlights how entrenched your child's noncompliance may be and that you will likely need some additional tools to help increase the chance that your child can and will comply more often.

Some level of noncompliance is a normal part of child development; as children grow older, they strive to be independent—which means they will test limits you set by being noncompliant. However, with strong-willed children, noncompliance to your instructions often becomes a continual affair. Helping your child to comply more consistently not only will decrease stress at home, but will help them thrive in other settings, including daycare and school. Toward this end, another tool or skill in your toolbox that will be effective is consequences for noncompliance as well as for some other more moderate or severe not-okay behaviors that we will address in Chapter 12. Before we tell you what we advise parents to use for consequences, let's look at what consequences parents typically use with their strong-willed children and why these often do not work as effectively as parents wish they would.

INEFFECTIVE CONSEQUENCES

The function of a consequence is to decrease the likelihood that your child does a not-okay behavior, such as noncompliance, again in the future. In our experience, most parents of strong-willed children have tried a variety of consequences for noncompliance and other problem behaviors. These consequences have ranged from overlooking noncompliance to reasoning to threatening to spanking. Some parents tell us that they have tried all these things. Other parents tell us that they stick to one even though it doesn't seem to be working very well, but they are unsure what else to try.

Let's start with overlooking your child's noncompliance. Importantly, parents are not always doing this intentionally, but rather the idea of a consequence just feels too hard or complicated to actually follow through. As a result, it is easier to pretend you didn't see or hear it. While we recommended "no look, no talk, no touch" ("Effortful" Ignoring, Chapter 8) for mild attention-seeking behaviors such as whining or tantrums, parents simply cannot Ignore noncompliance or some other not-okay behaviors like hitting a peer or sibling, breaking a rule (e.g., not climbing on the counter), or running off in a public place like a mall. If you Ignore these types of not-okay behaviors, your child is actually likely to do them more (rather than less) frequently because the behavior allows them to get their way, get out of doing something they do not want to do, or ineffectively communicate how they are feeling.

Let's look at noncompliance for a moment. If you Ignore the behavior after you give an instruction, your child learns that it is okay to avoid doing what you ask because at least some of the time you don't seem to notice (or care). As a result, noncompliance pays off and will occur more frequently. In a similar fashion, aggressive and destructive behaviors should not be Ignored, because these behaviors are dangerous and because "Effortful" Ignoring does not immediately decrease the likelihood of them happening again. The behaviors are too rewarding in and of themselves for "Effortful" Ignoring to work. As an example, a child wants a toy another child has and hits the child to get the toy. The aggressive behavior is reinforced by getting the toy. Your "Effortful" Ignoring of this act of aggression will simply not work.

Reasoning is what many parents would prefer to do. After all, if you could explain to your child why compliance is a good thing to learn, wouldn't your child be more likely to comply?

Unfortunately, reasoning rarely convinces young children to behave, in part because they do not yet have the cognitive ability to reason in the same way that adults do. Again, remember that young children are not necessarily thinking about how their behavior will impact others. Rather, the behavior of most children in this age range is motivated by learning—I do this behavior, and it achieves this response from Mom or Dad. Based on what I learned from my last experience, I will (or will not) do that behavior again. In addition to parents running the risk that children simply do not understand our adult rationales, reasoning actually functions to give your child attention for the not-okay behavior. Think about the times when you have tried to reason with your child. You are likely very earnest, leaning in to get their attention, talking in a soothing tone of voice, and perhaps placing your hand gently on their shoulder or back. In turn, your words and actions are following a not-okay behavior like noncompliance and increasing (rather than decreasing) the likelihood that your child will do the same thing in an hour, later tonight, or tomorrow.

When parents are really frustrated and when overlooking the behavior no longer seems possible and reasoning is simply not working, it is not unusual to threaten extreme consequences in the moment. For example, something like "You will never be allowed to use your tablet again as long as you live if you don't do what I say now!" might aptly convey how you are feeling, but it is unlikely that you will actually be able to or even want to follow through with this consequence in the future. So while such threats may get your child's attention and even stop the not-okay behavior in the moment, it is unlikely to have a lasting effect, as your child starts to learn over time that you do not or cannot follow through with your threat.

Some parents also spank their children. Often parents will tell us that they were spanked as a child and that it was effective for them. As a result, it is what they do with their child as well. There are a couple of issues with spanking. The first is that parents often spank out of anger or frustration and subsequently rarely feel good about doing it. Some of these parents even worry about taking it too far and accidentally hurting their child, which is, of course, a risk. Also, while spanking may have "worked" for you when you were a child, you probably decided to start reading this book because it doesn't seem to be working as well (or at all) in terms of changing your child's not-okay behavior. In part this may be because of your strong-willed child's temperament. And some research suggests that these children may be more responsive to positive attention than to punishment. So giving (e.g., Attending, Rewarding) and removing (Ignoring) attention may actually be more effective than things like spanking! Finally, spanking has the potential to teach children that the way to address not-okay behavior is to be physical, which is a message that we do not want to convey as we think about how we want young children to treat their siblings, peers, and pets.

So we suggest that you do not overlook, reason with, or spank a child who is being noncompliant or engaging in other moderate to severe not-okay behaviors (e.g., hitting, breaking rules, running off in a store). We therefore must have an alternative strategy in mind, right? We recommend *Time-Out*, which is a technique you may have tried unsuccessfully already. However, we believe Time-Out works very effectively when used appropriately. Nevertheless, we should note that Time-Out has received a fair amount of criticism in the popular press and media, which may discourage parents from trying it again or using it the first time. We will address these common misconceptions and describe why Time-Out (rather than Time-In) is a way to efficiently and effectively decrease not-okay behaviors like noncompliance and other problem behavior.

TO USE TIME-OUT OR TIME-IN: THAT IS THE QUESTION

Although there are various definitions and examples of Time-Out in the media, our definition of Time-Out simply refers to putting your child in a quiet, ideally boring spot for a few minutes while doing your best to practice your "Effortful" Ignoring skills—no look, no talk, and no touch. In other words, rather than overlooking the behavior, reasoning with your child, punishing your child with something like spanking, or threatening your child in a moment of frustration, you are letting your child know the not-okay behavior (e.g., noncompliance) will not receive any attention. Indeed, research has demonstrated that the Time-Out procedure that we present here is an effective way to decrease noncompliance and other problem behavior, but we admit it is not an easy skill to learn. Our research indicates that immediately after our five-week program, parents find Time-Out to be relatively difficult to use with their child and only moderately useful. However, over the following two months, parents report that Time-Out becomes significantly easier to implement and more useful in dealing with their child's strong-willed behavior. So we will ask you to use it exactly as we suggest here, as even slight variations can decrease the effectiveness of Time-Out significantly! This means you need to learn and continue to use the Time-Out procedure for it to be effective, which, like most parenting, takes time, practice, and consistent use.

As we mentioned earlier, we realize that we may be asking you to use a procedure that you heard criticized in the popular press. There are various reasons for this unfounded negative attention to Time-Out. The central idea behind much of this criticism is the notion that a parent's removal of attention (i.e., no look, talk, or touch) by using Time-Out can or will have a lasting negative effect on the quality of the parent-child relationship, as well as the child's emotional security, self-esteem, and well-being. Critics have pointed out that this may be particularly true for children with a history of maltreatment or other trauma, given the potential perceived risk of confusing or frightening or making the child feel abandoned. As a result, these critics have suggested doing the opposite, which is sometimes called "Time-In," or sitting with and engaging the child to talk about their thoughts and feelings. We absolutely do not want to minimize the concerns about using Time-Out versus Time-In, which is why we are addressing them here. Importantly, there is no research to date that suggests that Time-Out is detrimental to the adjustment of young children, including young children with trauma histories. Instead, theory and research suggest that Time-Out, in combination with the other skills you are learning in this book, creates a sense of predictability for children, helping them to learn what behaviors are adaptive and to do those behaviors more frequently. It also produces a context in which children can learn to regulate their own feelings and behaviors. Moreover, we fully support parents talking with their children about their thoughts, feelings, and behaviors as parents are told to do with Time-In; however, we recommend having these conversations *after* (but not immediately after) the consequence (Time-Out) in order to decrease the likelihood that parental attention is not inadvertently increasing rather than decreasing the likelihood that the not-okay behavior occurs in the future. So let's take a look at some of the important components of Time-Out.

PICKING A TIME-OUT SPOT

As we noted earlier, our suggestions regarding Time-Out will be quite specific, as they will be based on what has been shown to work in research, as well as in our own clinical experience with children and families. First, choose a location where you will do Time-Out in your home. There are a number of things you need to consider in choosing this place. It should be away from toys, people, windows, televisions, radios, and anything else your child enjoys or will likely find stimulating or engaging. Remember, using Time-Out as a consequence means your child is receiving *no* positive attention from you or anyone else or anything else. Second, nothing breakable should be nearby. Why cause more stress by putting your child in Time-Out next to a valuable lamp? Table 10-1 summarizes locations that are suitable and unsuitable for Time-Out. Let's explore these.

TABLE 10-1   Choosing a Time-Out Location

BEST OPTIONS
Hallway
Kitchen corner (for two- and three-year-old children)
Parents' bedroom
LEAST DESIRABLE OPTION
Child's bedroom
NOT OPTIONS
Bathroom
Closet
Dark room

One good place for Time-Out can be at the end of a hallway. This is typically a place away from people and other enjoyable activities (for example, watching television). If you use a hallway for a Time-Out area, we recommend keeping an adult-sized chair in the Time-Out place. This can serve several useful purposes. First, it can remind your child that this is the Time-Out area. In addition, it helps you define where your child should be during a Time-Out (that is, in the chair). Also, an adult-sized chair will keep your child's feet off the floor, so it is harder to get up and leave the Time-Out area or scoot the chair backward. Be careful not to put the chair so close to the wall that your child can continually kick the wall, perhaps putting a hole through it.

A bedroom is also a possible location. Your child's bedroom may contain too many enjoyable activities, however. If it does and you absolutely must use your child's bedroom as the Time-Out area, remove all toys from the room. Your own bedroom may be a preferable location because it probably contains fewer things to entertain your child. Just make sure there are no breakables in the room.

For children who are two or three years old, a corner in the kitchen may be a good option. You can keep an eye on your child during the Time-Out. Be sure, however, not to make any contact (visual, verbal, or physical) with them.

Some parents identify a bathroom as a Time-Out area. This can be dangerous if it contains medicine, razor blades, or other potentially harmful objects. Consequently, we do not recommend using a bathroom.

Whatever location you select, never turn off the lights as part of giving a Time-Out. This will only scare your child. For the same reason, never use a closet or small enclosed area for a Time-Out. The purpose of giving a Time-Out is to remove your child temporarily from attention, not to frighten.

DOING TIME-OUT

When you use Time-Out for your child's noncompliance, you need to follow an exact sequence to maximize its effectiveness and to decrease the likelihood that your child is noncompliant. The steps to use are summarized in Table 10-2. Once you know the steps and before you actually use them, specify for your child exactly what behavior (e.g., "not doing what you are told to do") will result in a Time-Out as well as how it works. You should walk your child through the entire sequence, from giving a "pretend instruction" to which your child does not respond at all or in the way you requested, to going to Time-Out, to issuing the "pretend instruction" again. Remember, practice makes perfect! You can also go through each step of the Time-Out procedure and ask your child, "What will happen next?" The more your child understands Time-Out, the more cooperative your child will be when you use Time-Out, and the fewer times you will actually have to use it.

TABLE 10-2 Time-Out Sequence for Noncompliance

1. Issue an effective instruction and Attend to/Reward compliance to the instruction.
2. If your child does not begin to comply within five seconds, issue a Warning: "If you do not _____, you will have to take a Time-Out."
3. If your child does not begin to comply within five seconds, state, "Because you did not _____, you have to take a Time-Out." Attend to/Reward compliance to the Warning.
4. Lead your child to Time-Out without lecturing, scolding, or arguing.
5. Ignore shouting, protesting, and promising to comply.
6. Tell your child to sit in the Time-Out chair.
7. When your child is sitting quietly, set the timer for three minutes.
8. When the time is over, including their being quiet for the last 15 seconds, return to the chair and tell them Time-Out is over.
9. Restate the original instruction.
10. Implement the Time-Out procedure again if your child does not comply.
11. Be consistent—consistent (as possible) use of this procedure is important.

Let's detail the Time-Out procedure. Remember, this is complex; as a result, don't expect to "learn" it with one quick read. We encourage you to read the material, summarized in Table 10-2, in this section carefully and to practice it, ideally with another adult.

When you have given a simple and clear instruction (as you learned to do in Chapter 9), wait five seconds for your child to begin complying. If your child does comply, use your Attending and Rewarding skills: "You did what I told you to do the first time!" (Attending) "Great job!" (Rewarding). If your child does not comply the first time, give one and only one Warning: "If you do not _____ you will have to take a Time-Out." Issue this Warning in a matter-of-fact voice without yelling or becoming angry. Wait five seconds. If your child begins complying, increase the likelihood that this happens in the future by Attending and Rewarding: "Thank you for doing what I told you to do." If your child does not comply after the Warning, take your child by the hand and say only, "Because you did not _____ , you have to take a Time-Out." Say this only once and in a calm but firm voice. Do not lecture, scold, or argue with your child, and do not accept any excuses. Remember, your goal is to minimize attention to the not-okay behavior. Then lead your child by the hand to the Time-Out place and set a timer (yes, it is very helpful to have a timer and to use it) for three minutes. Do not talk to your child during the Time-Out, and practice your "Effortful" Ignoring to any shouts, protests, and promises to comply.

When you tell your child to take a Time-Out, a couple of things may happen. For one thing, your child may immediately begin complying in an attempt to avoid the Time-Out. If this happens, do not give in, but move ahead with the Time-Out. This is difficult, because after all, your child did at least start to comply. However, think about what message this would give to your child: "I don't have to comply until my mom gives me an instruction and a Warning and then starts to take me to Time-Out." Obviously, this is not your goal.

A second possibility is that your child may resist going to the Time-Out chair. If this occurs, you have several options. First, you can stand behind your child, put your hands under your child's armpits, lift your child up with your child facing forward or away from you, and then take your child to and put your child in the Time-Out chair. Second, you can tell a child who is five or six years old that they will lose a privilege. (See the section "Overcoming Common Time-Out Challenges" later in this chapter for more information.) Third, you can tell your child that you are going to add three more minutes to Time-Out (six minutes instead of three minutes). Then try again to lead your child to Time-Out, and set the timer for six minutes. If you still cannot get your child into the Time-Out chair, do not keep adding three minutes. Try either the first or second (if your child is five or six years old) option. When you reach the Time-Out chair, tell your child to sit down. When your child is quiet, you can set a timer and tell your child to stay in the chair until the timer sounds. A timer can provide your child with a cue about the length of the Time-Out. Place the timer where your child can see but not touch it. Set the timer for three minutes (unless you lengthened it to six minutes).

Beyond the initial three-minute period, the length of the Time-Out should depend in part on a requirement that your child be quiet before you end the Time-Out. When you first begin using Time-Out, require your child to be quiet for the last 15 seconds of the Time-Out. If your child is screaming or kicking the wall at the end of the Time-Out period, wait until your child has been quiet for at least 15 seconds beyond the Time-Out period before ending the Time-Out. After several weeks of using Time-Out, you can change the requirement so that your child has to be quiet for the last minute of Time-Out. You can gradually continue to lengthen the time your child has to be quiet before leaving Time-Out. In this way your child will learn that good behavior in Time-Out is important and is required for leaving Time-Out. Do not end the Time-Out until your child is quiet!

After the Time-Out period is over, return to the chair and tell your child it is time to get up. Since your child had to go to Time-Out for not following an instruction, return to the scene where the initial noncompliance occurred, and give the original instruction again. You must do this, or your child will learn that a Time-Out is a way not to have to comply. For example, if your child goes to Time-Out for refusing to pick up toys and you pick them up during the Time-Out, your child will learn to avoid picking up toys by taking a Time-Out. Once your child is out of Time-Out and you have given the instruction again, follow the same sequence leading to Time-Out if your child does not comply.

The flowchart in Figure 10-1 shows the different pathways and consequences for each pathway that you should apply depending on whether or not your child complies with your instructions. Remember, after giving a Time-Out, you always return to giving the instruction again. Theoretically, you could stay in the sequence forever if your child never complied. However, we recommend that you continue this sequence only until your child complies or reaches their eighteenth birthday (just kidding!). Seriously, you must stick with it until compliance occurs, Reward that compliance, and in turn teach your child that compliance (not noncompliance) is what gets your positive attention.

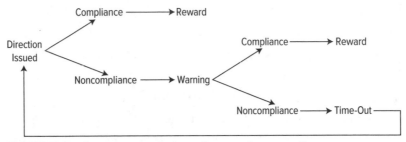

FIGURE 10-1 Consequences for compliance and noncompliance

Some parents worry this process may take "forever" or never work. We totally understand this concern because based on your experience with your child this may feel very likely. That said, in our experience if parents follow these recommended steps, do it every time, and genuinely do not give a child unintended attention for the not-okay behavior, it will extinguish more quickly than they expect. The issue too often is that parents do not realize how much attention they are giving the not-okay behavior even when they are trying not to.

As an example, one of us was walking in a park where there were a number of children's soccer games going on across multiple fields. We saw something like this: A parent was walking his child over to a fence where he placed a lawn chair to do a Time-Out. While the steps the parent were following looked spot on from afar (i.e., a chair, an isolated spot), a closer look revealed that the parent was muttering under his breath (attention) when taking his child to Time-Out, occasionally shouting to the child during Time-Out about how much time they had left (attention!), and then walking back and forth between the game and the child's Time-Out spot when the child yelled something or got up (attention!). Then the game ended, and the parent ended the Time-Out before the child's time was up. Needless to say, the child's behavior is unlikely to be changed by this experience during which the child received lots of attention and the end of the Time-Out was not tied to the child's behavior. Of course, it is easy to watch from afar and point out everything this parent was doing wrong, which is why getting Time-Out right is going to take a lot of practice. We talk more in the subsequent sections of this chapter about this and other common challenges to using Time-Out.

Some parents want to spend time discussing in detail with their child why Time-Out was used, their love for the child, and how horrible it made them feel to have to give a Time-Out. Other parents want to have a discussion with their child in order to induce guilt over not complying and to receive an apology from the child. Neither of these two types of discussion is desirable or helpful. A brief comment, such as "You had to go to Time-Out because you did not do what Mommy told you to do," but no more, is acceptable immediately after Time-Out. Earlier, we talked about using Time-In after Time-Out has been completed. Our recommendation is to wait 30 minutes afterward to discuss why Time-Out occurred and the child's feelings. If you choose this approach, one Warning: Don't use this time to browbeat your child or to induce guilt.

Finally, let's turn our attention to an important point: Use Time-Out consistently. So if you tell your child that noncompliance will result in a Time-Out, use this sequence every single time noncompliance occurs. In order for consequences to be most effective, parents must use them *every time* a child fails to follow directions. If you do use consequences every time, then your child will learn that you are not going to give attention to not-okay behaviors such as noncompliance. In other words, there will be no motivation for your child to test your limits if your response (a consequence!) is the same every time!

Why aren't more parents consistent with their use of consequences? Well, use of consistent consequences can be challenging and time-consuming. Parents are busy, managing a lot of things at one time, and each hour, let alone each day, can feel like a flurry of activity balancing work inside and outside the house, family, and other activities (see Chapter 3). So one day you may respond to your child's refusal to take a bath by saying, "You are going to take a bath now, and I mean it!," while on another day you may find yourself saying, "Okay, just be dirty if that is what you want." While there may be reasons for your flipping back and forth (e.g., whether it is a school day or weekend; your mood or stress level), your child doesn't necessarily know that there is a method to the madness and instead comes to learn that limits (e.g., bathtime) can be successfully tested. In turn, it is not surprising that once a limit is successfully challenged, children will test it again—and again and again.

Let's consider an example from your world. As adults, we can think about the times when we have driven over the speed limit. You may have been pulled over at some point in your life for speeding. If so, the embarrassment of getting pulled over, the financial burden of paying the ticket, the time commitment of going to court, and the points on insurance likely dramatically decrease the likelihood that you will speed again—at least for a while. But there are likely lots of times you have gone over the speed limit and not been pulled over, so you may start to quite literally test the limit, and you find yourself going over the speed limit more frequently because there is no consequence.

Now what if instead you knew that every time you were going over the speed limit, you were pulled over by the police, you automatically received a fine, and your car insurance rates went up. If we knew that these consequences would happen every time, not just some of the time, we would likely change our behavior and speed less or not at all. Children are the same! Any inconsistency in your reaction to their not-okay behaviors like noncompliance increases the likelihood of further non-compliance because you have left open the possibility that your response will be no response at all or may even earn them lots of attention. In contrast, consistently using a specific consequence and using it every time decreases the likelihood that not-okay behaviors like noncompliance will occur again or at least as frequently because children learn there is no option in terms of how you will respond!

The message should be clear by now: Just like Rewarding compliance consistently, using Time-Out consistently for non-compliance is important. However, please remember, we as parents are *not* perfect. Your goal is to be as consistent as possible, but realize you will not be totally consistent—no one is!

OVERCOMING COMMON TIME-OUT CHALLENGES

As we have already alluded to, you may encounter several challenges when using Time-Out. One of the most common is that your child may not stay in the Time-Out chair when you tell them to do so. If this happens, you have several options. First, if your child initially refuses to sit or stay in the chair, you say that the Time-Out period will not even start until your child sits down in the chair. A second option for refusing to stay in the chair is to add three minutes to the Time-Out (six minutes instead of three minutes). As with refusal to go to Time-Out, do not keep adding minutes to Time-Out each time the child leaves the chair. Instead, set the timer for six minutes each time your child is returned to the Time-Out chair. A third option is that you can place your child in the chair again, say something like "Stay in the chair," and place your hand on your child's leg to encourage staying seated. A fourth option for children who are five years of age or older is to say that there will be a loss of a privilege if the child does not return to the Time-Out chair. For example, you could say in a calm voice, "If you get up again, you can't ride your bike the rest of the day." Remember, if you say it, do it! Removing privileges will not work with children younger than five because they have difficulty bridging the gap in time between what is happening now and enjoying the privilege later.

Another common problem is that your child may say things in Time-Out that are meant to get your attention. Some of these may be painful for you to hear. Let's look at some examples that Mr. Gonzalez, whom we met earlier in the book, told us that Emily said while they were beginning to use Time-Out as a consequence:

- "I have to go to the potty."
- "I don't love you anymore."
- "I'm going to run away."
- "I hate you."
- "I like Time-Out better than being with you."

Ms. Williams, whom you also met earlier in the book, told us that Jacob said similarly hurtful and even scary things, like:

- "You are ugly and mean."
- "I wish I was dead."
- "I am going to call 911."
- "I wish you were not my mommy."

These sorts of statements will be difficult for you to hear, and it will be really challenging not to try to soothe your child.

We tell parents to predict these sorts of behaviors so that they are not surprised when the behaviors occur and to be prepared to practice "Effortful" Ignoring with these types of statements. And remember, you can talk about anything that your child says during Time-Out 30 minutes afterward, but you cannot talk about it until Time-Out ends. Once again, you want your attention to be your superpower, so giving attention to what your child is saying before or during Time-Out will increase the behaviors you do not want to see (or want to see less).

Some parents also report a lot of movement in the Time-Out chair, including things like slowly moving the chair farther from the wall or outside the Time-Out spot. As we noted earlier, this is one reason for using an adult-sized chair in Time-Out—it makes it more difficult for your child's feet to touch the floor and move the chair or kick the wall. If either of these behaviors does occur, follow through with one of the four options we previously presented for handling a child who leaves Time-Out.

Sometimes a child refuses to come out of Time-Out when it is over. If this occurs, tell your child that they need to take another Time-Out. After all, refusing to leave Time-Out is another case of not complying. Set the timer for three minutes again. When the timer goes off, return to the Time-Out area and again tell your child it is time to leave Time-Out. If your child still refuses to come out of Time-Out, start the timer again. Do this until your child comes out of Time-Out and follows the instruction you originally issued. You will get there—it just may take practice for you and your child!

Table 10-3 summarizes these and other Time-Out problems and solutions. One or more of these problems will likely occur—so get ready. Also, as you now know, giving Time-Outs is a complicated procedure, so you will need to practice it before using it with your child and then go over it with your child, including walking through the entire procedure. In the next section, we will spell out how to learn, practice, and use Time-Outs for noncompliance.

TABLE 10-3 Time-Out Problems and Possible Solutions

PROBLEMS	POSSIBLE SOLUTIONS
Refusing to sit in the chair	Do not start the Time-Out until your child is seated.
Leaving or moving the chair	Stop the timer until your child sits down.
	Add three minutes to Time-Out, and reset the timer for six minutes.
	Place your child in the chair, tell your child to stay, and place your hand on your child's leg.
	Remove a privilege if your child does not return to the chair (for children aged five years old and up).
Insulting you verbally	Ignore the insults.
Yelling and crying	Ignore the yelling and crying.
Refusing to leave Time-Out	Start Time-Out over.
A sibling interacting with your child while the child is in Time-Out	Put the sibling in Time-Out in another location.

PRACTICING YOUR TIME-OUT SKILLS

Worksheet 10-1 summarizes your daily assignments for using Time-Out with your child's noncompliance during Week 5. As you carry out these assignments, remember to continue at least one 10-minute daily practice session in Attending, Rewarding, and "Effortful" Ignoring.

WORKSHEET 10-1 Assignments for Week 5: Using Time-Outs

TASKS	DAYS						
	1	2	3	4	5	6	7
1. Select Time-Out place.	❏						
2. Memorize the steps of Time-Out.	❏						
3. Practice giving Time-Outs with another adult and without your child.	❏	❏	❏				
4. Tell your child about Time-Outs for noncompliance.			❏				
5. Begin giving Time-Outs for failure to comply with one instruction.			❏	❏	❏	❏	
6. Begin giving Time-Outs for failure to comply with all instructions.							❏

Remember: Attend to/Reward your child's compliance!

Let's look at Worksheet 10-1 in a little more detail. Start on Day 1 by selecting a Time-Out place and memorizing the Time-Out procedure. On the first three days of this week, learn the Time-Out procedure by studying and practicing as described below. Plan to allow at least 30 minutes a day. Remember, Time-Out is challenging, especially at first as you learn to do it the way we suggest here, which may be different than what you have tried before! Reread this chapter; in particular go over Tables 10-2 and 10-3. Practice Time-Out with your spouse or other co-parent or adult by completing the following:

1. Describe where and why you selected a particular place for Time-Out.
2. Describe Time-Out step-by-step as presented in Table 10-2 and earlier in this chapter.
3. Describe how you will handle problems that arise in Time-Out (see Table 10-3).

4. Walk the adult through Time-Out as presented in Table 10-2. Note any questions or "wrong turns" you make, and recalculate.

5. Do the walk-through again, but this time have the other adult do one or more of the problem behaviors that you anticipate being a challenge and problem-solve how you will navigate those together.

On Day 3, go over Time-Out as described in Table 10-2 with your child. Walk your child through Time-Out so your child knows exactly what to expect, and ask questions such as "What do you think will happen next?" Tell your child about two important rules that must be followed when in Time-Out: (1) Stay in the Time-Out chair and (2) remain quiet.

Select an instruction that you often give and your child often fails to follow. Tell your child that Time-Out will occur every time noncompliance occurs. Then following the Time-Out sequence from Table 10-2, give a Time-Out whenever your child does not follow the instruction. After using Time-Out with this behavior on Days 3 through 6, tell your child that all failure to follow instructions at home will result in Time-Out. Begin using Time-Out with all such noncompliance.

Here is an additional thing you can do that helps many parents. Post two things on the wall where you will see them every day: a copy of the Time-Out procedure in Table 10-2 and a calendar. Refresh your memory daily by reading the Time-Out sequence. On the calendar, record each time you use Time-Out and the behavior for which you used it. This will help you keep track of how often you use Time-Out and whether your child's strong-willed problem behaviors are changing.

Learning the details of the Time-Out procedure will take your full attention. In fact, you will have to be a little strong-willed yourself in order to learn and use it effectively. And as our research indicates, it takes time for you to feel comfortable with the use of Time-Out and for it to be effective. However, if you are attentive to your child and Reward compliance, you should not have to use Time-Out very often, and as time goes by and you consistently use Time-Out, you will need to use it less and less often. Be careful not to revert to focusing only on your child's problem behaviors. Attending and verbally Rewarding will build the positive relationship you want to have with your child.

For this week we will not present a Time to Reflect, as we have given you a lot to learn and use. Nevertheless, we encourage you to reflect on what you have been using as a consequence for your child's noncompliance and how you can use the "new" Time-Out procedure we have presented. Most of all, we encourage you to practice! After all, as we said earlier, practice makes perfect (well, as close to perfect as you can become considering you are a parent!).

CHAPTER 11

REVIEWING AND INTEGRATING THE FIVE SKILLS

First and most importantly, congratulations! You completed our five-week parenting program! You have learned skills to increase your child's okay behavior or behavior you want to see or see more. These skills, which are summarized in Table 11-1, include Attending and Rewarding. As a reminder, Attending is a sort of running commentary of your child's okay behavior without instructions, questions, or teaching. This can be in the context of playing with your child, and as a parent you are Attending to your child's play behavior such as "You are putting the red block on the blue block." We do want you to continue to look for all kinds of opportunities to practice your

Attending during your child's play, but also throughout the day. For an example, let's circle back to Mr. Gonzalez in a scenario where Emily wants to go outside to play but needs to put on shoes first. In this situation, Mr. Gonzalez's Attending to Emily might look something like this: "You are looking at your shoes! Now you picked up your right shoe! You are wiggling your right foot into your right shoe!" So as you see, Mr. Gonzalez is simply describing what Emily is doing, but the exclamation points convey that he is not just describing Emily's behavior but also communicating lots of enthusiasm about Emily's behavior.

You also learned Rewarding in our five-week program. Rewards can be verbal, either labeled or unlabeled, as well as physical. Ideally, parents want to use Attends and Rewards in combination, with the use of Attends being more liberal (remember, Attends are the pennies!) and Rewards used more judiciously to really emphasize to your child the very specific behavior you like and want to see more. So if we go back to Emily who is putting on shoes, Mr. Gonzalez may follow those Attends with "Great job putting on your right shoe!" (Labeled Verbal Reward), and then pat Emily on the back (Physical Reward). As you can see, Mr. Gonzalez did a great job using Attends to shape each of Emily's behaviors that led up to ultimately putting on the right shoe and then saved the Rewards for once the shoe was on.

Now let's imagine that in this example once the right shoe is on, Emily starts to get distracted and off task. Emily is playing with the left shoe, sort of kicking it around on the floor, then picking it up and tossing it from one hand to the other. Knowing what you know now, what would you want to see Mr. Gonzalez do here? If you answered "Effortful" Ignoring, you are right! So yes, we want Mr. Gonzalez to respond to Emily's off-task behavior with "Effortful" Ignoring, or no look, no talk, and no touch. Then once both Mr. Gonzalez and Emily start to get the hang of this, Emily will realize sooner and sooner that the on-task behavior (e.g., putting on the shoes) gets lots of positive attention from dad and the off-task behavior (i.e., anything but putting on shoes) doesn't get any attention at all. So let's presume Emily picks up on this and bends over in the chair to start to put on the left shoe. What do you want Mr. Gonzalez to do? If you answered start Attending and Rewarding, you are right! It may look something like this: "You are bending over to put on your left shoe!" (Attending) "You are wiggling your foot into your left shoe!" (Attending) "You put on your left shoe!" (Attending) "Thank you so much for putting on both of your shoes before you go outside!" (Labeled Verbal Reward).

The use of Attending, Rewarding, and "Effortful" Ignoring while playing with your child and throughout the day will be helpful in and of itself, but practice will also prepare you for those moments when you tell your child to do something and you need them to do it the first time. So let's take putting on shoes again, but this time Mr. Gonzalez says, "Emily, we need to leave for school. Please put on your shoes." As you may remember, this is a Clear Instruction—Mr Gonzalez gets Emily's attention by saying "Emily," gives the explanation first, and then give his instruction (and only one instruction). If Emily starts putting on the shoes within five seconds, what would we tell Mr. Gonzalez to do? If you said Attending and Rewarding, you are right! "You picked up your right shoe!" (Attending) "You are putting on your shoe!" (Attending) "Thanks for putting on your shoe!" (Rewarding). If instead Emily doesn't start putting on the shoe within five seconds, Mr. Gonzalez would say what? If you answered give a Warning, you are correct! So he may say something like "Emily, if you don't put on your shoes, you will have to go to Time-Out" and then wait another five seconds. If

Emily complies with the Warning, Mr. Gonzalez would then say what? If you answered Attending and Rewarding, then you are getting the hang of this! "You are putting on your shoe!" (Attending) "Thanks for putting on your shoe!" (Rewarding). If instead Emily fails to start putting on the shoe within five seconds after the Warning, then Mr. Gonzalez needs to follow through with the consequence, Time-Out. Mr. Gonzalez would say something like "Emily, you did not put on your shoes, so you have to go to Time-Out." As a reminder, Time-Out should be in a designated spot that is free from distraction or opportunities for attention and that lasts for three minutes, and your child needs to be quiet and still for the last 15 seconds or so. At the end of the Time-Out, what would Mr. Gonzalez say to Emily? If you said that Mr. Gonzalez should reissue the Clear Instruction, then you are right! So Mr. Gonzalez may say something like "Emily, your Time-Out is over; now put on your shoes."

TABLE 11-1 The Assessment Process and Five Parenting Skills

ASSESSMENT PROCESS
Does your child's behavior need to change?
Does your child often display problem behaviors common among strong-willed children?
Is your child's behavior a problem in daily situations?
Does your child score poorly on the Compliance Test?
Are you often frustrated with your child's behavior?
SKILL 1: ATTENDING
Describe your child's okay behavior.
Imitate your child's play behavior.
Reduce directions, questions, and attempts to teach.
Practice!

SKILL 2: REWARDING
Continue to describe and imitate your child's okay behavior.
Verbally Reward your child's okay behavior by labeling the desired behavior.
Practice!

SKILL 3: "EFFORTFUL" IGNORING
Decide which behaviors you can Ignore.

When your child misbehaves in a way that can be Ignored:
    No look.
    No touch.
    No talk.

Practice!

SKILL 4: GIVING CLEAR INSTRUCTIONS
Get your child's attention and make eye contact.
Use a firm, but not loud or gruff voice.
Give a Clear Instruction that is specific and simple.
Use physical gestures when appropriate.
Reward compliance.
Practice!

SKILL 5: USING TIME-OUTS
Choose a Time-Out location.
Memorize the steps of Time-Out.
Practice without your child.
Tell your child about Time-Out for noncompliance and other problem behaviors.
Begin giving Time-Out in the home.
Begin giving Time-Out outside the home.

RULES OF THUMB AS YOU USE AND INTEGRATE THE FIVE SKILLS

Of course, using and integrating your new skills is easier said than done, and we realize that. As a result, we have a few useful rules of thumb that can help increase the likelihood that you remember to use the skills and increasingly feel like you are using them and using them effectively:

1. **Positive attention increases okay behavior.** As parents (and humans in general!), it is easy to "let sleeping dogs lie" because we feel like we are getting (and perhaps need!) a break, but by doing so we miss lots of opportunities to shape behavior. In the case of your child, it will take an investment of your time, energy, and attention up front to think about, notice, and Attend to and Reward behaviors you want to see or see more. But once your child starts to learn that the okay behavior is the type of behavior that is getting attention (and that mild not-okay behavior is not), then you should start to see a shift in their behavior as well. So try to remember to start each day thinking about what behaviors you want to see or see more, let your child know in advance that you really like when you see those behaviors, and Attend to and Reward those behaviors immediately and every time they occur. Okay behavior is incompatible with not-okay behavior, so in theory your child cannot engage in not-okay behavior if they are engaging in okay behavior. Returning to the shoes example, if Emily is putting on shoes, she cannot be distracted or off task. So give lots of positive attention to move your child in the direction of looking at, putting on, and wearing their shoes, which decreases the likelihood over time that putting on shoes to get out the door (or any other behavior) is a battle.

2. **Plan ahead and use your parenting superpower positive attention accordingly.** Often parents (and all humans!) are reacting, in this case to your child's

not-okay behavior (e.g., not putting on shoes) rather than being proactive. So if you know that in 10 minutes you need your child to put on shoes to get out the door quickly, do not wait until the last minute to start Attending and Rewarding. Instead, start Attending and Rewarding 10 minutes before to see if you can get your child on track and keep them on track right on through putting on their shoes and going out the door into the car. If we go back to Mr. Gonzalez and Emily, this may look something like: "You are eating your cereal!" (Attending) "You are doing such a good job chewing before you put the next spoonful in your mouth!" (Rewarding) "You finished the last bite!" (Attending) "Nice job putting your bowl in the sink!" (Rewarding) "You are walking over to the coat and shoe rack!" (Attending) "Now you bent down to put on your shoes!" (Attending) "Great job putting on your right shoe!" (Rewarding) "Now you are tying your shoe!" (Attending) "Now you are tying your other shoe!" (Attending) "Great job putting on your shoes!" (Rewarding). As you can see in this example, Mr. Gonzalez didn't wait until Emily was supposed to be putting on the shoes to think about using the parenting superpower positive attention. It was used early and often to keep steering Emily in the right direction.

Now the example we just gave is loaded (to say the least!) with Attending and Rewarding. In an ideal world, you as the parent would use these skills a lot. However, we recognize that "life happens" and you have many other responsibilities. What is important here is to overlearn and then overuse Attending and

Rewarding initially. As time passes, you will gradually use them less—which is natural and fine. However, our goal is to strengthen okay behavior, and that will require a lot of effort on your part initially. Besides, you will be reinforced by positive changes in your strong-willed child, which may lead to your continual skill use.

3. **You can give positive attention, and you can and should also (temporarily) take it away.** Just as your child will begin to learn what earns your positive attention (Attending and Rewarding), so too will they learn what gets no attention at all. It is precisely this difference, or *Differential Attention*—putting shoes on (Attending and Rewarding), tossing shoes from one hand to another ("Effortful" Ignoring)—that will help your child begin to learn how to "recalculate" their behavior (to return to the use of a common GPS phrase many of us know all too well when we deviate from the directions that our car or phone is giving us). "Effortful" Ignoring, even when effortful or intentional, may not feel good in the moment, but we remind parents that becoming frustrated, repeating yourself, and even yelling are behaviors that probably don't feel good either. Moreover, we give children a clear road map by telling them which behaviors will result in you using "Effortful" Ignoring, or no look, no talk, and no touch. "Effortful" Ignoring is also temporary and should only last as long as the not-okay behavior is occurring. That is, as soon as another behavior begins to occur that merits positive attention, you should use your Attending or Rewarding skills. So if Emily is tossing the shoes from hand to hand and

Mr. Gonzalez is using "Effortful" Ignoring, then the moment Emily pauses the tossing, Mr. Gonzalez may jump in and say something like "You are holding your shoes!" (Attending) "I like how you are using gentle hands with your shoes!" (Rewarding). By using this Differential Attention, it will become clear to Emily that putting on the shoes is what receives attention from dad.

4. **Clear Instructions can give you confidence that your child heard and understood when you told them to do a task and give you reassurance that a consequence like Time-Out is appropriate.** By getting your child's attention, giving one instruction at a time, and giving an explanation before the instruction, you can feel fairly confident that your child has heard and should have understood you. By giving the Warning, you have a built-in check that you gave the instruction clearly and that your child heard and understood you. With this in mind, you are more likely to approach Time-Out with confidence as well, using a firm (not gruff) tone and a no-nonsense style to communicate that this is the consequence for noncompliance each and every time no matter what. It is precisely your firm tone, no-nonsense style, and predictable behavior that will help your child to learn that there are consequences for not-okay behavior including noncompliance and that in the future alternative behavior (i.e., compliance!) may be the choice that leads to more desirable outcomes (i.e., your positive attention!). There are other consequences than Time-Out, of course, but as we talked about in Chapter 10, Time-Out is evidence-based (i.e.,

tested in research), effective (e.g., shown to reduce noncompliance), and brief (three minutes).

You can talk to your child about their noncompliance and other behavior or their thoughts and feelings about Time-Out or anything else after the following three things have occurred: (1) The Time-Out is over, (2) you have given the Clear Instruction again, and (3) your child has complied. Talking about thoughts and feelings is wonderful and encouraged—we just want you to pause that only briefly during the Clear Instruction, Warning, and Time-Out sequence so that your child has a chance to learn that particular behaviors (e.g., noncompliance) will result in a temporary pause in your attention as a consequence. As we said earlier, talking about your child's thoughts and feelings can occur approximately 30 minutes after the Time-Out. This gives both of you time to calm down. This will take time and practice, but remember that your positive attention is a superpower, and pausing it, if only briefly, can be incredibly effective!

WHAT IS NEXT?

At this point in this book, you have a better understanding of your child's strong-willed behavior, including the role of your child's temperament (Part I). You can consider your child's temperament as a sort of barometer of how much effort will be required to decrease not-okay behavior and increase okay behavior. The more challenging you find your child's temperament in such areas as persistence, reactivity, adaptability, and emotionality, the harder you will have to work to use your new skills.

Indeed, if you are a parent of a child whose temperament is especially strong-willed, resulting in lots of challenging behavior, this does not mean that change cannot occur. Rather, the degree of change may be less or take more effort on your part than a parent of a child with less challenging behaviors. We say this not to disappoint parents, but instead, we have learned over the years that the more reasonable parents' expectations are, the more effectively they can learn, apply, and tailor our five-week program skills (Part II) based on their own child's temperament and behavior. Indeed, this point makes it even more critical that you keep reading even though you may be thinking, "I have read all that I need to" and may be considering putting the book on your shelf or in the drawer of your bedside table. You have worked hard up until this point and are to be commended for all the changes that you have tried and made, but you are not done.

In Part III, we will help you think about specific types of behaviors that parents think about and talk to us about and how to apply your skills to those behaviors. We wove some examples throughout Part II, but Part III will include more specifics on using skills with a broader range of not-okay behaviors, including things like rule breaking and lying. We will also cover how to use your new skills with your child's day-to-day activities and routines, such as mealtime, bathtime, and bedtime. A fairly recent daily activity for many children is screen time. This can be a daily hassle (How much screen time? When should screen time occur?) for parents of these children. Therefore, we have added a chapter by two experts on using your skills with screen time. Finally, we will focus more on some okay behaviors, such as social skills and self-esteem, that you want to see and see more in order to shape positive aspects of your child's identity.

PART III

USING YOUR NEW SKILLS EARLY, OFTEN, AND CONSISTENTLY!

In Part I, you gained a greater understanding of your strong-willed child's behavior and that you have a parenting superpower—your positive attention—that can help you to shape their behavior. In Part II, you learned and practiced a set of new skills that are particularly useful for parents of strong-willed children, including skills to increase okay behaviors, or behaviors you want to see more, and ways to decrease and more effectively respond to not-okay behaviors. As you learned, the key to using those skills effectively is realizing that by being intentional about how you use your superpower of positive attention, you can improve the quality of the relationship that you and your child have and, in turn, change your child's behavior. We included lots of examples of not-okay behaviors in Part II and provided suggestions for ways you can use your skills to respond to those not-okay behaviors, including things like whining, yelling, and throwing tantrums. In addition, our focus in the latter weeks of our five-week program was on helping you address your child's noncompliance, as it has been identified as a critical or keystone behavior.

In Part III we turn to how you can use the skills learned in our five-week program to improve various aspects of your strong-willed child's behavior and your effective parenting. Included in this part of the book is the following: how to cope with additional challenging behaviors like aggression (Chapter 12); how to use your skills to address problems of daily activities like mealtime (Chapter 13); how to address a relatively recent daily challenge for many parents of young children—screen time (Chapter 14); and finally, how to use your skills to enhance positive aspects of your child's behavior, including emotion regulation, self-esteem, and social skills (Chapter 15). Positive youth development is what we as parents most want!

We should note that we called on two experts in technology and children's screen time to guide you through the difficult process of how to manage screens with young strong-willed children. Even if your child is not yet spending a lot of time on screens, it very likely may occur as they grow older, considering the prevalence of screens at home, in school, and at friends' houses. This is your opportunity to be thoughtful about how best to navigate screen time, given your child's temperament and behavior.

CHAPTER 12

AGGRESSION, RULE BREAKING, AND OTHER CHALLENGING BEHAVIORS—OH MY!

You have probably watched the *Wizard of Oz* or, if not, heard Dorothy's oft-quoted "lions and tigers and bears—oh my!" Indeed, the yellow brick road to Oz was fraught with many challenges, which may feel familiar to parents of strong-willed children. In fact, one parent described the experience like playing the game Whac-A-Mole in that she would feel like she was making progress dealing with one behavior when a new one would pop up or another would get worse! We aren't minimizing the challenges—they are real and can be frustrating and disheartening and require a lot of time and energy to change.

That said, you have made it through Part II of this book, which means you have made progress on one key not-okay behavior—noncompliance. We start there because noncompliance is a hallmark of the behavior of strong-willed children. So you want to continue to work on and make progress on that front. But once you have practiced all the skills in combination including Time-Out for noncompliance (Chapter 10) for two weeks, then you can begin to work on applying your new skills to other not-okay behaviors as well. These include behaviors that you decided you could not Ignore (Chapter 8), including aggression and rule breaking. So let's get started thinking about how to use your new skills with these kinds of not-okay behaviors and how to use those skills when these kinds of behaviors occur in public places. But first an important reminder: As we will emphasize in the next section—use your superpower of positive attention early and often!

USE ATTENDING AND REWARDING EARLY AND OFTEN

Aggression and rule breaking are not-okay behaviors that are quite common among children with a strong-willed temperament. Now that you have learned Time-Out and are beginning to find it helpful with noncompliance, it would be easy to want to start applying it to other problem behaviors as well—and you will. But ideally you are being thoughtful about how to use your superpower of positive attention even *before* these not-okay behaviors occur. So if aggression is a problem for your child or you know that your child may behave aggressively with certain people (e.g., siblings) or in certain situations (e.g., the playground), we want you to start thinking about how you can decrease the likelihood that these more challenging not-okay behaviors, like hitting or kicking or biting, will occur when your child is around siblings at home, with friends on the playground, or even perhaps with you.

The old saying "An ounce of prevention is worth a pound of cure" certainly applies to your child's not-okay behavior. By thinking about and planning how to prevent not-okay behavior by using your new skills, you will be more successful with your child!

TIME TO REFLECT

Imagine that you are getting out of the car in the playground parking lot. You can see the same children playing who were there earlier in the week when your child got upset and hit one of them.

- How can you use the power of positive attention to decrease the likelihood that your child hits (or kicks or bites) one of these children today?
- What skills could you use?
- When would you start using them?

Were you thinking that you would start using your skills even before you get out the car? If you were, that is spot on! We want you to use your power of positive attention early and often and long before the not-okay behavior has the chance to occur if possible. Were you imagining yourself using Attends and Rewards? Yes, you are getting the hang of this! You want to start Attending to and Rewarding any okay behaviors that you see as soon as possible with the goal of filling up your child's reserves before you even get to the playground. You may also be using "Effortful" Ignoring if your child is whining about who is or is not there or complaining about wishing you had brought snacks, for example. But remember, "Effortful" Ignoring those not-okay behaviors should always be sandwiched in between Attending and Rewarding

Now let's see an example with Ms. Williams and Jacob, whom you have already met in Parts I and II:

MS. WILLIAMS: We are here!

JACOB: [Peeking out the window to see who is on the playground]

MS. WILLIAMS: You are looking at the playground! (Attending)

JACOB: I see Drew!

MS. WILLIAMS: You are telling me you are excited to see Drew! (Attending) I really like how you are staying in your seat until I can come around and let you out! (Rewarding)

JACOB: Daisy isn't here. *Why* isn't Daisy here today? (Whining)

MS. WILLIAMS: [No look, talk, or touch]

JACOB: [Gets out of the car after his mom opens the door, and takes her hand]

MS. WILLIAMS: Wow! Thank for taking my hand! (Rewarding) I love when you use gentle hands! (Rewarding)

JACOB: Let's go to the playground!

MS. WILLIAMS: You are telling me you are ready to go play! (Attending)

The goal here is for Ms. Williams (and you!) to see if she can increase Jacob's reservoir of positive behavior in order to decrease the likelihood that mild not-okay behaviors, like whining, as well as more challenging not-okay behaviors, like aggression, occur. Again, how does Ms. Williams do this? Right, by increasing her positive attention to okay behavior.

BEST-LAID PLANS

Presuming you use your skills as we describe above, you too will decrease the likelihood that your child will get to the playground and hit a child again. You have filled your child up with positive attention from you, which is a great way for them to approach playtime with friends. This will take some practice—try increasing the Attends and Rewards; try ramping them up even earlier than arriving at the playground, for example as soon as you get in the car to drive to the playground; and try changing your tone of voice and affect (e.g., more enthusiasm) to see if by filling your child's reservoir with your positive attention you can help them steer clear of not-okay behaviors (at least some or most of the time!).

That said, sometimes parents use the skills in just the way that we recommend, and these more challenging not-okay behaviors still occur. You Attend and Reward from the minute you get in the car until your child runs off to play with friends on the playground. You do the Attending and Rewarding with lots of enthusiasm, and you smile and act like you are enjoying every minute of it immensely (and although you may not be really enjoying it, your child believes you!). And yet you walk onto the playground and within minutes your child hits or kicks or bites the same (or a different) child. This is embarrassing—we know that, but try to remind yourself in that moment that you already have a skill in your toolkit. What is it? You guessed it—Time-Out!

TIME-OUT FOR AGGRESSION AND OTHER CHALLENGING BEHAVIORS: THE STANDING RULE

The most effective response to not-okay behaviors like aggression and other challenging not-okay behaviors such as destruction of property and rule breaking is a Time-Out procedure similar to the one you learned in Part II for noncompliance. Similar to Time-Out for noncompliance, you should explain the Time-Out procedure to your child in advance. Specifically, you should tell your child in advance that you have a standing rule about hitting (or whatever challenging not-okay aggressive behavior you are working on). So if we continue with the example of hitting, you would say something as simple as, "If you hit [or kick or bite] other children [or your siblings or Mommy or Daddy], you will go to Time-Out." However, Time-Out for these more challenging behaviors will differ in several important ways from what you learned in Part II: First, tell your child only one time that this behavior will not be tolerated. Tell your child that if the behavior *ever* occurs again, there will be no Warning but rather an automatic Time-Out. Tell your child that this is a standing rule and one that remains in place. You may also want to post the standing rule in a prominent place in the kitchen such as on the refrigerator or in your child's room. Write it on a piece of paper and/or use a picture if your child cannot yet read or read well.

Let's look at how a parent could use a standing rule for hitting. But first let us remind you that once the standing rule is established and your child violates it (e.g., hits you, a sibling, or another child), then you *do not* give a Warning like you did with noncompliance. Rather, you use Time-Out immediately. Let's go back to Ms. Williams to see how she explains this to Jacob:

MS. WILLIAMS: Jacob, I have something I want to tell you, so please turn off the TV. (Clear Instruction)

JACOB: [Pouts but turns off the TV]

MS. WILLIAMS: [No look, talk, or touch related to the pouting] Thank you for turning off the TV the first time I told you! (Reward)

JACOB: [Moves closer to his mom on the couch]

MS. WILLIAMS: Do you remember how upset I was when you hit Drew on the playground?

JACOB: You yelled at me!

MS. WILLIAMS: Hitting is not okay, so no hitting is now going to be a standing rule. If you hit another child, one of your siblings, or Mom or Dad, then I will lead you to Time-Out and you will have to sit there for three minutes. You will not get a Warning before you go to Time-Out for hitting.

JACOB: Aw, Mom! That is not fair! [Jabbing fists in the couch cushions while talking]

MS. WILLIAMS: [No look, talk, or touch until Jacob calms]

MS. WILLIAMS: We are going to practice Time-Out after breaking a standing rule like no hitting. [They practice the procedure just described.] Do you have any questions?

JACOB: No [Pouting]

MS. WILLIAMS: [No look, talk, or touch during the pouting]

JACOB: How will I remember the standing rule? What if I forget?

MS. WILLIAMS: Those are really good questions, Jacob! (Reward) The standing rule is written on this piece of paper with pictures to remind you of the rule. The standing rule is "No hitting." So anytime you hit someone, what will happen?

JACOB: I will go to Time-Out.

MS. WILLIAMS: Yes, great job remembering that! (Reward) That's right; you immediately will have to go to Time-Out. Tell me what the rule is.

JACOB: If I hit you, or my siblings, or my friends, I will go to Time-Out.

MS. WILLIAMS: Very good job listening and remembering! (Reward) Now I am going to put the rule here on the refrigerator. Every morning I will remind you of it.

JACOB: Okay.

MS. WILLIAMS: Okay, let's head out to the playground.

Depending on your child's age, adapt this approach to the rules and needs of your own household. We recommend starting with one not-okay behavior; then once you start seeing that behavior lessen (or you don't see it at all), you can add one or two more not-okay behaviors. However, we recommend never having standing rules for more than three behaviors at a time. For young children, it is just too much to remember.

Let's think for a moment of some other challenging behaviors besides aggression that can be addressed with standing rules. These include:

- Destruction of property such as their own or other children's toys
- Rule breaking
- Lying
- Safety-related behaviors like running into the street

Explain the new behavior and the consequence to your child each time you add one to the list of standing rules using the same sort of script that Ms. Williams used with Jacob above. This increases the likelihood that your child knows the rules in advance and you can feel that you are being fair. Then remind your child each day by reading or pointing to the pictures describing the standing rules. This is very important for you to do!

At the end of a Time-Out for breaking one of the standing rules, say, "You had to go to Time-Out because you broke a standing rule. Which rule did you break?" If your child responds correctly, then you say, "That's right!" (Reward) "Don't _____ again." If your child responds incorrectly or does not respond, briefly present the rule that was broken. Next immediately try to involve your child in some sort of activity (such as helping you do a task) so you can give Attends and Rewards! It is critical that you Attend to and Reward your child when the problem behaviors are *not* occurring! You can take your child's hand and then say, "You took my hand!" (Attending) "I really like when you use gentle hands!" (Rewarding) "You are walking with me to the kitchen!" (Attending) "You are helping me set the table!" (Attending) "You are such a good helper!" (Rewarding).

TIME TO REFLECT

- What are some other not-okay behaviors of your child that call for a standing rule?
- How can you devise a standing rule for one of these behaviors?
- How will you implement the standing rule?

CHALLENGING BEHAVIORS OUTSIDE THE HOME: USING TIME-OUT

In Part II, we talked about using Time-Out for noncompliance, and those examples were in the home. In the example we have in this chapter, you may be thinking to yourself, "Do I have to do this in public?" The answer is yes—not because we are trying to embarrass you or make your life complicated, but because it is most likely to work if you use it every time the not-okay behavior occurs (no matter where you are!). The main difference in using Time-Out outside the home is that you have to be a little more thoughtful and often creative about where you are going to do Time-Out. So ideally you want to pick a spot that is a little bit out of the way from people or activities (away from attention) and somewhere safe where you can stand close by while trying not to look, talk, or touch as much as possible.

What kinds of places are we talking about? Well, in our playground example, you would look for a spot away from playground structures, activities, and other children—maybe in a corner of the playground, or under a tree, or on a bench. If instead you are shopping or in a restaurant for example, you can similarly find a corner in the store or restaurant or bench out front. It can be hard for parents not to give any attention to the crying, yelling or kicking that may occur, especially in these public places. We understand this is embarrasing and we are not minimizing that

If you are using Time-Out for noncompliance in public, then follow the same steps you did in Part II including the Warning. As an example, your child may be trying to climb up the front of the slide on the playground, and it is preventing other children from sliding down. You would say, "Other children can't slide down the slide, so please walk up the steps to slide." (Clear Instruction) Then wait five seconds. If your child complies, say, "Thank you for walking up the steps!" (Reward) If instead your child continues to try to climb up the front of the slide, say, "If you don't use the steps, you will go to Time-Out." If your child complies, Attend and Reward! If your child does not comply, initiate Time-Out. Follow the procedure exactly as you did in Chapter 10 for noncompliance. Specifically, the length of Time-Out is the same as when you do it at home, three minutes, during which you are trying to give your child no or as little attention as possible. Then tell your child Time-Out is over. Then repeat the Clear Instruction: "Walk up the steps of the slide."

If your child is breaking a standing rule, such as hitting on the playground like in the earlier example with Ms. Williams and Jacob, then the Time-Out is automatic. After the Time-Out, remind your child, "Hitting is not okay," and lead your child back to what you were doing before the not-okay behavior while looking for any opportunity to use your Attends and Rewards—walking (not running), using an inside voice (instead of yelling), holding your hand (instead of running ahead).

Parents usually have two big concerns about using Time-Out outside the home. The first is just as we said earlier—using Time-Out in public places can be embarrassing. We hear you but also remind you that your child behaving aggressively or breaking rules or destroying property in public is also probably embarrassing. So you will feel the same either way, but by doing Time-Out you are also decreasing the likelihood that the behavior will occur again (or as often). The second is that someone will hear your child whining or yelling in response to the Time-Out and have lots of thoughts and feelings about your competence as a parent. You are right—others may think negatively about you (or your child). Take deep breaths. Count to 10. Or take a page out of a playbook witnessed by one of us in a store. A mother was doing a great job with not looking at, touching, or talking with her screaming child, but told everyone who passed by, "I am practicing Time-Out." Her plea for grace was met with kind thumbs up and gentle smiles as the rest of us continued to shop.

Let us return for a moment to two things we said earlier in this chapter: Plan ahead, and use lots of Rewards and Attends early in and throughout the process for okay behaviors. If you do, Time-Out will only be an occasionally used backup!

TIME TO REFLECT

- What will be your first standing rule?
- Is this not-okay behavior likely to occur only in the house, or is it likely to occur outside the house as well?
- If outside the house, where is it likely to occur, and what ideas do you have for Time-Out spots in those spaces?
- What are your biggest concerns about doing Time-Out in public, and how will you cope with those?

CHAPTER 13

USING YOUR SKILLS THROUGHOUT THE DAY (AND EVERY DAY!)

In this chapter we are going to focus on how you can also use your skills throughout the day to help with your child's day-to-day routines, such as going to bed, taking a bath, eating meals, getting dressed, and making transitions. It can be hard for all parents to shepherd their children through these day-to-day routines, but this can be particularly challenging for parents of children with strong wills, given they are more likely to have big emotions, may have difficulty navigating change, and are more likely to (or at least try to) take charge!

TIME TO REFLECT

- What day-to-day activities do you find to be the biggest challenge for your child?
- What strategies have you tried to make those activities more manageable?
- How well and how consistently have those strategies worked?
- Are the strategies based on those you learned in our five-week program?

If you are like most parents with whom we have worked, you struggle with at least one day-to-day activity and perhaps feel some days are harder than others. Parents with whom we work tell us they have tried a range of strategies to get their strong-willed child through the daily tasks, from "begging" (e.g., "*Pleasssssssse* put on your shoes for me"), to "nagging" (e.g., "Sit down at the table to eat . . . Please turn off the television and, like I said, sit down at the table to eat . . . please sit down so that we can eat"), to "guilt" ("It would really make my day if you would pick up your toys"), to eventual frustration and (sometimes vague) threats (e.g., "If you don't get in the bathtub, I will _____"). It is especially easy to fall into these less than helpful patterns when parents and families are busy and you feel like you don't have time to deal with your strong-willed child doing anything but what you need them to do. Let's quickly look at some of the "busy" activities you may have on your schedule. You are working, often both inside and outside the home. You may be transporting multiple children to different schools and activities at different times and in different parts of town. You are grocery shopping and cooking meals with the hope that you all may sit down in one place at one time for dinner. For everything to go well, you need your family to be a well-oiled machine, which can be a challenge sometimes with a strong-willed child.

While you may be frustrated with your child (and yourself!), we have good news: You already have the special parenting superpower that will make all of this easier—your positive attention! And now that you have lots of practice with the skills in our five-week program, you can think about how to change both your and your child's behavior throughout the day to make things easier. As with other things in this book, finding this new normal in your day-to-day activities will take time, energy, and effort up front. Of course, it may not be easy at first because you are implementing change, and as you well know by now, change can be hard, particularly at the beginning. But your investment up front can lead to real shifts in how you behave and how your child responds, which will save you time, energy, and effort in the long run!

In this chapter, we will cover a few examples and encourage you to think about how to use your parenting superpower—your positive attention—in combination with your other skills to address these day-to-day activities. As our primary example, we will focus on mealtime behavior and then briefly summarize a few strategies for some other behaviors of daily living (i.e., dressing, bedtime, chores). Remember, the aim is to help you use your attention to increase behaviors you want to see more (okay behaviors) and decrease behaviors you want to see less or not at all (not-okay behaviors). While positive attention is your superpower, you also have other skills in your toolkit to consider using.

MEALTIME

Mealtime is important, as it can be the one time during the day when everyone is together in one place and you all can catch up on the day with each other. Families that are in the habit of eating meals together experience lots of positives, including more opportunities to talk about children's day-to-day experiences and their thoughts about those experiences. Some parents will turn this into a game like Roses and Thorns, and everyone at the table takes a turn highlighting a positive, as well as perhaps a challenge, from the day.

Mealtimes can also be very stressful. Parents are often trying to make food and get the meal on the table, and it is rarely an easy feat to coordinate everyone in the house being in the same place at the same time with jobs, school, and activities. Mealtimes can be even more challenging if your strong-willed child is doing one or more not-okay behaviors. Common not-okay behaviors during mealtime that parents of strong-willed children tell us about include everything from refusing to come to the table in the first place, refusing to eat certain things on their plate (like vegetables!), trying to leave the table early to go back to their tablet or television, or doing things at the table that at best are not helpful (e.g., putting their carrot sticks in their ears and making funny faces) and at worst disruptive (e.g., throwing or spitting out food).

We suggest parents treat mealtime like everything else we have talked about in this book: Try to be proactive! That is, plan ahead and use your skills to increase the likelihood that you see okay behavior rather than being reactive to not-okay behavior and, in turn, often giving attention to the very behaviors you want to decrease. So let's move beyond some of the not-okay behaviors noted in the preceding paragraph and list what not-okay behaviors make mealtime a challenge. We will mention those we hear commonly, but we encourage you to list on the three blank lines below any that you are dealing with at your table as well.

Not-Okay Mealtime Behaviors

- Refusing to come to the table (noncompliance)
- Refusing to eat certain (or all) foods
- Eating off others' plates
- Tipping or rocking the chair
- Playing with food
- Throwing food
- Spitting food out (on plate or at someone else)
- Attempting to leave the table early
- _____
- _____
- _____

Now let's think about what okay behaviors you would want to see instead. Let's take one at a time. We will do some for you to provide examples, although you may come up with other okay behaviors as well! Then we encourage you to finish the list for any not-okay mealtime behaviors that you added.

NOT-OKAY MEALTIME BEHAVIOR	OKAY MEALTIME BEHAVIOR
Refusing to come to the table	Coming the first time "Dinner!" is called
Refusing to eat certain (or all) foods	Willing to try a bite of each item on plate
Eating off others' plates	Keeping hands to self
Tipping or rocking the chair	Keeping four legs of the chair on the floor
Throwing food	Keeping food on the plate
Spitting food out (or at someone else)	Keeping food in the mouth
Attempting to leave the table early	Staying at the table until excused

Great! Now you have a list of behaviors you want to see or see more at the dinner table, which positions you to—you guessed it—use your parenting superpower—your positive attention! So before dinner even starts, you want to be thinking about how to use Attending and Rewarding to increase attention to okay mealtime behaviors, as well as "Effortful" Ignoring in order to give no attention to mild (i.e., not safety-related) not-okay behaviors. Remember, if the behavior truly gets no attention (no look, no talk, and no touch) from anyone at the table, then it should start to decrease in frequency and eventually go away (especially if your child is getting positive attention for okay behaviors). This will take time, but it will be worth it in the long run.

You can also start to think about how you can use Clear Instructions and Time-Out in response to your child, for example, not coming to the table when called to dinner. Or you could consider making a standing rule for a mealtime behavior that occurs often and is really annoying to you. For example, you may consider a standing rule for behaviors like tipping in the chair (if you are worried about your child falling) or spitting or throwing food. Of course, having to think about Clear Instructions, Time-Out, or standing rules may feel aversive to you in the short term because you just want to sit down and have a relaxing meal. We get it! But you are reading this book in general and this section in particular because all too often, mealtime is likely not relaxing. So again, remember that as we have said, this will take time, energy, and effort up front, but if you can recalculate the balance of your attention and reshape your child's behavior, you have a good shot at changing mealtimes in your home!

Because all of this is, of course, easier said than done, let's provide an example. To do so, we will turn to Ms. Williams, who is using her Attending, Rewarding, and "Effortful" Ignoring in order to increase the likelihood that Jacob exhibits more okay and less not-okay behavior during mealtime. We also provide in our example an opportunity for her to turn to Clear Instructions and Time-Out skills.

> **MS. WILLIAMS:** Jacob, you have been doing such a nice job playing quietly with your toys! (Rewarding) You are putting the red block on the blue block! (Attending) You are building such a big tower! (Attending)
>
> **JACOB:** Do you like it?
>
> **MS. WILLIAMS:** Yes, I think you have done a great job! (Rewarding) We are getting ready to eat dinner now though, so I would like you to leave your toys there and come to the table. (Clear Instruction)
>
> **JACOB:** Ahhhhhh, Mom, but I am playing!
>
> **MS. WILLIAMS:** [Counts silently to five] Jacob, if you don't come to the dinner table, I will take you to Time-Out. (Warning)

JACOB: Okayyyyyyyyyy. [Walks to table while stomping feet]

MS. WILLIAMS: [Using "Effortful" Ignoring in response to the stomping] Thank you for coming over to the table with us! (Rewarding) And now you are pulling out your chair and sitting down! (Attending) Tonight we are having hamburgers and baked potatoes.

JACOB: But I like french fries better! [While putting fork into the baked potato]

MS. WILLIAMS: You are digging right into the baked potato! (Attending) I love when you eat what I made for you! (Rewarding)

JACOB: Potatoes are okay, but I like french fries better! [Flicking a piece of potato off fork and onto the plate]

MS. WILLIAMS: ["Effortful" Ignoring]

JACOB: [Taking another bite]

MS. WILLIAMS: You are taking a nice big bite of your baked potato! [Attending] You are eating like such a big kid! (Rewarding)

You have probably had dinners at your house that have gone something like the example between Ms. Williams and Jacob, but what is likely different is seeing how Ms. Williams used her skills more effectively to increase the likelihood that Jacob did more okay behaviors and fewer not-okay behaviors (or at least addressed the not-okay behaviors when they occurred). Too often at mealtimes and during other day-to-day activities like bedtime and bathtime, strong-willed children receive lots of (too much!) attention for the not-okay behaviors. As you now know, this increases the likelihood that the not-okay behaviors will continue or become worse. In our example, Jacob saw instead that it was the okay behaviors that were going to get his mom's attention and the not-okay behaviors were going to get no attention at all or risk consequences! If Ms. Williams uses these skills consistently and proactively (rather than reactively) during day-to-day activities, then both she and Jacob will experience less stress, as their daily routine will be more predictable!

We also should note that it is often the transition from one activity (e.g., playing) to another (e.g., mealtime) that is associated with the most not-okay behavior. Therefore, it is important for you to carefully plan beforehand how you will use your skills to handle this transition.

OTHER SUGGESTIONS FOR NAVIGATING DAY-TO-DAY ACTIVITIES

We won't go through each day-to-day activity that you have with your child, but for each we encourage you to do the same thing we did with mealtime. That is, list the not-okay behaviors that are making a particular activity challenging; then beside each put the okay behavior you would like to see instead. Next start to think in advance how you will use your new skills to increase the likelihood that your child does the okay behavior and what you will do in response to the not-okay behaviors when they occur. In particular, as we have just stated, you can start to think about how you will use your new skills to handle the transition to the daily task (e.g., mealtime) that you selected to change.

Although we will not go through all the day-to-day activities, let's briefly summarize some things to consider with three tasks that many parents find difficult.

GETTING DRESSED

Getting dressed is a very common challenge that parents of strong-willed children face. And there are likely some strengths emerging in your strong-willed child's behavior when picking out clothes that may include a very keen sense of style! In fact, it is not unusual for us to work with children sporting what may at first appear to be mismatched shirts, sweaters, pants, and skirts (sometimes all at once on the same child!), but we quickly come to learn that the outfit was actually very carefully curated by our little budding fashionista. Results aside (and presuming parents can "lean into" their strong-willed child's fashion choices), getting a child dressed at the start of the day (or undressed and into pajamas at the end of the day) can be challenging for many parents (and sometimes parents tell us they can't keep clothes on their child at all!). Given this is such a common challenge, we offer some guidance:

- **Have appropriate developmental expectations.** By age two to three, most children show interest in wanting to dress themselves. By age three, most children can put on large articles of clothing like shirts or pants. By age four, children usually do things like fasten large buttons. By age five, they can typically dress themselves save for more intricate things that require finer motor skills such as fastening small buttons.
- **Decide on and lay clothes out the night before.** If mornings are busy—and they are for many families—pick clothes out the night before. Use your skills to increase the likelihood the process moves along efficiently. You may say something like "You are picking the blue shirt!" (Attending) "You are picking

the polka dot pants!" (Attending) "I really like the outfit you picked out for tomorrow!" (Rewarding).

- **Give your child choices.** It is developmentally appropriate as children grow and develop that they want to make choices. So to balance wanting to give them choices with also wanting them to pick out their clothes fairly efficiently, you can narrow the range of their choices. For example, if your child has five pairs of pants, you can lay two pairs on the bed and say, "Will you wear the pink or blue pants tomorrow?" "You picked the blue pants!" (Attending) "Great job picking out your pants!" (Rewarding).
- **Set a timer.** If your child is four years old or older, consider turning getting dressed into a game of "beat the clock." At first, give your child more time. Attend and Reward each step of the way until your child is dressed and then celebrate. The next day, give your child a little less time although keep Attending and Rewarding to help keep them focused and moving toward the finish line. If you do this consistently, you will likely be able to give them a bit more independence as they get dressed because a routine will be established!

BEDTIME AND SLEEP PROBLEMS

There are more and more data to show that sleep is likely associated with physical and mental health, and children's behavior is no exception. Just as with mealtime and dressing, you can increase the likelihood that your child sleeps enough by considering the following:

- **Stick to the same bedtime every night and the same waketime every morning.** We know this isn't always possible, but the more your child can have a set bedtime and waketime all seven days of the week, the more likely they will quickly fall asleep and feel more rested when they wake up.

- **Have a bedtime routine.** You can do lots of things to signal to your child that it is nearing bedtime (e.g., turn the television off) and pair those with bedtime rituals that you do each night to quiet and soothe your child. These likely include having a snack, taking a bath, brushing teeth, putting on pajamas, arranging stuffed animals, and reading a bedtime story. Of course, you should Attend and Reward as they progress through this routine to keep them engaged, focused, and moving along toward bedtime!

- **Predict any challenges.** Many children will wait until "goodnight" hugs and kisses have been given and the lights are out to ask for a glass of water or tell you they need to use the bathroom. If you see this pattern, start to anticipate and respond to it in advance. For example, take a glass of water into the bedroom, or make using the bathroom the very last step in the bedtime routine.

- **Be ready to handle difficulty falling asleep.** If your child has difficulty falling asleep once or twice, that is normal. If you see a pattern developing, consider things like making the bedtime a bit later to see if your child falls asleep more quickly. If this works, keep the bedtime later for a little while; then back it up earlier and earlier using 15-minute increments until you are back to the bedtime you had in mind. Also, try to avoid your child taking a nap while you are doing this!

- **Be ready to handle coming into your room.** Many children will wander from their own bed into their parents' bed soon after they are tucked in or sometime in the middle of the night. To decrease the likelihood this happens (or keeps happening), think about how your child may be getting your attention for behaviors you want to see less or not at all. So if you are having your child climb under the covers with you (attention!), or you are talking with your child about why they can't sleep (attention!), or you are negotiating how to get them back into bed by reading one more book (attention!), you are increasing the likelihood that they will come in tomorrow night, the next night, and the night after that. Instead, tell them the next morning that from now on you will take them back to bed. Then when you do that, try to give them as little verbal and nonverbal attention as you can. Simply pick them up, gently put them in bed, and firmly say, "You need to stay in your room." No soothing or cuddling. This may not feel good in the short term, but again you are teaching your child the rules that will help you both in the long run to get your sleep!

- **Pause before responding to calls for you.** Some children are afraid of the dark. Some children have bad dreams. Some children don't like to be alone. All these reasons can lead your child to call out to you after you put them to bed. The first time your child calls, wait a few minutes before checking. If you check and your child is awake, try to avoid lots of talking or cuddling in bed with them. You simply want to reiterate that it is bedtime, tell them goodnight, and leave. If your child calls out again, wait a bit longer (5 to 7 minutes) the

215

next time to respond. When you do respond, avoid lots of talking or cuddling. Try to see if you can build up to waiting 10 to 15 minutes before going in—this way you are teaching your child important self-soothing and self-regulation skills that are critical to effective bedtime and sleep routines. Similar to taking your child back to bed if they come in your room, this can be hard for parents who often report feeling like they are hurting their child's feelings or causing their child distress, especially if the child starts to cry. But remember, you are using your attention and skills to shape their behavior in the short term so that they are more well adjusted, including their sleep, in the long run!

- **Use your superpower.** And always use your superpower (your positive attention!) to reinforce even small gains. This will lead to bigger and bigger gains in the long run. Attending and Rewarding are very important with this behavior (and any behavior) of your child!

CHORES

As your child grows older, they can also start to do more chores independently. Nevertheless, you can start to engage and reinforce even young children for helping with household jobs.

- **Start by doing a chore with your child.** If you are sweeping the floor, give your child a play broom (or dust brush and pan) and have them do it alongside you.
- **Use your skills of Attending and Rewarding.** Describe what your child is doing, such as "You are brushing

the dust on the floor!" (Attending) "Wow! You made a big pile!" (Rewarding) "You are brushing the dust into the pan!" (Attending) "I love when you help me clean!" (Rewarding).

- **Tell your child you need assistance.** Remember, your superpower of positive attention! Therefore, chances are if you offer to do something with your child, they are going to take you up on it. And if you act excited about the activity and give them lots of positive attention for helping you, it is even more likely they will enjoy it and want to do it in the future. As with so many things we discuss in this book, this will make the task take longer than if you just did it yourself. But your investment in the short term will foster positive things. For example, your child's self-esteem will increase when they have a chance to contribute to the family, and their problem-solving ability will increase when they have a chance to see how you tackle various tasks and problem-solve when challenges arise.

SUMMARY AND NEXT STEPS

As we said at the start of this chapter, we are only providing examples of day-to-day activities that many parents of strong-willed children face. Our hope is that these examples can give you some ideas to help problem-solve and implement strategies to address problems you may be having with not only these day-to-day activities but others.

Nevertheless, we believe it is important to give you some expert advice on one particular activity many parents are experiencing in recent years: screen time. Children's use of screens has become more and more typical since the COVID-19 pandemic when learning and recreational activities had to pivot to online learning. For better or worse, screen time will likely be a part of children's lives moving forward as technology takes an increasingly central role in our daily lives. As a result, we have asked two experts to contribute the next chapter on the challenges parents of young children face with screen time and some potential solutions.

CHAPTER 14

I SCREAM, YOU SCREAM, WE ALL SCREAM WHEN IT COMES TO NAVIGATING SCREEN TIME!

Wesley Sanders, PhD, and Justin Parent, PhD

Screen time is a significant challenge for most families! In the past decade, children, on average, have tripled the amount of mobile media time spent each day. Recent surveys suggest young children spend, on *average*, about four hours per day using screens. However, these numbers can be a bit deceiving because families differ greatly in how much screen time they allow their young children to have each day. In fact, the average range is likely between an hour and 6½ hours per day. Regardless, screen time is often a *big* part of a child's day (even for young children!), and many children spend more time on screens than any other activity! Clearly, this is a challenge for parents, particularly those of strong-willed children.

While concerns about screen time and media are not new—in fact, they date back over many generations and forms of media—the rapid technological changes over this past decade and the integration of these devices into our everyday lives has created an unprecedented stressor for families. Gone are the days of debating about having a TV in the bedroom or whether video games are bad for kids. The TVs are now portable and come in all shapes and sizes; video games have evolved to include virtual reality; and school may be face-to-face with screen-based assignments and homework or entirely remote with children on screens for much of the day. Thus, it is important to note that based on the last point, screen time in some contexts can be educational.

You may be asking what is important to know about screen time. Parents often first want to know "How much is too much?" and then "What do I do about that?" In this chapter, we will try to give you some information about both questions and help you feel empowered to use your new skills learned in the five-week program to manage your child's screen time without needing your own personal IT support.

So how much is too much? That's a tricky question without a straightforward answer. (Sorry!) What we do know is that too much of anything can be harmful, and this applies to screen time, likely regardless of the content of the videos your children watch or the games they play. Many people have attempted to come up with a golden number of how much screen time is the right amount. But unfortunately, there is no Goldilocks amount that is perfect for all kids. We know that research shows that very high amounts (think over eight hours a day) can start to impact children's well-being by disrupting their sleep or causing physical health issues through not having enough physical activity. Also, lots of time spent on screens can sometimes make strong-willed behaviors worse, increasing not-okay behaviors (e.g., tantrums)—often when they are the least convenient (like when needing to leave the house for an activity or to start getting ready for bed).

Finally, some children may be more sensitive than others when it comes to screen time. You may have found that even a little bit of screen time may cause your child to become irritable or more defiant (maybe both), whereas other children in the family or community may seem just fine with spending hours on these devices. Why is this? The best answer is that it depends on the particular child (think temperament!) and their ability to make transitions or perform nonpreferred tasks (which do *not* include screen time). Children who have difficulty transitioning from one task to another or have difficulty with compliance to parental instructions can be more negatively impacted by screen time than other children. Also, beyond the question of how much screen time is right for your child, the content they are exposed to can make a difference. For example, some children may be susceptible to specific media content that shows aggression or violence.

So there are a number of factors that can influence the answer to "how much is too much" screen time. What we do know is that the average levels of screen time have been increasing over time. If these increasing amounts of screen time are left unchecked, a child's sleep, physical activity, emotions, and behavior can be harmed.

All this sounds a little scary, but the good news is that *now* is the perfect time to help your child develop healthy screen time habits. We know that the amount of screen time children typically have increases as they get older. For example, average levels of child screen time increase by 20 percent between pre-school and middle school and then *double* in the teenage years! Also, the complexities of the potential problems that screen time causes worsen as children get older, especially during sensitive developmental stages like when they go through puberty. What is great to know, though, is that you are ahead of that curve! Now is the time to help your young child develop healthy habits, at least in part because it's the easiest time for parents to manage screen time content and limits (at least compared with parents of teens). So if your two- to six-year-old child has too much screen time daily in your opinion, now is the time to address the issue. On the other hand, if your child is limited in screen time currently, you can prevent this from becoming a problem as they increase in age.

In the following sections, we will help you understand how to assess media use in your home (an important first step!), offer some screen time limits you can consider implementing, and give you tips for implementing the limits (a plan!) to change screen time. And of importance, the new parenting skills you learned in Chapters 5 to 11 will help you to use your new screen time plan effectively.

TAKE INVENTORY!

In order to make longstanding changes around screen time in the home, it's important to assess *everyone's* media use, not just your children's. All the skills you learned and practiced in Chapters 5 to 11 are powerful tools for shaping behavior, including screen time! But another powerful influence—socialization—can affect your child's behavior without your even knowing it. For example, children who grow up in a household with parents who read are more likely to read themselves. Why is this? Parents who read are modeling (demonstrating) the kinds of behaviors they want to see in their children. They may have more books in the home, and reading may be more front of mind when thinking of ways to engage with their children. Screen time is no different; in fact, research shows that as parents' screen time use increases in the home, so does their child's. It is especially important then that as you consider the rules and boundaries around screen time for your child in the home, also consider how closely they line up with your *own* screen time use.

TIME TO REFLECT

Screen time has become such an embedded part of daily life that we often don't notice how often we are using it. As you begin to examine your own media use, consider these questions:

- How often are you using your screens while with your children?
- When you're spending time with your children, how often do you become distracted by a text message or email?
- Are you giving instructions to your children in the other room while watching TV?

Sometimes we are so busy trying to get the kids ready for daycare/preschool/school, grab our breakfast, and respond to emails that screen time becomes an automatic feature in our own routines and an entertainment device for our children at these times. These behaviors send messages to our children about what we should prioritize and how frequently we use media. Another common way we engage in screen time around children is when stressed or tired. It can be such a relief for us to sit down and enjoy a favorite episode of television (oops, that's screen time!) after a long day. Furthermore, we sometimes use screen time as a way to relieve parenting stress. Do you give your child a tablet to watch YouTube when they get cranky? Have you ever given in to a temper tantrum and handed over the digital device so your child can play that smartphone game? It's completely understandable and happens from time to time, but it's also important to consider the message this sends to your child about coping. It reinforces the idea that screen time is the solution to stress. And while it certainly can be, consider how you might be reinforcing this message in the home and look for other possible solutions as well—like some calming music, a relaxing activity together, or another form of play.

Finally, it is also important to consider *where* you take your screen time and what messages this might communicate for your child. Decades of research have found that media use in the bedroom can negatively affect our sleep, and it's not just about the "blue light" effect. Watching TV or movies keeps our brain activated and stimulated at a time when we are trying to accomplish just the opposite. You also might even find your child coming into your bedroom to watch TV with you. Similarly, having screen time at family gatherings, like a family meal, can send the message that screen time is appropriate in this setting. For example, if you find yourself checking messages at the dinner table, it can make it all the more difficult to change those behaviors for the rest of the family.

With screen time so ubiquitous for families, how do we know if our efforts to place rules around them are working? The first step is simply to gather more information over the coming week. Take an inventory of your technology devices in the home for a week. How many tablets, phones, TVs, or video game consoles does your child have access to? Write down the devices, and estimate to the best of your knowledge how much time your child uses each device daily. The time of day and location are also important: Is your child most likely to pick up the tablet for example during particular routines (such as morning or bedtime), times of the day (such as after daycare or school), or locations (such as their room)? It's also important to note that some of this use may be for educational purposes. If so, make your best estimate of this time separately. In addition to timing, consider also the type of content your child is exposed to. Is your child restricted only to educational media, or are they playing video games with action/violence? Are they co-viewing with Mom or Dad, and if so, what kind of content do you all watch together? We have provided you with a sample weekly screen time inventory in Table 14-1. Feel free to change it in any way that best suits you. And do not be surprised if the information you record is surprising (shocking?) to you!

After taking your screen time inventory, next consider what feels like too much. If you notice there are times when screen time use really interferes with completing daily routines, doing homework, or just getting out the door some days, these are all good signs that further limitations might be needed.

You've likely already had some rules or expectations in place within the home. How have they been going? It's helpful to take stock of these rules in light of the helpful information gathered over the past week. For example, if you set a time limit for screen time each day, does your child ever exceed the time limit? What gets in the way of you adhering to the time limit? Have you thought about using your superpower of positive attention

TABLE 14-1 A Sample Weekly Screen Time Inventory

DAY	NUMBER OF SCREENS YOUR CHILD HAS ACCESS TO	LIST SCREENS AND NUMBER OF HOURS CHILD USES EACH DAY	TIME OF DAY AND LOCATION SCREEN WAS USED BY CHILD	IS SCREEN EDUCATIONAL?
Sunday		1. _____ 2. _____ 3. _____ 4. _____	_____ _____ _____ _____	_____ _____ _____ _____
Monday		1. _____ 2. _____ 3. _____ 4. _____	_____ _____ _____ _____	_____ _____ _____ _____
Tuesday		1. _____ 2. _____ 3. _____ 4. _____	_____ _____ _____ _____	_____ _____ _____ _____

Wednesday

1. _____
2. _____
3. _____
4. _____

Thursday

1. _____
2. _____
3. _____
4. _____

Friday

1. _____
2. _____
3. _____
4. _____

Saturday

1. _____
2. _____
3. _____
4. _____

to try to reduce screen time? What about a standing rule? All of these are important questions that our five-week program and earlier chapters in this book should help you address.

Let's first reflect on some assessment questions and then consider some forms of limits you could place on screen time if you believe your child is spending too much daily screen time.

TIME TO REFLECT

- Does your child have access to too many screens?
- Does your child spend too many hours per day on screens?
- Does your child use screens only in some locations at home?
- Is at least some of your child's screen time educational?
- Do you believe your child needs to reduce access to the number of screens, number of hours on screens, location of screen use, and/or content of screens?

SUGGESTED TYPES OF SCREEN TIME LIMITS IN THE HOME

It's important that you carefully assess media use in your household, and then develop a screen time plan that is specific to the needs of your child, your home, and your preferences around media use. Now that you've spent some time gathering all the information you need, here are a few possible limits for you to consider in order to support changes in screen time for your family:

- **Specific amount of daily time.** One option is to pick an amount of time you feel comfortable allowing your child to have screen access per day. For example, maybe for an hour after dinner or from 5 to 6 p.m. Once everyone agrees on this time, you would need to make sure that you have backup plans in case that time becomes unavailable one day. For example, if everyone arrives home late in the evening from hockey practice, would you let your child still have their hour, or would it be given up for the day? Make sure these expectations are clear before that day comes, however, so you can avoid these conflicts before they happen. As we have said, an ounce of prevention goes a long way in solving problems! You also might want to reread Chapter 9 on making instructions clear and be sure to reinforce (Chapter 7) your child for complying with whatever rules you set up (Chapter 12). In other words, use the skills you learned in the five-week program.

- **Specific type of screen time activity.** Some parents may not be concerned about the total amount of time, but are concerned about the types of activities, such as time on video games or on social media video activities like YouTube or TikTok. If this is you, instead of a total screen time limit as described earlier, set a limit for time allowed on a specific screen time activity. For example, if you are worried about your child's defiant behavior being worse when they have too much video game time, you could set a specific limit—like 30 minutes of video games on weekdays and maybe an hour on weekends. There is no just-right or "correct" amount because it depends on your child and how they cope with specific types of screen time—some children play hours of video games with no issues, while others have a tantrum after only a few minutes. You may also want to combine a total time limit with a time limit for specific screen time activities such as no more than one hour total on weekdays with up to 30 minutes of that time on video games. Keeping track of this can get tricky, so using a timer or using screen time limits on their device can help with tracking and setting limits when the time is up.

- **"Time-of-the-day" limits to promote healthy sleep.** A common type of limit is to make rules about *when* your child can use screen time. In particular, setting limits to ensure your child gets enough good-quality sleep each day is often a top priority. As mentioned above, as screen time right before bed can make it hard for children (and parents) to fall asleep, setting limits on the amount or type of screen time allowed before bed can be helpful. For example, you could choose to have no screen time in the hour before bed. However, if that isn't a good fit for your family, you could instead only allow calming screen time before bed, such as nature videos, and avoid exciting, scary, or action-focused screen time activities. One useful way to help set this type of limit is on the device or devices your child uses since tablets and phones typically have a downtime or sleep time option in the settings that will turn off most apps or features of the device after the "bedtime" you set on the device. Regardless of whether you limit the amount of time or type of content before bed, the most important way to limit sleep-interfering screen time is to remove devices from bedrooms at night.

- **No weekday devices.** No screen time devices on weekdays? Some parents have busy schedules, with after-preschool or -school care, sports teams, and homework taking up most of the evening. If this is the case, you might just want to kick out the gadgets and TV until the weekend. This still leaves you with some leverage since you can negotiate expectations during the week that will allow your child to have screen time on the weekend, but also keeps some of the stress off monitoring their access during the week.

- **When-then rules.** For some parents, while technology use isn't a big problem, they believe homework always should come first. If this is the case, maybe establishing screen time under a simple "when-then" statement would be helpful. That is, "*When* you finish your homework, *then* you can play video games/watch TV." This statement makes it clear what your child must do (finish homework) and puts the onus on them to accomplish these tasks if they want screen time. Please note that you have had some practice already with when-then rules both in Warnings before Time-Out (if-then statements) and in the standing rules you set up.

- **Educational only.** With respect to video games, some parents don't want their child accessing them at all but understand the value in the educational component. If this is the case, you might simply limit your child's game time to educational games that you approve.

- **No devices?** What about banning screen time devices altogether? This one we would caution against, as the strategy prevents your child from learning about these devices in the safety of the home, and they will likely start exploring them on their own at friends' houses or in school. Knowing how to operate mobile devices and computers is becoming increasingly important in our everyday life and future careers, so having the opportunity to explore them in a safe environment where you can monitor their use will benefit your child and give you more control over what they see.

The main point here is that you carefully assess screen time use in your home and then consider what limits you need/want to impose. These are important first steps if screen time is a challenge in your home or if you want to prevent it from becoming a problem. Next, you should always think, "How can I use the skills I learned in the five-week program to implement my plan regarding screen time?" In the next section we not only draw on some of those five-week skills but provide you with some additional ideas.

TIPS FOR IMPLEMENTING YOUR NEW PLAN

Now that you have decided on how you will limit screen time for your child, there are a few things to consider when starting this new plan:

- **How will you set limits?** There are lots of types of limits but really just two main ways to follow through with the limits you choose. The "old-school" method that is tried and true involves setting a timer (a kitchen timer, your phone, a device like Alexa/Google/Siri) and then physically removing access to the devices when the time is up. This usually involves having a go-to spot to store devices or game controllers that only parents can access. The "new-school" method takes a bit of time to set up and practice but has the advantage of using technology to make it easier to track screen time and turn the device off when time is up. There are lots of ways to set technology-based limits on devices, including ones that are free. These are usually in the settings, such as Apple Screen Time or Google Family Link. These methods work by using the device to track how much time your child uses the device or a specific app, and then it turns access off to that app once your child has used all their time. A common concern is that children will "hack" their way around these limits, but companies like Apple and Google are pretty good at these settings, so the most common way a child could hack the device is through getting the screen time password from you or someone else in the home. (So be careful—strong-willed children can be very persuasive.) The key to success for this method is using a screen time passcode or password that is different from the one used to open the device and keeping the screen time passcode for parents' eyes only!

There are also other ways to set limits using paid devices or services like Disney's Circle or using your internet provider or Wi-Fi. Most of these kinds of screen time–limiting technologies change often, but you can usually find instructions for how to set them up online from websites like Common Sense Media or how-to videos on YouTube.

- **Planning ahead with your child.** Does your child know the rules? This may sound odd, but it happens! Sometimes we enforce our own internal idea of screen time simply by putting a stop to the screen time when it feels like too much. It's helpful to be clear with your child how much the limit is and when they will reach the limit. A standing rule about screen time, posted on the refrigerator and reviewed on a regular basis with your child, is a recommended procedure (see Chapter 12 for further information on standing rules). Also, give them warnings when they are nearing the limit and set visible timers, as young children have not yet internalized how long "a few minutes" might be.

- **Planning ahead with co-parents.** Do you *and* any co-parents or other caregivers know the rules? Sometimes multiple caregivers have different perspectives on screen time in the home, or maybe screen time rules change from day to day, given our mood, schedule, or child's behavior. It's important to set realistic and consistent expectations in the home. As we learned in the five-week program, the more predictable the environment is, the easier it is for your child to know what's expected of them. As you introduce suggested screen time expectations in the home, have a family meeting with your child and other caregivers to make sure all are on the same page about when and how digital devices can be used in the home.

- **Screen time as a Reward.** As discussed in Chapter 7, Rewards encourage the behaviors we want to see more. Many parents express exasperation with their child *always* wanting more screen time! Well, this is a great opportunity to harness that desire by using screen time as a Reward for positive behaviors or activities. Screen time can be used as a Nonsocial Reward (Chapter 7) on the spot by, for example, offering it for immediate compliance. You could start with an instruction, e.g., "It's time to put your toys away so we can get ready for your bath," and offer screen time as a way to encourage more immediate action: "If you put your toys away *right now*, you'll get five minutes of extra screen time after your bath!" Or as another example, you might say, "*When* you get your shoes on, *then* you can play on the iPad until we have to go." However, as you learned earlier in this book in Chapter 7, it's important to pair Rewards like screen time with praise whenever possible ("I love how you got your shoes on so quickly! You really earned that extra five minutes of screen time!").

Screen time can be embedded into larger Reward systems as well. If your child is old enough for daily chores like making the bed, putting away their belongings, or cleaning the dishes, these behaviors can be reinforced with screen time. Consider the maximum amount of screen time or different types of content of screen time as described earlier in this chapter and work backward; if you want to limit your six-year-old's screen time to two hours per day, for example, then two hours is the maximum pool of screen time minutes your child can earn. Perhaps they earn 30 minutes for making their bed, or 30 minutes for taking a bath. In this way you can assign a value of screen time as a form of digital currency to encourage positive behaviors. But again, pair your superpower of positive attention (praise) with this Nonsocial Reward.

- **Loss of screen time for a consequence.** Just like screen time can encourage positive behaviors, it can also be utilized to discourage negative behaviors in the home. For example, less screen time can be a natural consequence for noncompliance during time-sensitive moments. Perhaps you allow for a short bit of TV time in the mornings after everyone is ready but before you have to head out for the day. If your child is being fussy about getting dressed, eating breakfast, or getting their shoes on, a natural consequence might be to miss out on that TV time.

In this instance it's important to pair the consequence with the behavior by explaining, "Because you took too much time to get dressed, we don't have enough time left over for you to watch a TV show this morning." Watch out too for situations where screen time might undermine your efforts to establish consequences in the home. So when you use your "Effortful" Ignoring skill (Chapter 8) or implement a Time-Out (Chapter 10), be sure to check that all TVs are off and that your child doesn't have access to digital devices. These parenting skills are all about the removal of reinforcers, and that includes screen time!

TIME TO REFLECT

- How will you follow through with the screen time limits you set?
- Does your child and do other caregivers know the screen time limits?
- Have you considered using screen time as a consequence (either gaining or losing screen time)?

SUMMARY

Screen time is an issue for many parents of young children or, unfortunately, will become an issue as your child grows older. We have suggested that you assess how much screen time is currently occurring (including your own!), decide on how much screen time you will allow your child and when it can occur, develop a plan and make it clear to your child and other caregivers, and stick to it. Remember, in Chapters 5 to 11 you learned a set of skills for interacting with your young child. It is important to use these skills when setting your screen time plan into motion! For more information on screen time, see the American Academy of Pediatrics and the American Academy of Child and Adolescent Psychiatry websites in the Appendix.

CHAPTER 15

POSITIVE PARENTING GROWS HEALTHY AND HAPPY KIDS!

In earlier chapters in Part III we talked about applying the new skills you learned in our five-week program to a wider range of child problem behavior and to the daily activities of your strong-willed child, including screen time. While most parents reading this book want to decrease challenging behaviors and make daily activities run smoother, we also know that is not enough. Rather, you also want to increase the likelihood that your child is behaving in ways that make them feel good about themselves and make other people like and enjoy their company. The good news is that by harnessing your parenting superpower (positive attention), as you learned in Part II, you are also increasing what we and others call "positive parenting"—that is, you are increasingly learning to balance warmth and support through skills like Attending and Rewarding as you give your child more and more attention for behaviors you want to see and see more and balancing this with clear and consistent consequences for their not-okay behavior (this balancing is the very definition of positive parenting!). As you continue to use your new skills and work to achieve this balance, we also want to help you to think about how to continue to nurture positive aspects of your child's development. So, for example, talking in an inside voice (instead of yelling!) is a good first step, but we also know there is more to nurturing a happy and well-adjusted child. To start you on this next step in your journey, we turn next to thinking about how to use your new skills to help your child identify and regulate emotions.

EMOTION REGULATION

Very simply put, emotion regulation is the process by which children (and their parents!) learn to become aware of, label, monitor, regulate, and manage both positive (e.g., happiness, excitement) and negative (e.g., sadness, anger) emotions. Children learn emotion regulation by watching how their parents and others regulate their own emotions (i.e., modeling), as well as how parents and other adults talk to children about the emotional experiences that they are having (i.e., emotion socialization). Parental modeling can include things like using words to describe your own feelings. For example if your child sees you crying, do you say something like "I am crying because I am sad," which begins to help children label feelings and the types of verbal and nonverbal cues that accompany those feelings. Or do you brush the tears away and say, "Oh, no, I was just cutting onions," which may feel more comfortable in the moment; however, this explanation not only is untrue but fails to help your child learn to label emotions. Besides being honest about your emotions, you as a parent can also give examples of what you do to manage those feelings. Continuing with the example above, by saying, "I am feeling sad so I am going to go for a walk" (assuming there is another adult home for childcare) teaches your child a label for the feeling, as well as serving as an example of a way that you cope when you are feeling sad.

TIME TO REFLECT

- Do you label your own feelings in the presence of your child?
- Do you show your child some of the different ways that you manage your feelings?
- Do you help your child to identify and label what they are feeling?
- Do you find ways to validate what your child is feeling?
- Do you help your child find ways to manage their feelings?

Parents of strong-willed children often describe their children by saying things such as the child has a "quick temper" or is "sensitive" or has "big feelings." All these descriptions suggest that parents of strong-willed children have lots of opportunities to help their children become more aware of, label, and regulate their positive and negative emotions; yet this can be easier said than done. That is, parents of strong-willed children often respond to their child's big feelings, particularly negative feelings like sadness or anger or frustration, by missing an opportunity to label and manage the feeling or by focusing only on the feeling and overlooking the behavior that follows the feeling. Let's explore these potential reactions a little more.

Parents of strong-willed children sometimes respond to a child's big feelings by saying things like "Oh it isn't that bad" or "That shouldn't upset you so much" or "Stop crying." While these sorts of responses may help parents to manage their own distress (at least in the short term), it not only invalidates the child's feelings but is a missed opportunity to teach them more about their feelings and how to manage or regulate those feelings. We as parents need to realize feelings are not right or wrong but just are—it is how we respond to those feelings that is most important. Ideally, we need to accurately acknowledge the feeling, but *only* after first addressing the behavior that is your child's reaction to the feeling.

Let's look at an example. Say your child hits another child on the playground. You know (we hope!) from our five-week program that the recommended response to that would be an automatic (i.e., no Warning) Time-Out based on a standing rule that you had established. So you first address the behavior; however, what often happens instead is the parent gives lots of attention to the child's not-okay (hitting) behavior (and increasing the likelihood it will happen again!) by focusing on what feeling they think led to the hitting.

It may go something like this. The parent crouches down on the playground to get at eye level with the child, takes the child's arms, and pulls them in gently for a nose-to-nose talk. Then the talk begins: "Oh, my gosh! Why did you hit your friend? Are you mad? Are you upset? Please tell me how you are feeling. It isn't good to hit your friend. How would you feel if your friend hit you?" While we want you to help your child to figure out what was upsetting and how to handle it differently next time, we highly recommend waiting to have these sorts of

242

conversations until *after* you have addressed the not-okay behavior (hitting a friend on the playground). So let's look at how Ms. Williams appropriately handles this with four-year-old Jacob:

MS. WILLIAMS: Jacob, you hit your friend, so you have to go to Time-Out. [Gently takes her child's arm and leading Jacob to the corner of the playground]

JACOB: *But* my friend pushed in front of me on the slide! [Starting to cry]

MS. WILLIAMS: [No look, talk, or touch]

JACOB: You are mean . . . this isn't fair. [Yelling]

MS. WILLIAMS: [Keeping track of three minutes on her watch as she puts Jacob in the corner of the playground for Time-Out]

JACOB: [Starts to calm down a bit, becoming quiet and calm in the corner of the playground with Ms. Williams standing close by]

MS. WILLIAMS: You can come out of Time-Out now, Jacob. You went to Time-Out because you are not allowed to hit.

JACOB: But my friend cut in front of me on the slide! [Starts to cry again]

So Ms. Williams immediately addressed the behavior, and now has the opportunity to address the emotion by further using the skills she learned in our five-week program. First, Ms. Williams can use Attends by just focusing directly on what Jacob is telling her. For example, Jacob's mom could say, "You are telling me that your friend cut in front of you on the slide." Ms. Williams could also use Attends to observe and describe and, in turn, begin to help Jacob label the feelings: "You are feeling sad [or frustrated or angry]." Jacob's mom can also use Rewards. Let's imagine Jacob says, "No! I am not sad. I am mad because my friend cut in on the slide, and it was my turn. My friend always cuts." In turn, Ms. Williams may say something like "You are telling me that you feel mad because your friend did not wait their turn!" (Attending) "I really like how you shared what you were feeling with me!" (Rewarding). By dealing with the not-okay behavior first, however, the consequence (the Time-Out) decreases the likelihood that hitting will occur again. Then by next focusing on any emotions that may have come before the not-okay behavior, Ms. Williams can begin to teach Jacob other strategies for dealing with anger and frustration. Here's how Ms. Williams does this:

> **MS. WILLIAMS:** You were really mad at your friend for not taking turns on the slide! (Attending) I am really happy you told me how you were feeling! (Rewarding)
>
> **JACOB:** I was really mad!
>
> **MS. WILLIAMS:** Being mad is okay. We all get mad sometimes. You didn't go to Time-Out because you were feeling mad. You went to Time-Out because you hit your friend.
>
> **JACOB:** Okay.
>
> **MS. WILLIAMS:** Let's back up to figure out if there is a better way to deal with feeling mad in the future. How did you know you were feeling mad?
>
> **JACOB:** I don't know.
>
> **MS. WILLIAMS:** Let's try to figure it out. Did your body feel any different?
>
> **JACOB:** I did this with my fists. [Clenching them]

MS. WILLIAMS: You are telling me that one way you know you are mad is that you clenched your fists! (Attending) I am really impressed that you figured that out! (Rewarding)

JACOB: And I yelled at my friend.

MS. WILLIAMS: You are telling me that when you are mad, you clench your fists and yell! (Attending) You are really good at figuring this out! (Rewarding)

JACOB: Yeah.

MS. WILLIAMS: Now let's figure out if there is anything else you can do the next time instead.

JACOB: I could walk away.

MS. WILLIAMS: [Gives Jacob a high five] (Rewarding) Yes, you are telling me you can walk away the next time! (Attending)

JACOB: Or come to you.

MS. WILLIAMS: Jacob, I am so impressed by the things you are coming up with to do instead of hitting! (Rewarding) You are telling me that you could walk away or come tell me! (Attending)

In this scenario, you can see how Ms. Williams first gave a consequence for Jacob's not-okay behavior (Time-Out), then circled back to talk about feelings and how to respond differently next time. In this way, Jacob's mom decreases the likelihood that hitting occurs again because it is the removal of attention (Time-Out) that immediately follows the not-okay behavior. Then, and only then, Ms. Williams focuses on Jacob's feelings and problem solving around managing those feelings.

Using your skills to help your child become more aware of, label, and manage their emotions is key to emotion socialization and, in turn, your child's ability to effectively regulate the range of feelings that are a very normal part of childhood, adolescence, and beyond. Children who are good at regulating their emotions tend to be less vulnerable to subsequent emotion and behavioral difficulties, do better in school, and also have higher self-esteem, which is a topic we will talk about next.

SELF-ESTEEM

Like emotion regulation, self-esteem begins to develop early in life, and parents can play a critical role in the process. Although how we define self-esteem becomes more nuanced as children grow older, with young children we are talking about the match or fit between what your child finds important, interesting, or valuable (e.g., school, sports, peers) and how comfortable and competent they feel in each of those domains. It is important for parents to focus on the development of self-esteem for *all* children but especially so for strong-willed children. Unfortunately, as we have discussed, their not-okay behaviors are often met with negative reactions from siblings, peers, and adults, including parents, other family members, and those outside the home such as daycare providers and teachers. One of the things you realize fairly quickly when you work with strong-willed children clinically is that these reactions are not lost on them—in fact, they are often acutely aware that others are not enjoying their company, but they can't necessarily figure out on their own what to do differently. Such a process does not lead to a child having positive self-esteem.

So by embarking on and using our five-week program, you have already taken a major step toward improving your strong-willed child's self-esteem because you quite literally taught them the rules (okay behavior!) that will earn your positive attention (Attends and Rewards). With time, practice, and experience, your child will then feel more and more comfortable and confident, given that their interactions with you are predictable (i.e., okay behaviors earn Attends and Rewards; not-okay behaviors earn no attention or a consequence such as Time-Out). This confidence can begin to spill over into their interactions with others as well, including daycare providers, teachers, siblings, and peers. That is, the more your child learns that okay behaviors are what earns positive attention, the more likely they are to use those same behaviors with others as well. Then once they learn that okay behaviors are met not only with less negative attention in those interactions but also with more positive attention, their confidence and, in turn, self-esteem will continue to build. As you can see, our five-week program has direct implications for how your child will feel about themselves.

You can also use your skills to increase the likelihood that your child's comfort and confidence are growing. Here are some examples of ways that parents like you can begin to do this with your child:

- **Use your skills to encourage your child's interests and abilities.** For example, if your child seems to enjoy coloring, look for opportunities to use your Attends and Rewards while they are coloring or doing other creative activities. Sit down next to them, lean in, smile, ramp up the enthusiasm in your voice, and say something like "You are using the red crayon now!" (Attending) "You are doing such a good job coloring in the lines!" (Rewarding)

"You are making such a colorful picture!" (Rewarding) Then do not hesitate to post your child's artwork on the refrigerator or another central spot in the house!

- **Use your skills to encourage your child to make decisions.** Choices and the ability to make decisions about the choices in our life increase our sense of self-control and bolster our sense of self and self-esteem. Of course, you only want to offer choices if the decision is one that you can leave up to your child to actually make, but examples may include "Do you want an apple or a pear for a snack with your crackers?" or "Do you want to wear the red shirt or the blue shirt today?" or "Do you want to play with the football or basketball?" When your child makes a decision, try to go with it (even if it isn't what you would have picked!) and give their decision-making positive attention: "You picked basketball!" (Attending) [High five!] (Rewarding)

- **Use your skills to begin to allow your child to take (small) risks.** Parents, of course, want to protect their children, but some risk-taking allows children to push their limits, build their confidence, and feel better about their skills and abilities. You can start with really small risks that happen every day around the house. Let's say your child tells you that they do not want to use the "baby cup" at dinner anymore, but instead wants a big cup. In your mind, you are thinking, "*No,* because you will spill it in two seconds!" but you also know that spilling a glass of water isn't the worst thing that can happen. So instead you may say: "You are telling me you want to use a big cup!" (Attending) "That is so brave of you to try something new!" (Rewarding) "Here you go." [Gives child big cup (with only a small amount of water in it).] As your child uses the cup, you can continue to give positive attention: "You are lifting that big cup to your mouth to take a drink!" (Attending) or "You are being so very careful with the big cup! (Rewarding) Of course, there is a reasonable possibility that the first time your child uses a big cup it will spill accidentally, and if (when!) that happens, you don't necessarily want to give the spilling positive attention, but rather focus on other things. For example, "We all spill our water sometimes. It can be easy to get upset when that happens, but accidents happen and you stayed nice and calm!" (Attending) "We will clean it up and refill your glass." A suggestion is warranted here: How you react will have a big influence on how your child reacts. So you need to stay calm also.

• **Use your skills to shape successive approximation.** We touched on successive approximation in an earlier chapter, but let's give several examples here as it is important. Think about when your child was a baby trying to roll over for the first time or a little later when you child was working toward crawling or taking their first steps. Chances are you were cheering on anything that looked like they were trying to roll over, crawl, or walk—you were smiling; you were coaching; you were clapping! That was using your positive attention to shape successive approximations of the behavior you ultimately wanted to see (rolling over, crawling, and walking!). You can do the same as your child continues to grow and develop. Let's use schoolwork as an example. Maybe early on you are using your Attends and Rewards to give lots of positive attention to the fact that your six-year-old child is simply sitting down to do homework: "You sat right down with your homework!" (Attending) "You are getting out your papers!" (Attending) "I love how you got right to work!" (Rewarding). As this routine becomes more established, you use your Attends and Rewards to reinforce their effort toward working on something, regardless of whether they get it right or not. For example, "Wow, you are really working hard to figure out the answer to that question!" (Rewarding) Finally, you may start Attending and Rewarding to getting the right answer by doing something like giving a high five (Rewarding) and saying, "You worked really hard and came up with the answer!" (Attending and Rewarding) As you can see, you gradually shape the behavior (getting the right answer), which is the ultimate goal.

These are just some examples of the ways in which you can use your skills to build your child's self-esteem. You can probably think of others!

TIME TO REFLECT

What are ways that you can use your skills throughout the day to build your child's self-esteem?

- Are there particular times of the day when your child can use a boost in confidence?
- Are there particular activities that your child seems to enjoy or look forward to?
- Are there particular things you would like your child to try or try more?

Higher self-esteem is also linked to social skills. This is a bit of a chicken and egg question—that is, does higher self-esteem increase the likelihood that children feel more comfortable and are more competent in their interactions with adults and other children, or is it that more interactions lead to greater self-esteem? The answer is probably both, so let's turn to your child's social skills now.

SOCIAL SKILLS

As we talked about earlier in this chapter, children who are strong-willed often have difficulties in their interactions with adults and other children, including peers and siblings. Their not-okay behavior at best can be mildly annoying to those who don't understand them and at worst can lead others to not want to spend time with them at all. As with emotion regulation, you can teach your child social skills by modeling how you interact with others. You can also use your skills to catch and reinforce times their successive approximation leads to socially skilled behavior. Behaviors you may look for include:

- **Getting someone's attention.** This can be hard for strong-willed children who may be more likely to do things like interrupt or demand attention. So if you happen to notice times at home in their interactions with you or their siblings when your child waits for a pause in the conversation to speak, you could say, "I really like how you waited your turn when you really wanted to tell me about your day!" (Rewarding) You can also suggest that your child say "Excuse me" if they are trying to enter into or engage in a conversation or get someone's attention, and be sure to notice and Attend and Reward when they do!

- **Waiting your turn.** Turn-taking can be incredibly challenging for children who are strong-willed, particularly those who struggle with hyperactivity, impulsivity, and/or inattention. So be sure to catch any moments when you see your child waiting patiently, whether it at home (e.g., waiting for lunch) or in places like the playground (e.g., standing in line for the slide). For example on the playground you may say, "You are doing such a good job waiting for your turn on the slide!" (Rewarding) Remember, the more positive attention that you give your child for the okay behavior (or something that is moving in the right direction of the okay behavior), the less likely they are to do the not-okay behavior (pushing or shoving in line). You can also help your child think of things to do while waiting, including saying the alphabet or counting as high as they can in their head!

- **Sharing.** Sharing can be challenging for strong-willed children, who often are more impulsive and inattentive, for many of the same reasons that turn-taking is. So work really hard every day to notice, Attend to, and Reward anything that remotely looks like sharing with you or others. Imagine you sit down with your child who is coloring. Your child is rearranging their coloring books on the table and happens to slide one of the books in front of you. You may say something like "You are moving your coloring books around and put one in front of me!" (Attending) Now imagine that your child looks pleased by this and slides some crayons your way too. "You are giving me some crayons too!" (Attending)

Now let's imagine your child says. "Color with me!" and you may say, "You are telling me you want me to color with you!" (Attending) "Thank you for sharing your coloring book and crayons with me!" (Rewarding)

In addition to using your skills to reinforce social skills like getting someone's attention, taking turns, and sharing, you can also do some role plays with your child. We recommend using the following guidelines:

- **Explain the skill.** In the example of getting someone's attention, you may say something like "We are going to play a game. I am going to pretend that I am reading a book. While I am pretending to read the book, I want you to try to get my attention by saying, "Excuse me, Mom."

- **Model the skill.** If we continue with this example, the next step would be modeling "Excuse me." So you may say, "Let me show you how it is done." You hold the book and pretend like you are reading. "I say, 'Excuse me, Dad.'"

- **Have your child role-play the skill.** Using this example, you will then do the role play. You will get comfy on the couch with your book and pretend to be reading intently. Then prompt your child to say, "Excuse me, Mom."

- **Provide feedback.** Presuming this example goes well, you would use your Attending and Rewarding skills: "You said 'Excuse me!'" (Attending) "Very nice job getting my attention!" (Rewarding) You can also give corrective feedback to your child, which will be important as they learn to do this better and eventually well. So if they were pulling on your sleeve while saying

"Excuse me, Mom," you may Attend to and Reward the words ("Excuse me, Mom") to give them positive attention, but then say, "Okay, let's try it again, but this time I want you to keep your hands at your side." Then repeat the role play and Attend to and Reward their words and their gentle hands!

- **Encourage your child to practice their new skill**. You can help your child think about situations at home and at school or other places where they may want to get someone's attention, and encourage them to say, "Excuse me" and let you know how it goes. Of course, if you see it, give lots of positive attention!

———————

Promoting positive development of your child requires a lot of thought and work on your part, particularly if you have a strong-willed child. However, using the skills you learned in our five-week program can serve as the base for building emotion regulation, self-esteem, social skills, and other positive skills!

PART IV

(DE-)STRESSING YOUR PARENTING

To this point, we have discussed the following topics: why strong-willed behavior develops; strategies for improving okay behavior with our five-week program; and how to apply the skills you learned to decrease a variety of not-okay behaviors, improve your child's daily routines, and increase certain pro-social behaviors, like social skills. By using the skills learned in our five-week program, you can enjoy your time with your child more while also setting them up for success outside the home with peers, at school, and beyond. But being an effective parent also requires that you take good care of yourself and your relationships with other adults in your life, both of which are a foundation for optimal child development as well. So in this final part of the book, Part IV, we turn to two important topics—the first is self-care. In Chapter 16 we start by presenting some self-care strategies for you to use to reduce the stressors you may experience in your life. Then in Chapter 17 we turn to the way you think about stressors, particularly the stress of parenting a strong-willed child. Believe it or not (and you probably do), how you think about stressors in your life, particularly how you interpret your strong-willed child's behavior, can influence how you parent. Both reducing the stressors you experience and changing the way you think about your child's behavior should help you implement the skills you learned in our five-week program. Finally, we conclude this final part of the book by extending our focus on self-care to how you care for and navigate your relationships with other adults in your life. We focus Chapter 18 on your relationship with your co-parent or the person(s) who helps you with raising your strong-willed child. This may be a spouse, partner, relative such as your own parent or sibling, or friend. Talking about these relationships is important because we know how adults navigate child-rearing *together* affects their parenting and, in turn, their child's behavior (including strong-willed behavior).

CHAPTER 16

SELF-CARE

PUT ON YOUR OXYGEN MASK FIRST

f you have boarded an airplane, you have heard this preflight reminder: "In the event of a loss of cabin pressure, oxygen masks will fall from the panel above your head. Reach up and pull the mask toward you and place the strap behind your head. Pull the ends of the strap to tighten your mask. Breathe normally and note that oxygen is flowing even if the bag does not inflate. If you are traveling with your children, or someone who needs assistance, place your own mask before helping others."

Nobody wants to ever be in the middle of a flight and hear this announcement, but the message is clear—you have to help yourself in order to be in a position to help others, including your child. This preflight announcement is an oft-used example in self-care as well, and self-care related to parenting is no exception. That is, the skills you have learned in this book require an immense amount of your dedication, time, and energy, as we have acknowledged repeatedly throughout. That said, to be able to offer so much of yourself to your child, you must be thoughtful about self-care as well.

Now we acknowledge at the outset that "self-care" has become quite a buzzword at this point in the popular press and on social media. As such, you may be rolling your eyes as you are reading this, thinking something like "I am a parent—I don't have time for self-care!" We also realize that self-care can sound quite privileged—that is, pampering yourself may be the last thing on your mind if you are working long hours, balancing work and family, and stressing about if and how well you are going to be able to get it all done. So let us clarify: We are not necessarily talking here about things that cost a lot of money or even take a lot of time (although if you have the time and resources, then why not!). Instead we are simply talking about how you treat yourself in the context of the very real day-to-day stressors of parenting in general and parenting a strong-willed child in particular, which can be taxing even for the most skilled parent! So in this chapter we are focusing on those stressors, the feelings you may have in the context of those stressors, and ways to prevent those feelings from seeping into your interactions with your child by taking good care of yourself first!

THE REALITY OF PARENTING STRESS

Parents have always experienced stress, although society has never done a great job of acknowledging this truth. Think about your conversations with other parents or how you hear other parents, including on television and in social media, talk about being a parent. Often you hear things like becoming a parent is "life-changing," that it "puts everything else in perspective," that it is the "most important thing" that someone can do, and that it is "better than imagined." Then pair these superlatives with carefully selected social media posts of perfectly dressed and well-behaved children enjoying the company of one another and their parents. How does this make you feel as the parent of a strong-willed child? We bet that it does not feel good. It makes you feel like you are not the perfect parent 100 percent of the time and you must be doing something wrong. We are here to tell you that is simply not true! While parenting is likely one of the most rewarding things you have done, it is also likely exhausting, sometimes messy, and often challenging. Even the best parents have at least fleeting thoughts of wanting to throw in the towel and run off to a desert island with only sunscreen and a good book or magazine. In fact, one of our children recently said as their child was throwing a tantrum: "I can't wait until my child grows up and has children!"

So rather than pretending that parents are or should be happy all the time, we instead want to acknowledge that as a parent, you will experience a range of emotions. Some of your feelings will be linked to things that have nothing to do with your child, including your health, work, world events, or your relationship with other adults. We know that feelings about any kind of stressor can affect how we behave in general, including how we interact with our child. It is also the case that you likely feel stress related to your child's behavior. Parenting any child in the two- to six-year-old age range can be challenging, given that it is developmentally appropriate that they are asking questions (lots of questions!) and testing (and retesting!) limits. Parenting a child who has a strong-willed temperament can add another layer of stress, as the not-okay behaviors are likely more frequent and often more extreme than for other children in the same age range.

So it is not uncommon for parents of strong-willed children to feel anxious about their child's behavior and what that behavior means. Similarly, parents of strong-willed children can feel anger at the child's behavior, especially if the child is doing things like being noncompliant or aggressive, and then parents feel guilty that they felt angry. Parents of strong-willed children can also feel sad and hopeless because they worry that things won't improve. Finally, parents of strong-willed children can feel embarrassment or shame that they cannot better manage their child's behavior or that others will think that they are not a good parent.

These feelings are totally normal among all parents, but parents of strong-willed children simply have more opportunities to have these types of feelings. Add your feelings about your child's behavior to the other types of stressors that you are feeling as a function of being an adult who is perhaps working and taking care of a family in a world that often feels uncertain, and it is not surprising you may be less patient, have less energy, and have less enthusiasm for doing the skills in our five-week program. You may know the skills and even know how to implement them, but perhaps you Attend to and Reward positive behavior less often. Or perhaps you fail to Ignore some minor negative behaviors and instead yell at your strong-willed child when these occur. Or maybe you let more serious not-okay behavior slide by saying, "I just do not have the energy to go through the whole Time-Out sequence." Any or all of these things can happen when you feel stressed.

So what can you do to be kinder and gentler with yourself about parenting (and other) stress? These stressors are important in their own right in terms of your mental health. However, even beyond this, they will negatively impact the way you use our five-week program and interact with your child. In this chapter we will present some basic strategies for you to use to improve your own self-care. These strategies for most of us really come down to managing the stressors in our life. When we are able to identify and manage the stressors, whether they be job-related (e.g., a boss who demands too much), home-related (e.g., too many tasks to be completed in a day, a strong-willed child), or society-related (e.g., tragic event in the news), we will be more effective with our strong-willed child by consistently implementing the skills learned in our five-week program (Part II).

Let's look at some ways you can cope with stressors in your life. By using these techniques, you will reduce the stress in your life and, as a result, more effectively implement the five-week program.

IDENTIFY AND REDUCE STRESSORS

Unfortunately, we cannot eliminate all the stressors in our lives. (Sorry!) In reality, life would perhaps be boring if we did not have some (but not too many!) challenges. We must usually accept and work around stress factors such as health problems and job responsibilities. However, if you are like most people, there are probably numerous small stressors in your life that you can eliminate or reduce.

The first step is to identify what contributes to your stress. Make a list of all the stressors, big and small (we sometimes call these "daily hassles"!), that affect you. Then go through the list and mark the stressors that you can change or eliminate. For instance, some people become stressed by overcommitting themselves. If this is true for you, resolve to start being more assertive and reducing your commitments.

Keep in mind that not only the "big" things, like finances, cause stress. For some people, the daily hassles of life build up to cause the most stress. If this is the case for you, try to minimize the small hassles. *Remember:* Organization is the key. Try to plan out each day. For example, by developing a daily plan, you may be able to do all your errands in one trip rather than two or three. This can be a big time-saver and reduce stress.

In sum, the initial step is to identify the stressors you can change. The next step is to decide exactly what changes to make. Then do it!

TIME TO REFLECT

Big Stressors

- List all the big stressors in your life.
- Put a check by those you could change.
- Put a second check by the one stressor that you want to begin working on.
- Then get started!

Daily Hassles

- List all the daily hassles in your life.
- Put a check by those you could change.
- Put a second check by the one that you want to begin working on.
- Then get started!

TAKE A BREAK OR CHANGE GEARS

If you were to list the most stressful occupations, you might list jobs like police officer, firefighter, or doctor. While these occupations are stressful, the people doing these jobs have time away from work to recuperate. They rarely work 24 hours a day, and if they do, they usually have periods of time off from work to recover.

Now think about being a parent—especially the parent of a strong-willed child—and realize that the small stressors of life often have the biggest impact, which is especially true when we have little relief from these ongoing small stressors. From this perspective, being a parent is at once one of the most rewarding *and* most stressful jobs in the world. We are parents 24 hours a day, seven days a week. Many parents of young children have little time off from the daily hassles of being a parent.

As the parent of a strong-willed child, you therefore need to take breaks from your parenting role. How you do this can vary greatly. Regardless of how you do it, the main goal should be for you to spend at least several hours a week doing something you really enjoy. Your activity might be something you consider relaxing, such as taking a nap, reading, taking a walk, doing a craft, going to a movie, or being with friends. Other kinds of breaks also can be helpful. For some people, just changing gears and doing something different from the routine of parenting is most helpful. For example, volunteer for an hour or two outside the home, sit by the window in the coffee shop to drink your coffee or tea so that you can people-watch rather than racing back to your car or bus and on to your next appointment, or find and go to a free exhibit or show. The point is to do something that you enjoy doing so that you can have a regular break or change of pace from the daily demands of parenting.

TIME TO REFLECT

What are some ways that you like to (or would like to!) take a break or change gears?

_____

_____

_____

Make a plan for doing one of these.

LEARN HOW TO RELAX

When most people become really stressed, they show signs of physical tension. Common symptoms are tense muscles, headaches, rapid and shallow breathing, and increased blood pressure. One way of managing stress is learning how to relax in order to reduce such physical tension.

Many people believe they already know how to relax. However, effective relaxation is more than just sitting down in front of the television, taking a coffee break, or having a beer or glass of wine with friends. These activities may distract a person from stress or help the person cope, but they generally do not reduce physical tension.

One effective technique for combating physical tension is to learn and practice specific relaxation exercises (see the box "Sample Relaxation Exercise"). There are many types of relaxation exercises. Some involve learning to tense and relax specific muscle groups, while others involve breathing and visualization techniques. For these relaxation exercises to be most effective in reducing physical tension, you must practice them daily.

SAMPLE RELAXATION EXERCISE

The technique described here involves visualization and breathing exercises. This brief description alone cannot provide you with the skills necessary to achieve the level of relaxation necessary to significantly reduce your physical tension. However, we hope it will give you an idea of what relaxation training can involve.

Before practicing this technique, lie down or sit in a comfortable chair that offers support for your head. Eliminate distractions by turning off the television, radio, computer, and all cell phones. Then choose a quiet location and a time you will not be disturbed.

Start by placing yourself in a comfortable position where all parts of your body, including your legs, arms, and head, are supported. Keep your legs uncrossed. Close your eyes. Try to focus initially on blocking out all other thoughts and concentrate solely on your breathing. Slow down your breathing. Take deep, relaxing breaths. Make your breathing smooth; that is, breathe in slowly and out slowly. Try to create a smooth rhythm to your breathing.

After your breathing becomes relaxed and rhythmic, imagine a small amount of tension in your body leaving through your breath each time you exhale. Imagine the tension being sucked out of your body each time you exhale. Imagine the tension leaving your feet, legs, back, shoulders, neck, and elsewhere in your body. Each time you inhale, imagine a small wave of relaxation spreading throughout your body from your head to your toes.

Try to continue this exercise for several minutes. Then daydream about a relaxing situation. For some people, it might be lying on the beach; for others, it might be lying in a field looking up at the clouds. The exact scene is unimportant as long as it is relaxing to you. (You should decide on the scene before beginning the relaxation exercise so you do not have to waste time and energy deciding on a scene when you are relaxed.) The most important thing to remember as you are daydreaming about your scene is to try to involve all your senses. Imagine that you are really there. Imagine not only the visual aspects of the scene but also the sounds, smells, and sensations. For example, if you imagine yourself at the beach, imagine the sounds of the surf, the birds, and the children playing in the distance. Imagine the smell of saltwater and perhaps suntan lotion. Also, imagine the sensation of the sun's warmth on your skin and the feeling of the wind as it blows across your body. Try to actually put yourself at the beach mentally.

After you have practiced daydreaming for at least five to ten minutes, you can slowly open your eyes and focus on how relaxed you feel.

You can use such relaxation exercises as brief respites from the daily stressors in your life. They can be viewed as brief catnaps that relax and refresh your body. Over time, and with training, many people learn how to use such techniques to quickly put themselves in a relaxed state during times of tension.

There are many ways to learn relaxation techniques. Mental health professionals often teach them individually. Your local hospital, community college, church, or other organization may offer classes in relaxation or stress management. Or you can learn on your own with one of the many books and audiotapes or CDs on the subject that you can purchase at a bookstore or online.

TIME TO REFLECT

- What is an effective relaxation technique for you?
- What is a good time and place for you to use the technique?

LEARN EFFECTIVE PROBLEM-SOLVING STRATEGIES

Problems in our lives, whether at work or at home, can cause stress. They can cause extreme stress when we do not know how we should handle them and, as a result, become overwhelmed. You are less likely to feel overwhelmed if you learn and practice a strategy for solving problems. One problem-solving process involves the following steps:

1. Try to relax and remain calm.
2. Clearly define the specific problem.
3. Generate a list of possible solutions.
4. Evaluate the solutions on the list.
5. Choose what you think is the best solution.
6. Implement the solution and evaluate the outcome.

To use this problem-solving process effectively, try to remain relaxed. The more tense and upset you become, the less clearly you will think, and the less effectively you will address the problem. When you are calm, try to clearly define the problem. Many times we do not effectively address problems because we look only at the symptoms instead of defining the exact problem. Once you have specifically defined the problem, generate a list of possible solutions. At this stage, do not think about whether each is a good or bad solution or even if it is realistic. You just want to brainstorm and come up with as many potential solutions as possible.

After you have exhausted your thoughts on potential solutions, it is time to evaluate the solutions on your list. Review each potential solution and decide whether it is at all possible and whether it would produce the desired result. Also, think about the negative repercussions of each solution. After evaluating all the possible solutions, choose the solution that you think is best, all factors considered. Some people never can make a decision because none of the options is ideal. If you are one of these people, remind yourself that most problems do not have an ideal solution (just as there are no ideal children!) and that you must choose the best possible solution for you. Typically, if you fail to select and implement a solution, you perpetuate stress. Finally, at some point after implementing the solution you selected, evaluate the outcome and how you did in making the decision. Make sure you Reward (e.g., praise) yourself if the solution you selected was a good one. If the selected solution was not a good one, use the experience as a time of learning. Think about other solutions that might have been more effective.

And here is another thought. Isn't this problem-solving approach exactly how you want your strong-willed child, as they get older, to approach problems? Assuming the answer is yes (why else would you be reading this book?), there are two ways to help them achieve this goal. First, as we have discussed often in this book, you modeling appropriate behavior is critical. If you engage in problem-solving skills, your child will see you use the skills and slowly acquire the same skills. Second, by you consistently using the skills you learned in our five-week program, your strong-willed child will know what to expect after their okay and not-okay behavior. This will lead to your child learning what works and what doesn't work to solve issues. What could be better for your child and for your own self-care?

TIME TO REFLECT

- What is one issue you can identify with which to use the problem-solving strategies?
- Can you give it a try and see if the issue diminishes?

GET ENOUGH REST

Everyone is tired at times, but frequently or constantly feeling tired is a problem. If you are like most people, you have less patience when you are tired. You may have difficulty seeing things objectively and using problem-solving skills and our five-week program. You may have a greater tendency to overreact to certain situations. Being tired creates problems that result in even more stress. If stress is a problem for you, you must get enough rest to effectively deal with the stressful situations you face.

Try to establish a consistent bedtime that will allow you to sleep sufficiently. Staying up past midnight every night and rising at 6 a.m. allows too little sleep time for most people. In the end, you will be able to achieve more (especially in terms of quality) if you have enough rest than if you regularly stay up late to complete things. One way to do this is to have consistent times for going to bed and rising.

If you have difficulty falling asleep, you might want to try using one of the relaxation techniques discussed earlier in this chapter. Also, try to limit the use of your bed to sleeping. Avoid watching television, doing paperwork, eating, or reading in your bed. Do these things in another room. In this way you will associate your bed only with sleeping, which may decrease the amount of time it takes for you to fall asleep when you go to bed. Remember, if you sleep enough, you will feel rested, view things in a more positive light, and be more effective at implementing our five-week program.

TIME TO REFLECT

- Are you stressed in part because you don't sleep enough?
- How can you address this situation?

EAT A WELL-BALANCED DIET (OR AT LEAST ADD SOME FRUITS AND VEGGIES!)

You have probably heard the saying "You are what you eat." You can argue the merits of this saying, but there is no denying that what you eat and drink influences your body's ability to function optimally. A balanced diet provides your body with the nutrition required to have the energy and health necessary to function well, including your being a good parent. A poor diet can result not only in a lack of energy in implementing our five-week program but also in an inability for your body to fight off illness.

That said, we know that the pressure of eating a "well-balanced diet" can feel overwhelming at best and at worst just plain unattainable. You are busy. You are trying to find reasonably healthy foods that your child will eat. Your meals may most days consist primarily of eating leftovers off your child's plate—or spoons of peanut butter as you make their peanut butter sandwich! No, don't worry; we are *not* watching you—we just know and work with lots of parents, and eating a nutritious meal is rarely first on their list of priorities (even if it technically should be).

Indeed, one of the major problems with stress and diet is that many people tend to eat less nutritious foods when they are under stress. Eating more junk food when under stress can establish a vicious circle. The more stressed you become, the poorer your eating habits; the poorer your eating habits, the less able your body is to help you deal with stress. So make an extra effort to eat balanced and nutritious meals, especially when you are under stress.

One way to make your nutrition something that feels more feasible amid everything else that is going on is to start small, see how it goes, and adjust until you find yourself eating even a little bit better each day.

TIME TO REFLECT

- What is one meal that you could begin to incorporate some changes into?
- If you are not eating during that meal at all (e.g., skipping breakfast), what is a relatively simple, healthy option you could try to weave into that time of day?
- What are one or two more nutritious foods you could weave into your daily meal or snack rotation? Think about fruits and vegetables you like, whole grains, or nuts and seeds, for example. And if your answer is "Spinach!," then maybe you don't need to start with a big spinach salad, but instead perhaps put some spinach on your otherwise vegetable-less sandwich and go from there!

GET ACTIVE (OR AT LEAST MORE ACTIVE!)

Just as nutrition is important to your general well-being, so is being active. The more active you are, the more physically fit you are likely to be, and the better your body will be able to handle the very real physical demands of stress. Unfortunately, when we are under stress, most of us are less, rather than more, physically active. The less physically active you are, the less physically fit you become. As a result, the physical effects of stress will be greater.

Now similar to our caveat in the section above on nutrition, we know that the idea of exercise can feel aversive (who wants to put on a coat and walking shoes if you can just snuggle on the couch and watch television!) and overwhelming (especially if you think exercise = running a marathon!). So we really encourage you to get creative in the ways you think about getting active. It could be running a marathon, joining a gym, or buying the latest and greatest form of exercise equipment. Any and all of those are fine *if* you do them, find some enjoyment in them and, in turn, will continue doing them! Being active, however, can also be as simple as any of the following: putting on your shoes and taking a brisk walk around your neighborhood or the local mall; choosing the stairs instead of the elevator or escalator; parking your car at the far end of the parking lot rather than driving around for 20 minutes looking for a closer spot; or getting off one bus stop earlier so that you have to walk just a bit more (presuming the weather cooperates). Step counters on our smartphones and watches have made it easier to keep track of how many steps we are taking and to set goals and try to break them with one or a combination of these daily activities. And while not all of us may find exercise fun, we may find ways that being active can be satisfying and even brighten our mood. For example, meet a friend or neighbor for even a short walk. Or break out your old roller/ice skates, go for a bike ride, or go for a swim/take swimming lessons.

Many people who regularly exercise or work out claim that it helps them manage stress. There is also growing scientific evidence that exercise provides benefits beyond general physical fitness. For example, endorphins (the body's "feel-good" hormones) are released after a certain level of physical activity is reached. Once you are moving more on a regular basis and doing things that you enjoy, you will likely find it easier to weave them into your day. Many people exercise when they feel stressed. You too may find it is an effective way to reduce the stress of parenting a strong-willed child!

TIME TO REFLECT

What are one, two, or even three things that you do (or will do) to get your body moving to help you to decrease stress?

_____

_____

_____

DEVELOP SUPPORT SYSTEMS

Don't try to do it alone! Life can be very difficult and stressful at times, and you need to be able to turn to others for support. This may mean having relationships with people you can talk to when life is stressful. Or it may mean building relationships with people who can offer more tangible support, like looking after your child occasionally so you can have a break. Remember the saying "It takes a whole village to raise a child." Don't be afraid to reach out to others. Of course, an effective support system needs to go in both directions. Make sure you reciprocate by supporting those who help you, or your support system will collapse.

Who are people you can reach out to when you need either emotional or tangible support? You likely can identify them, but maybe you have not thought of some of the ones listed below. We listed several common possibilities and left several blanks for you to fill in other people you might rely on.

TIME TO REFLECT

- Spouse/significant other
- Neighbor
- Friend
- Coworker
- _____
- _____

- Teacher
- Coach/instructor
- Parent
- Sibling
- _____
- _____

And remember, a human is not necessarily required for support: A pet can offer a lot of emotional support and comfort for many people.

One word of caution: We would encourage you not to rely on your child for support. Young children are not an appropriate source of support for a parent. It is your job to provide support to your child, not vice versa.

MAINTAIN A SENSE OF HUMOR

When people are under stress, they tend to lose their sense of humor. They may fail to see any of the humor in what is going on in their life. This is unfortunate because humor can be a very effective way to manage stress. Laughing about things and about ourselves can really help us maintain a more realistic perspective about what is happening to us. Laughing also makes us feel good, and it can break tension. So try not to take yourself too seriously, and look for the humor in the situation or for other opportunities and excuses to build laughter into your day such as listening to a funny podcast, or watching a silly TikTok video, or calling a funny friend. Sometimes laughter really can be the best medicine, especially when you have a strong-willed child. Such a child truly can test your ability to use our five-week program.

TIME TO REFLECT

- When was the last time you laughed really hard, so hard that you cried? What were you doing? Whom were you with? What was so funny? Can you re-create that or create that more?
- Looking back over your day, week, or month, what is something that you could have done to allow yourself to laugh more? What got in the way? How can you increase the likelihood that you can (and will!) laugh next time?
- What could you build into your day that will make you laugh more? What is something easy, that won't take much of your time, but will have you laughing before you know it? In fact, you may already be laughing now just thinking about it!

A FINAL THOUGHT

By reducing the number of stressors in our life, we will have less difficulty implementing the five-week program more consistently. However, even the best of us as parents have times we lose control, particularly with a strong-willed child. If you do, cut yourself some slack, take a deep breath, try to implement one or more of the stress reducers we suggested, and resolve to return to using the skills you learned in our five-week program.

A TIME TO REFLECT

- Which of the behaviors summarized in the list below do you currently use to reduce stress in your life?
- Which of the behaviors in the list below could you begin using to reduce stress in your life?

Managing the Stress in Your Life

- Identify and try to eliminate (or at least reduce) stressors.
- Take a break (your own Time-Out!) or just change gears (even for a little while).
- Learn relaxation strategies like deep breathing or progressive muscle relaxation.
- Learn effective problem-solving strategies (brainstorm; consider the pros/cons; pick one to try).
- Get enough (or at least more!) rest (naps are for adults too!).
- Eat a well-balanced diet (or as well balanced as possible)— you sneak fruits and vegetables into your children's diet, so sneak them into yours too!

- Become more active—if you can't walk a mile, just walk a block, or park farther away from the store, or take the stairs instead of the elevator.
- Develop and maintain support systems—call a friend, get together with a family member for lunch, or join a parenting or other type of group with common interests.
- Maintain a sense of humor (laugh as often as you can!).

CHAPTER 17

I THINK, THEREFORE I AM (OR I THINK, THEREFORE MY CHILD IS)!

As we discussed in the preceding chapter, self-care involves reducing and coping with the stressors in your life; however, it is more than that—it is also changing the way you think about those stressors, including your strong-willed child's behavior. Children who are strong-willed often lead parents to have negative thoughts—both about their own parenting (as we talked about in Chapter 16) and, as hard as it can be to admit, about their child. These thoughts are important to acknowledge though, as they can affect how you apply our five-week program you learned in Part II.

Let's take an example. Some parents become upset over fairly minor events (e.g., their child spilling a beverage at the dinner table), whereas other parents are not upset by what seem to be fairly major events (e.g., their child breaking an heirloom vase). And whether you become upset or not (or even the degree to which you become upset) will influence whether you can consistently implement our five-week program. If you find yourself becoming upset (or more and more upset) by your child's behaviors, then it may be helpful to read the last chapter again to think about how you are navigating stress and if there are ways to help you alleviate some of your stress a bit more. As we discussed in Chapter 16, if you are traveling with children or someone who needs assistance, put on your own mask before helping others. As you continue to work on strategies for managing (and even reducing) stress in your life, another strategy is to pay more attention to what you think and how you think about those stressors, including your child's not-okay behavior.

In this chapter, we will focus on what you tell yourself about your strong-willed child and how this can help determine how you react to their behavior. In short, it is important in determining whether you blow up at your child or whether you can develop patience in addressing their strong-willed behavior. Let's begin by focusing on your patience with your strong-willed child.

DEVELOPING MORE PATIENCE (A *BIG* CHALLENGE)

Parents of strong-willed children often report that their patience is constantly tested. They have to deal not only with the typical stressors of parenthood but also with a child who can be very demanding. The constant demands would take their toll on almost any parent's patience! Therefore, it is normal to some-times lose your patience; feel upset, frustrated, or angry; and, as a result, not use our five-week program consistently.

Unfortunately, being the parent of a strong-willed child places you in a difficult dilemma. Your child's demanding behavior increases the chance that you will lose your patience, but your child needs you to be patient *more* than most other children do. Strong-willed children respond best to parents who can handle problems in a matter-of-fact way. When you lose your patience, you lose control of effectively managing your child's behavior.

Losing your patience, especially if it happens often, can create significant problems in the long run, even if it sometimes appears to have remedied the situation in the short term. The more patient you can be, especially in the face of your child's disruptive behavior, the more effective you will be as a parent implementing our five-week program. However, as you well know, this is not easy. And losing your patience with your child often leads to subsequent guilt on your part. This can be painful to you and something you want to avoid (how many times have you vowed you will *never* lose your patience again?). And as you know, this does not lead to good self-care.

In this chapter we will discuss the relationship between how you think about your child's behavior and how you react to it. Understanding this relationship will help you learn to become more patient and thus be a more effective parent in implementing our five-week program. After discussing this relationship, we will present ways to improve your reaction by changing how you think. Unfortunately, even after learning ways to increase your patience, you probably will lose control of your emotions again at some point. Therefore, we also will discuss what you can do when you feel you are at your wit's end. Remember that the number and type of stressors in your life (Chapter 16) also affect how you parent. Although how you think about stressors is important, when you are under constant or considerable stress, you may well not be able to implement our five-week program. Therefore, we encourage you to consider both the strategies in Chapter 16 for reducing stressors *and* how you think about stressors, including how you think about your strong-willed child's behavior. This is an act of self-care that will serve both your child and you well!

THE WAY YOU THINK ABOUT YOUR CHILD'S BEHAVIOR

When you are with your strong-willed child, you probably experience a wide range of emotions. Some are good; some are not so good. Most parents think those feelings are caused by their child's behavior. Suppose your child has a temper tantrum in a store, and you become upset. You might conclude that the temper tantrum caused you to become upset. However, the temper tantrum does not *directly* cause you to become upset. What causes you to become upset is the way you view the temper tantrum.

Let's look at some different ways you might view your child's tantrum. If your child begins a temper tantrum in public and you think that your child should always behave in this setting, you might view your child as bad or mean, which may lead you to become angry and start yelling. Or you might start thinking that others view you as a terrible parent for not being able to control your child. In this case, you might question your ability to be a good parent, start feeling depressed, and do nothing to address your child's tantrum because you lack the confidence to take action. A third, and more helpful, view may be that the tantrum resulted from your child's strong-willed temperament, or being overtired and needing a nap, or some interaction of those things.

In this case, you would probably not become very upset or feel bad about yourself but rather decide that it is time to go home so that your child can take a nap (and perhaps you too!).

THE CAUSE OF PARENTS' EMOTIONAL REACTIONS

As in the example we just provided, your child's behavior itself does not make you become upset. You cause yourself to lose your patience by the way you view the behavior. See Figure 17-1, which illustrates this important point.

Your child's behavior *does not* directly cause your emotional reaction.

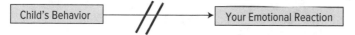

Your emotional reaction depends on how you think about your child's behavior.

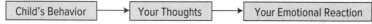

FIGURE 17-1 The cause of parents' emotional reactions

Certain common ways of thinking about a child's behavior often lead parents to lose their patience:

- "My child should never behave in certain ways."
- "I am a bad parent if my child behaves in certain ways."
- "It is terrible, and I can't stand it when my child behaves in certain ways."
- "My child behaves in certain ways to upset me."
- "My child should always behave well."
- "My child is always trying to get on my nerves."
- "I need to get angry to correct my child's behavior."

Becoming aware of these possible thoughts will allow you to identify whether you have similar thoughts, which put you at risk for your emotions determining how you react to your child's behavior. In addition, losing control of your emotions is not part of the self-care that is so important for effectively implementing our five-week program. So let's consider how you can change those negative thoughts.

CATCHING (AND REVISING) YOUR NEGATIVE THOUGHTS

All children are going to misbehave at times or do things that their parents do not like. Therefore, it is not terrible or awful when your child misbehaves unless you convince yourself that it is terrible or awful. This does not mean that you should be content with or condone your child's not-okay behavior. However, you do need to have a realistic perspective regarding your child's behavior, and you need to try really hard to avoid negative absolute thinking.

Negative absolute thinking occurs when you start thinking negatively in absolute ways about something and use terms that include "should," "must," or "always." For example, you might think, "My child should never misbehave." But all children are going to misbehave. If you think your child should never misbehave, you are setting yourself up to lose your patience, become angry when it happens, and, importantly, not use our five-week program skills to respond effectively. In addition, you probably will not feel good about yourself as a parent.

Many parents think in negative absolute terms. If you are one of these parents, try to challenge and change those thoughts. For example, if you tend to think that your child should never misbehave, try to think along more reasonable lines when your child does misbehave. You might say to yourself, "I don't like it when [your child's name] behaves like this, but I can handle it." Also, try to be realistic and acknowledge to yourself that all children misbehave and it is not terrible when your child misbehaves. You do not have to like it, but admit that it is going to happen and that it is undesirable—not terrible. *Terrible* is when a child is stricken with a life-threatening illness, not a temper tantrum at the shopping mall!

Let's look at another common way of thinking in negative absolute terms: thinking other people believe you are a bad parent when your child misbehaves. If you have such a thought, try to challenge it. A more realistic thought is that most parents have had similar experiences and probably empathize with you in such a situation. Even if they do not understand, you do not need the approval of strangers to know that you are a good parent and you are doing the best you can with a difficult, strong-willed child. Try to replace your negative absolute thinking with these more realistic thoughts. After all, remember that your worth as a parent is not based on your child's behavior in public places!

Some parents who are prone to negative absolute thoughts find it helpful to consciously start reciting more realistic and helpful thoughts to themselves when their children misbehave. Here are some sample statements:

- "My child will misbehave sometimes."
- "Getting angry will not help me effectively deal with my child."
- "It is undesirable and irritating when my child misbehaves, but it is not terrible."
- "I can handle this situation more effectively if I stay calm."

- "I am not a bad parent just because my child broke a rule. All children break rules."

This realistic self-talk helps avoid the trap of thinking negatively out of habit.

Another kind of negative thinking involves making negative assumptions about the intentions of your child's behavior. An example is assuming your child is misbehaving to get back at you for something you did. Although this may occasionally be the case, young children rarely misbehave in order to get revenge or to get on your nerves at least in part because they don't yet have the cognitive or emotional skills to understand what you are thinking and feeling and adjust their behavior accordingly. More likely, your child is behaving in a certain way because their strong-willed temperament increases the likelihood of that behavior (e.g., noncompliance), as we talked about earlier and throughout this book, *and* they have learned from experience that you will behave in certain ways in response to that behavior (e.g., giving them attention!). Indeed, in most cases young children misbehave to get something they want or to avoid something they do not want to do. Their motives are typically quite self-centered and do not include a desire to upset their parents. This may be hard to believe at times, but it is true! And by not assuming the worst and by putting their behavior in this developmental context that takes into account what they are capable of, then you are engaging in self-care of yourself and increasing the likelihood that you respond (or not respond!) in ways that are more helpful to them in the long run!

WHAT TO DO WHEN YOU LOSE YOUR PATIENCE

Almost all parents lose their patience at times. Even if you try really hard to change your negative thoughts, you are likely at some time to lose your patience and become angry. If you think in absolute terms that you should never lose your patience, that you should always be patient, and that it is terrible if you lose your patience, you may very well become upset or depressed when you do. This is *not* good self-care behavior on your part and will further interfere with you successfully implementing our five-week program.

Becoming upset or depressed when you lose your patience will not help you be more patient in the future. Instead, when you lose your patience, acknowledge that it is undesirable and unfortunate but also human. Expecting yourself to always be patient is unrealistic. Do not make excuses for losing your patience, but instead, acknowledge and understand that it is going to happen on occasion. And make a brief apology to your child such as the following: "I am sorry I _____. I will try to do better." It is important to keep it brief.

Since you probably will lose your patience with your child in the future, what can you do to minimize the negative effects? We recommend using the four Rs of damage control:

1. *Recognize* that you have lost your patience.
2. *Remove* yourself or step back from the situation.
3. *Review* the situation.
4. *Respond* to the situation.

The first step is to *recognize* as soon as possible that you have lost your patience. Since we all react somewhat differently, try to identify your personal signals that indicate you are losing or have lost your patience. Examples of such signals might be a hot flash, a clenched jaw, a clenched fist, a pounding heart, swearing, or starting to raise your voice. The key is to identify that you are losing (or have lost) your patience as early as possible so that you can regain control of yourself more easily.

The second step is to *remove* yourself from the situation as soon as you recognize that you are losing or have lost your patience. If you are at home or in public with another adult who can assume temporary responsibility for your child, walking away for a few moments may be most effective. Of course, no matter how mad you are, you should never leave your young child unattended in a potentially dangerous situation, such as alone in a public place. When you cannot physically leave the situation, try to step back—literally. Take a couple of steps away from your child, momentarily look at something other than your child, and try to regain your composure. Take some deep breaths, and try to calm yourself as much as possible. Recite to yourself realistic thoughts about your child's behavior, such as the ones suggested earlier. For example, say to yourself, "My child broke a rule. Getting angry and losing control will not help me effectively deal with this situation." This type of positive self-talk can be very effective in managing anger and regaining self-control, leading you to feeling better.

Think back about our five-week program. What we are suggesting you do here is very similar to using Time-Out with your child. You are ideally remaining calm as you place your child in Time-Out *and* you are giving them a few minutes to calm down. Your young child, of course, will not go through the self-control steps you are learning now, but they will see you model self-control and control of your emotions. And this can lead to them beginning to demonstrate some self-control. For example, we have seen children begin to learn self-control by placing themselves in a Time-Out chair when they become upset in order to allow themselves to calm down!

But let's return to you and controlling your thoughts and emotions. Once you have gained your self-control, pause and briefly *review* the situation to yourself. Think about what happened, how your thoughts led you to lose your patience, and how you can use the skills you learned in our five-week program to best handle the present situation. Then decide on what you think is the most effective response.

The final step is to confront the situation and *respond* in the way you have decided is most appropriate. Maintain your self-control while you are responding to the situation. If you sense that you are losing your patience again, start back at the beginning and go through the four Rs again: recognize, remove yourself, review, and respond.

Try to move through the four Rs as quickly as possible. When you remove yourself and review the situation, do not become caught up in all the details of the situation or all the possible ways of responding. If you take too long reviewing the situation, you may lose your chance to respond most effectively. After the situation has resolved, you can analyze it in greater detail and think about possible responses that you did not consider initially. Analyzing the situation later, when you are more relaxed, can lead to more creative ideas that might be helpful the next time you are confronted with a similar situation. At this time, ask yourself: "What do I like about the way I handled that situation?," "What would I do differently next time?," and "Did I use the skills I learned in the five-week program?"

And just as important as reinforcing your child when they engage in okay behavior, you should reinforce yourself when you gain self-control. In fact, as you learned with your child in our five-week program, don't wait until you have completed all four Rs, but reinforce yourself ("I did _____ very well!") for each step. Gaining self-control in the heat of the moment is no small feat—it takes continual practice, self-reminders, and self-reinforcement!

Parenting a strong-willed child is *not* easy! And when you are under stress or interpret events as stressful, it becomes even more difficult. But it is important both for tending to your own self-care and for parenting your strong-willed child to reduce the number of stressors in your life and how you think about those stressors, particularly when your strong-willed child's behavior is the source of the stress.

TIME TO REFLECT

- Do you find yourself frequently thinking about negative events that have happened or might happen in the future?
- What are some negative thoughts you have about your child's behavior?
- Pick one of these negative thoughts to change.
- How will you change it?

CHAPTER 18

IT TAKES A VILLAGE TO RAISE A CHILD

(AND REQUIRES THAT THE VILLAGERS TALK OPENLY AND OFTEN)!

The final part of self-care that we will discuss is your relationships with the other adults in your life. For the purposes of this chapter, we will focus on your co-parent(s) or the other adults who play an active role in raising your strong-willed child. This may include a spouse or domestic partner, your own parent or other family member, or a friend. The things we talk about in this chapter can also be extended to the other important adults in the lives of you and your child such as the teacher in your child's daycare/preschool class, for example. Here is one thing we do know: Research clearly shows that how adults in a child's life get along affects the ways in which those adults parent a child and, in turn, the child's behavior. This may operate through various family processes like conflict about child-rearing, inconsistency in how to approach particular parenting decisions, or different responses to various kinds of not-okay behavior. Importantly, one misconception is that divorce "causes" young children to increase their not-okay behavior. This is often not the case. Instead, what we know is that many divorced parents continue to argue about lots of things including child-rearing and often in front of the child and it is that arguing and inconsistency that is the problem (rather than necessarily the divorce).

In contrast, families that communicate effectively tend to have fewer problems, are more likely to address problems successfully when they do arise, and enjoy being with each other more than families that do not communicate effectively. Effective communication skills are a vital building block of successful functioning for your child, you, and your whole family, but communicating effectively can be the most challenging when—you guessed it!—parents and the other adults in their lives are stressed. Just like the demands of parenting a strong-willed child can increase your stress, they can increase the stress levels of other adults involved in your child's life and lead to the development and intensification of communication breakdowns in the family and those close to the family. Over time, poor communication can seriously erode family functioning through a vicious circle in which distress leads to poor communication, poor communication leads to greater distress, greater distress leads to even poorer communication, and so on. The result is that conflict increases and family problems worsen, and in this context, you are less likely to use the skills in our five-week program consistently and your child is less likely to benefit.

Having a strong-willed child influences communication among all family members but may be most detrimental to the communication between co-parents. Adults co-parenting together often end up arguing about discipline at home, problems at child care or preschool, and whom or what to blame for their child's behavior. Over time, the problems and distress that arise from having a strong-willed child influence the communication between co-parents on issues unrelated to their child. In extreme situations, this vicious circle of poor communication and distress can eventually cause the breakdown of family relationships, as illustrated in Figure 18-1. To avoid or at least minimize such family crises, co-parents must actively work on improving their communication skills.

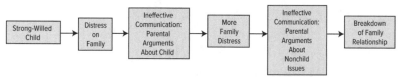

FIGURE 18-1   The strong-willed child and snowballing ineffective communication between parents

In summary, remember that not only can poor communication between co-parents increase not-okay child behavior, but the behavior of a strong-willed child can increase stress and poor communication with your co-parent. This is a double whammy and obviously can interfere with using the skills you learned in our five-week program. Let's next look at some communication problems and some potential solutions.

COMMUNICATION CHALLENGES AND SOLUTIONS

In this chapter, we present some common communication problems and recommend solutions to those problems. Changing communication styles can be very difficult, so like everything else in this book, we acknowledge that it will require a major effort on your part. Old habits are hard to break! We recommend identifying only one or two communication problems to work on at a time. Let your co-parent know specifically what skills you are going to work on. Ask your co-parent to help point out to you (very gently!) when you err and to offer positive feedback as you make progress. This process typically works best when your co-parent is also trying to improve communication because you can support each other. After all, communication is a two-way (not a one-way) street! A supportive atmosphere is essential to effectively change communication patterns. An atmosphere of criticism and finger-pointing will inevitably cause your efforts to fail and will be stressful not only for you but also for your child.

PROBLEM #1: INATTENTION

Most people would agree that you cannot have a meaningful conversation if one person is not paying attention to what the other person is saying. Although we all recognize the importance of paying attention to what is being said, inattention is the most common communication problem. Inattention can result from various external and internal factors. External factors include distractions such as interruptions by children, a phone ringing, a loud television, or the buzzing and beeping of text messages, email, and other alerts on our phones. Internal factors that prevent us from paying attention include fatigue, anger, anxiety, thoughts about something else that is pressing (such as being late for an appointment), or general indifference to what the other person has to say (which does happen to the best of us sometimes!).

Inattention to what another person is saying is easy to recognize if you observe the conversation, often through nonverbals alone. People who are not really listening are often looking away from the person speaking, or are making negative facial expressions such as sneers or smirks, or are even just gazing off into the distance with no affect at all. Inattention is also obvious from the verbal content of conversations. Conversations marked by inattention typically involve long lags before a response is offered, a response that is off topic or misses the point, or frequent interruptions that are at best questions or at worst criticisms. It is hard to feel that someone who repeatedly interrupts you is listening to you!

SOLUTION: BE AN EFFECTIVE LISTENER

Being a truly good listener is hard, but it is something that you can work on, practice with your co-parenting partner, and model for your partner and, in turn, for your child. It can require a lot of effort and practice! However, the payoff for becoming a good (or at least better!) listener makes it well worth the effort. Most people can accept differing opinions and disagreements as long as they believe that their perspective has been heard and their point of view understood. Since effective listening is considered to be the most important communication skill, we are devoting more attention to listening than to some of the other communication skills. To be an effective listener, you should develop a listening style that incorporates the following good practices.

Eliminate Distractions. When you make the effort to do this, you show the person who is talking to you that you are interested in what the person is saying. So, for example, turn off the show that you are watching or listening to (or at least turn down the volume), put down the newspaper/magazine/book, and put your phone face down on the table. If you cannot eliminate distractions immediately, indicate that you really want to hear what your partner has to say. Suggest another time (such as when the children are outside playing) when you will be able to discuss the issue without interruption.

Listen to Understand (Not Necessarily Agree). When people are discussing an issue, they often approach it with the goal of agreeing (or disagreeing). But what if that isn't the goal—or at least not the initial goal. Rather, what if the initial goal is simply to try to understand the other person's point of view (and for the other person to understand yours). What is your co-parent telling you? What thoughts are they conveying? What feelings are they conveying?

Reflect and Summarize What You Hear. How can you let your co-parent know that you have really listened and tried to understand? A useful way to do this is through reflection and summarization. *Reflection* refers to making comments during the course of a conversation that indicate you are really paying attention to what is being said. Let's circle back to two-year-old Ethan (introduced in Chapter 1) whose parents, Avery and Reese, are talking:

> **AVERY:** Ethan's daycare called me at work today. They said that Ethan cries and cries after drop off. They can eventually calm Ethan down by lunchtime, but then becomes really picky and just repeats "ice cream."

When they say no, Ethan gets very upset and they say inconsolable. I am going to lose it if they tell us Ethan can't go to daycare anymore—this is the second one we have tried!

REESE: You are really worried about Ethan's behavior and what will happen after your call with them.

Notably, it would be easy for Reese to jump in by dismissing Avery's worries (e.g., "Oh, it can't be that bad") or defending Ethan's behavior (e.g., "C'mon Ethan is a good kid!"), which likely misses the crux of Avery's concerns. Instead, Reese simply listened and tried to reflect what Avery was saying.

Another type of response that indicates attention, *summarizing*, involves stating *in a nonjudgmental way* the overall point the other person is making. It is particularly useful when discussing complex issues or after a lengthy discussion. Let's continue with the example above where Avery responds and then Reese summarizes:

AVERY: Yes! What will happen if Ethan gets kicked out. I mean we both have to work, and I don't have the time or energy to find another place—and that presumes another place would offer a spot, given Ethan's history at this point!

REESE: So it sounds like the biggest issue that we know about is the crying and eating, but we don't what they have tried or how willing they are to talk about options.

In this example, Reese did a nice job summarizing the highlights of what Avery is saying by just focusing on what they know and don't know.

Clarify to Reach Full Understanding. When you clarify, or ask pertinent questions about what another person is saying, you increase your understanding of their perspective, as well as indicate that you are listening. In clarifying, you express interest in trying to fully understand what the other person is saying. Although most of us ask questions for clarification in our jobs and other activities, we are much less likely to do so in our personal relationships, especially when conversations involve stressful family issues. However, the discussion of stressful family issues is perhaps the most important time to ask clarifying questions. So let's take the same example above and see how Reese clarifies in the next step of the conversation:

> **AVERY:** Right, just the crying and eating—although the message made it sound like a big deal!
>
> **REESE:** Okay, so it sounds like they are concerned enough to call, but we don't yet know if they are frustrated enough that they are thinking about asking us to find a new daycare for Ethan.

Again, Reese did a nice job conveying attention by pointing out the issue that needs to be clarified.

Use Receptive Body Language. Your body language can tell a great deal about how interested you are in what another person is saying. You clearly communicate your lack of interest in what is being said when you do not look at the person who is talking. When you look away, continue to read the newspaper, look at your phone, or watch television when your co-parent is talking to you, you send a strong message: What you are hearing is not important.

When you express disinterest and disrespect in such ways, the conversation more than likely turns to conflict or simply ends. Some ways of expressing interest through body language include maintaining eye contact, facing your partner, leaning into the conversation, nodding occasionally to demonstrate that you are following, and avoiding negative facial expressions (or other negative gestures). The nonverbal message you want to convey is "I respect you enough to listen and try to understand your perspective."

PROBLEM #2: MONOPOLIZING THE CONVERSATION

It is hard to carry on a real conversation when one person monopolizes it. We have all tried to have conversations in which the other person would not let us get a word in edgewise. A dominant talker may be fine in certain social conversations, but this behavior presents a problem when two people are discussing an issue of importance to both of them. If you monopolize conversations and are only interested in gaining support for your own views and opinions, your co-parent will probably begin to feel resentful, and their frustration will build. At this point, your co-parent is likely to become angry, and communication probably will break down.

It is important to note that a parent who consistently monopolizes conversations is modeling for their child exactly what we want the child to avoid doing. (Review Chapter 2 for a discussion of the importance of modeling in parenting.) Instead, we as parents want to provide our child with an example of balanced communication, with as much emphasis (if not more) on listening as talking. This is best taught by parental modeling. As a reminder, children learn best by what we do, not what we tell them to do.

SOLUTION: REQUEST FEEDBACK AND TAKE TURNS TALKING

Individuals who monopolize conversations tend to be more extroverted and talkative. If you are a "talker" and monopolize conversations, you may need to take steps to involve others more. This is especially true when you are talking to someone who tends to be quiet and introverted and who may be reluctant to interrupt you in an effort to express their views and opinions.

When you are discussing an issue with your co-parent, make a point to ask for their opinions and views. In doing so, avoid questions that encourage simple yes-or-no answers. For example, saying, "You agree with me, don't you?" encourages the other person to simply say yes. These types of questions are called "closed-ended questions," as they often close the line of communication. Instead, try to ask questions that promote dialogue. Questions that promote conversations begin with the words "how," "when," "what," or "why." Such questions are commonly referred to as "open-ended questions." These questions encourage the other person to express their views or opinions and open up the line of communication. For example, "What happened at work today?" will promote more conversation than the yes-or-no response you are likely to receive from a closed-ended question, such as, "Did you have a good day at work?" Again, when our children see us use this type of open communication style, they are more likely to use it themselves.

PROBLEM #3: SILENCE

On the opposite extreme from people who monopolize conversations are those who remain silent. Many of these people try to avoid conflict or disapproval by keeping thoughts and feelings to themselves during discussion. Not speaking does avoid conflict and disapproval in the short run. However, if you let feelings bottle up inside you, you are likely to reach a point at which you explode in anger. This certainly does not improve communication!

SOLUTION: SPEAK UP

You can avoid angry outbursts from bottled-up feelings by expressing your feelings and opinions as they arise during conversations. This is difficult for many people. If you are someone for whom speaking up does not come naturally, you will have to plan how to speak up before you actually can do it. Here is a plan for learning how to speak up in conversations:

- Think about the worst thing that can happen if you speak your opinion. It rarely is horrible.
- Think about the good things that can happen if you express your opinion. These include modeling effective communication and preventing bottled-up feelings that we can end up (unfortunately) expressing with our children.
- Plan to express your opinion in a conversation with one particular person, ideally someone who is likely to be supportive.
- Do it and evaluate the consequences, which will likely not be as bad as you think.

PROBLEM #4: BEING JUDGMENTAL

Many of us have very strong opinions about one (or more!) issues. If you are one of these people (a human!), your co-parent may be reluctant to express differing views. Your co-parent may believe you are not open to considering other views and will judge them negatively. In such situations, your co-parent may be more likely to withdraw from the conversation. As a result, resentment can build over time. This does not help the relationship or the development of effective communication between the two of you.

SOLUTION: EXPRESS OPENNESS TO LISTEN TO OTHER VIEWS

Although you may have strong opinions regarding certain issues, demonstrate a willingness to hear other opinions. This does not mean that you are going to change your opinions or agree, just that you are willing to listen and to try to understand what makes your co-parent see something differently. So here again you can use the skills above like reflecting, summarizing, and clarifying, all the while reminding yourself that your goal may not be to agree, but instead to understand. And not surprisingly, once you begin to better understand where your co-parent is coming from (and they you!), you may be able to find some more middle ground or points of commonality than you realized initially.

PROBLEM #5: DWELLING ON PAST PROBLEMS DURING CONFLICTS

When we are discussing a conflict, some of us tend to bring up past conflicts. For example, you might catch yourself saying, "It's just like when you . . ." When you do this repeatedly, it can make your co-parent feel hopeless or like there is no opportunity to change or recognition for change. This can lead to negative feelings and to a breakdown in communication.

SOLUTION: STICK TO THE PRESENT ISSUE

When discussing problems, try to focus on the problem at hand. Avoid bringing up past problems that are not directly related to the present. For a relationship to flourish, the people involved must be willing to focus forward and to forgive, if necessary. We all make mistakes. The hope is we can learn from them without having to be repeatedly reminded about them. This is a valuable lesson to teach our children. Mistakes are opportunities to learn, and we, as parents, will teach our children that this lesson is true by our own example—as we focus on the present.

PROBLEM #6: FOCUSING ON WHO IS TO BLAME

In our society, we often want to focus on who is to blame for a problem. This concern with assigning blame occurs at the national, local, and family levels. However, whether the problem is the federal budget deficit or a child's behavior, most major problems are the result of several factors and the interaction of those factors, not just one—if only it were that simple! Trying to identify or focus on who is to blame is rarely productive. Finger-pointing usually leads to hurt feelings, not solutions to a problem.

SOLUTION: FOCUS ON DEVELOPING SOLUTIONS TO PROBLEMS

Rather than assessing blame for a problem, it is much more effective to focus on potential solutions for the problem. For instance, if your child has been heard using a curse word at school repeatedly, it will be much more productive for you and your co-parent to focus on developing a united approach for dealing with the problem rather than blaming each other for the times each of you said the same word perhaps within earshot of your child. In such cases, it is certainly acceptable to discuss factors that may be playing a role, such as overhearing others using curse words, as long as the focus is on identifying solutions, such as not modeling the use of curse words as well as using the skills you learned in our five-week program to decrease the likelihood that curse words occur (e.g., Attending and Rewarding for kind words, "Effortful" Ignoring or Time-Out for curse words), rather than finger-pointing.

PROBLEM #7: CROSS-COMPLAINING

When someone complains about something you have done, a common reaction is to respond by complaining about something that person has done. For example, if you complain about your co-parent's lack of help with the housework, your co-parent may complain about your lack of affection. The philosophy behind such cross-complaining is that the best defense is a good offense. That is, the way to protect myself when verbally attacked is to counterattack. Unfortunately, instead of solving a problem, cross-complaining often escalates into an argument and deeper and deeper dissatisfaction.

SOLUTION: WORK ON THE CURRENT ISSUE

It is hard to accept another person's complaint about you or your behavior without getting at least somewhat upset. It is okay to notice your own feelings—they may be quite valid, but the key can be how you navigate those feelings. Instead of responding based on your initial emotional reaction alone, try to take a deep breath, give yourself a moment to pause, and then try to focus on the issue at hand. Start by reflecting, summarizing, and clarifying as we discussed in the section above to make sure you understand the behavior that is upsetting to your co-parent and why it is upsetting. If you disagree with what your co-parent is saying, discuss the issue from a problem-solving perspective and try to understand from your partner's point of view. During such disagreements, it may be less important to know who is "right," but rather to truly understand where the other person is coming from. Often once we understand our co-parent's point of view (even if we do not necessarily agree or see things the same way), we are more likely to be motivated to have productive discussions that lead to growth and positive change in relationships.

PROBLEM #8: MIND READING

At times, many of us assume we know what another person is thinking. Assumptions are especially likely among people who know each other well. If you start assuming you know what your partner is thinking, you are heading down a dangerous path. If you have not asked, you will never know for sure. When you say, "I know what you're thinking," or "I know you think . . . ," it puts your co-parent on the defensive. Over time, a lot of resentment can develop if you are repeatedly speaking your co-parent's mind.

SOLUTION: SPEAK ONLY FOR YOURSELF

During conversations, especially those that involve some level of conflict, speak only for yourself. Let your partner express their own opinions. You also may want to encourage your partner to express opinions by simply asking. Try to avoid interrupting when your co-parent begins to speak. Do not assume you know what your co-parent is thinking and is about to say!

PROBLEM #9: DISRESPECT AND PUT-DOWNS

Unfortunately, people tend to show less respect for loved ones than for casual acquaintances. Most of us are generally polite and respectful toward people we do not know very well. However, knowing someone well sometimes makes you feel as if you have permission to be less than respectful—especially when you are frustrated, hungry, and tired like so many parents are in just a typical day! This disrespect often includes using put-downs such as "You're lazy," "You're stupid," or even "You're worthless." These are hurtful words that chip away at a relationship.

SOLUTION: BE POLITE AND USE I-MESSAGES

If you treat the people you love with respect, you will greatly reduce the amount of conflict in your relationships. Make every effort to be as polite to those you love as you are to others. Try to express yourself rather than just vent your feelings. When you find yourself about to say something that could be a put-down to your partner, rethink the words you are about to use and present the message in a less threatening way. How can you do this?

It is more effective to describe how you feel about a problem than to hurl accusations. Describing how you feel is often referred to as the use of *I-messages*—that is, statements about yourself that begin with the word "I." These types of messages communicate your feelings or needs. *You-messages*, on the other hand, are about the person you are talking to—they begin with the word "you." Such statements often direct blame or criticism at the other person. Let's look at an example of these two types of messages:

> **YOU-MESSAGE:** "You are such a slob. You just throw your stuff all over the place, and you never help clean up."

> **I-MESSAGE:** "I get so frustrated about the house being such a mess. I feel like I constantly need to clean up, but I just don't have the time to do it myself. I really need some help."

Think about how much more willing you would be to help clean up after hearing the I-message than the you-message. Although I-messages cannot solve all communication problems, they can minimize conflict and encourage healthier patterns of communication.

PROBLEM #10: MIXED MESSAGES

Imagine your co-parent tells you they are interested in what you have to say but does not look at you when you are talking. Your co-parent's behavior is inconsistent with the words being spoken. When verbal and nonverbal messages conflict in this way, what message do you choose to receive? Mixed messages can be hard, if not impossible, to interpret.

SOLUTION: USE CONSISTENT VERBAL AND NONVERBAL MESSAGES

To be understood as well as possible, try to make sure your verbal and nonverbal messages are in sync. For example, if you are saying something positive, your nonverbal language also needs to be positive. Positive nonverbal language includes facial expressions (such as smiling and looking empathetic), body language (such as touching or leaning in toward the person), and tone of voice (for example, warm, joyful, caring, or happy).

PUTTING SOLUTIONS INTO ACTION

As we mentioned at the beginning of this chapter, changing your patterns of communication is often very difficult. To give you a handy reference, Table 18-1 summarizes the 10 communication problems and solutions we have discussed. Review them and decide which areas are problems for you. Also, get feedback from others. One way to do this is to ask your co-parent or another family member or friend to indicate which of the solutions in this chapter are strengths they have observed in you. You then may assume that the other areas are the ones on which you should focus.

After identifying specific problems and potential solutions using the problem-solving approach you learned in Chapter 16, you may need to establish a structured approach to learn how to use the solutions. This approach might include practicing with audio or video recording of the problem, role-playing with someone, or using planned discussions. Planned discussions involve selecting a time and place free from distraction where you can discuss specific issues with your co-parent or close friend in order to practice the communication skills you are trying to master. For example, when discussing how to implement one of the skills in our five-week program, select a time and place where your strong-willed child will not interrupt you (e.g., after bedtime, during daycare or school).

TABLE 18-1   Review of Communication Challenges and Solutions

PROBLEM	SOLUTION
Inattention	Give your full attention.
Monopolizing the conversation	Ask questions and take turns talking.
Silence	Speak up.
Being judgmental	Express openness to listen to other views.
Dwelling on past problems during conflicts	Stick to the present issue during conflicts.
Focusing on who is to blame	Focus on developing solutions to problems.
Cross-complaining	Work on one problem at a time.
Mind reading	Speak only for yourself.
Disrespect and put-downs	Be respectful and use I-messages.
Mixed messages	Use consistent verbal and nonverbal messages.

SUMMARY

In this chapter we present some negative communication styles and some solutions to these negative ways of interacting. Use these as your "Time to Reflect." Remember, you may have few of the negative communication styles with a friend but more of them with another adult living in your household or with your strong-willed child. Carefully assess with whom you primarily use a negative style and then begin working on changing one or two (not all at once!) of these styles of communicating.

For some suggestions of communication builders to incorporate in your planned discussions, see the box "Does Your Communication Style Need Improvement?" Try to apply these tips to all your conversations! These apply not only to your adult relationships but also to your conversations with your strong-willed child.

DOES YOUR COMMUNICATION STYLE NEED IMPROVEMENT?

Nobody is perfect, and that axiom applies to communication as well as to the other things we do. But there are some communication styles that can really turn people off. Pay attention to the way you talk to others this week. How often do you hear yourself using some of these negative communication styles?

- Nagging
- Lecturing
- Interrupting
- Criticizing
- Sarcasm
- Threatening

If you use some of these negative practices, work on improving your communication style. Focus on replacing the negatives with some of these communication builders:

- Be clear and specific in what you say.
- Use I-messages.
- Ask for feedback about what you are saying.
- Focus on positives.

- Ask questions that promote detailed responses:
  - "I'd really like to hear about . . ."
  - "Can you tell me more?"
  - "What do you think about . . . ?"
  - "Can you explain that to me?"

Being an effective communicator is difficult, but if you learn the skills presented in this chapter, you can improve your communication style. These skills will directly improve the behavior of your strong-willed child because you will communicate more effectively with your child. In addition, they will indirectly improve your child's behavior in two important ways: (1) You are becoming more effective in discussing concerns you have about your child or other issues, and (2) you are modeling good problem-solving behavior for your child. Providing a positive communication model is a gift to our children that can last a lifetime.

ADDITIONAL GUIDANCE FOR PARENTS AND PROFESSIONALS

As we said at the start of this book, parenting is both rewarding and challenging. The challenges can feel even bigger if you are a parent of a child who is strong-willed, given all the possible issues we talk about in this book. For some parents, this book may be all that you need to understand your child's behavior and, in turn, to respond to it differently with your new skills. Other parents may realize that what they learned in this book can only be a first step and they may need other resources. For those parents we suggest consulting the list of websites, organizations, and books that we provide below. Still other parents may decide that they need hands-on assistance (i.e., a therapist) from someone who specializes in children and parenting, and we include a section to guide you in identifying those in your area who can help in this way. Because many of those professionals look for self-help resources for the parents with whom they work, they also may find some of the resources noted below useful. In addition, professionals may be interested in the journal articles and chapters that support our parenting program. As a consequence, we provide some of these. Of course, there are many resources for parents and professionals. We cannot and do not list them all. Rather, we focus on some of those that we have used and suggested for parents as well as in consultation with other professionals.

WEBSITES

- **Center for Effective Parenting, parenting-ed.org.** This noncommercial website offers information on a variety of parenting topics. Go to the "For Parents" tab, which offers a variety of resources, including handouts, classes, and links related to the behavior problems of young children and the development of these children more broadly. The handouts may be especially helpful, as they address almost any problem young children may have.
- **Healthy Children, healthychildren.org.** This website is sponsored by the American Academy of Pediatrics for parents. It provides information organized by age of child, including topics such as child development, health, safety, and family issues.
- **Your Child: Parenting Guides and Resources, mottchildren.org/your-child.** This Mott Children's Hospital and University of Michigan Health System

website offers information on a wide variety of topics related to child behavioral, mental, and physical health.

- **National Center for Fathering, fathers.com.** This website offers a variety of information, research, and training opportunities that aim to increase engaged fathering. A Fathering Library is offered that provides information on fathering and parenting in general.

WEBSITES OF PROFESSIONAL ORGANIZATIONS

The following national organization websites contain information that may be of interest to parents. Most of them have large sections devoted to child, parent, and family issues.

- American Academy of Child and Adolescent Psychiatry (AACAP), aacap.org.
- American Academy of Pediatrics (AAP), aap.org.
- American Psychological Association (APA), apa.org.
- Association for Behavioral and Cognitive Therapies (ABCT), abct.org.
- Centers for Disease Control and Prevention (CDC), cdc.gov/parents/essentials/index.html.
- Society of Clinical Child and Adolescent Psychology (APA Division 53), sccap53.org/.

BOOKS

The following books offer additional information for parents and professionals who work with parents on selected topics included in or related to *Parenting the Strong-Willed Child*:

- Barkley, R. (2020). *Taking Charge of ADHD: The Complete, Authoritative Guide for Parents* (4th ed.). New York: Guilford Press.

- Bertin, M. (2015). *Mindful Parenting for ADHD.* Oakland, CA: New Harbinger.
- Chronis-Tuscano, A., O'Brien, K., and Danko, C. M. (2021). *Supporting Caregivers of Children with ADHD: An Integrated Parenting Program: Therapist Guide.* New York: NY. Oxford University Press.
- Dadds, M. and Hawes, D. (2006). *Integrated Family Intervention for Child Conduct Problems: A Behaviour-Attachment-Systems Intervention for Parents.* Bowen Hills, Queensland: Australian Academic Press.
- Emery, R. E. (2016). *Two Homes, One Childhood: A Parenting Plan to Last a Lifetime.* New York: Penguin Books.
- Gottman, J. and Schwartzman Gottman, J. (2022). *The Love Prescription: 7 Days to More Intimacy, Connection, and Joy.* New York: Penguin Books.
- Lebowitz, E. (2021). *Breaking Free of Child Anxiety and OCD: A Scientifically Proven Program for Parents.* New York: Oxford University Press.
- Long, N. and Forehand, R. (2002). *Making Divorce Easier on Your Child: 50 Effective Ways to Help Children Adjust.* New York: McGraw-Hill.
- Mindell, J. A. (2005). *Sleeping Through the Night: How Infants, Toddlers, and Their Parents Can Get a Good Night's Sleep* (rev. ed.). New York: HarperCollins.
- Ollendick, T. H., White, S. W., and White, B. A. (eds) (2018). *The Oxford Handbook of Clinical Child and Adolescent Psychology*, Oxford Library of Psychology. New York: Oxford University Press.
- Weisz, J. R. and Bearman, S. K. (2020). *Principle-Guided Psychotherapy for Children and Adolescents:*

The FIRST Program for Behavioral and Emotional Problems. New York, NY: Guilford Press.

OTHER RESOURCES

This book focuses very specifically on understanding and shaping strong-willed behavior in your child, as well as primarily family-level factors associated with strong-willed behavior and parenting. That said, we realize there are a lot of topics that we did not cover that may be of interest to parents of young children, including strong-willed children. Suggestions for such topics are mentioned here, but parents should also consult trusted members of their support systems, which may include other parents, teachers, or your child's pediatrician:

- Anxiety and depression, https://www.cdc.gov/childrensmentalhealth/depression.html.
- Anti-racism, https://www.apa.org/monitor/2021/06/anti-racist-children.
- Bullying, https://www.stopbullying.gov.
- Feelings, https://www.verywellfamily.com/how-to-teach-kids-about-feelings-1095012.
- Gender identity development, https://www.healthychildren.org/English/ages-stages/gradeschool/Pages/Gender-Identity-and-Gender-Confusion-In-Children.aspx.
- LGBTQ youth, https://www.hopkinsmedicine.org/health/wellness-and-prevention/tips-for-parents-of-lgbtq-youth.
- Talking to kids about the news, https://kidshealth.org/en/parents/news.html.
- Racial socialization, https://www.apa.org/pi/families/resources/newsletter/2015/08/racial-socialization.

- School and community violence and media, https://www.nasponline.org/resources-and-publications/resources-and-podcasts/school-safety-and-crisis/school-violence-resources/talking-to-children-about-violence-tips-for-parents-and-teachers.
- Technology and social media effect on children and adolescents, https://technosapiens.substack.com/
- Transgender kids and gender dysphoria, https://childmind.org/article/transgender-teens-gender-dysphoria/.

SEEKING PROFESSIONAL HELP

While the information in this book and the resources we provide here may be helpful, some parents may be thinking they cannot do it alone. There is absolutely no shame in that realization, and in this section, we provide some information to help you begin to identify the support that you need.

- **Who provides assistance to parents of strong-willed children?** A variety of professionals provide assistance to parents of strong-willed children, including those at some daycares, pediatricians' offices, and schools. As a consequence, we recommend starting by asking for guidance and direction from those with whom you have a relationship and can feel comfortable acknowledging the challenges your family is experiencing. Others who provide services to families of strong-willed children include psychologists, counselors, and social workers.
- **What type of help am I looking for?** Consistent with the five-week program we share in this book, we recommend professionals who work with parents to improve the behavior of their young children.

Professionals who provide these sorts of services may refer to it as "behavioral parent training," "behavioral parenting intervention," or "parent management training" among other terms. The key is that, as we do in this book, they work directly with the parent to change the way they respond to the child's okay and not-okay behavior.

- **Are there parenting programs you recommend?**
This book is an extension of one such program called Helping the Noncompliant Child (HNC). HNC is just one of a group of programs that have a common rationale and teach skills that are very similar to the types of things you learned in this book. The main thing is that in these types of programs parents have a professional providing hands-on assistance as they learn the skills and practice them with their child. Other programs you can look for or ask professionals if they provide include Parent Child Interaction Therapy (PCIT), Incredible Years (IY), Defiant Child (DC), the Community Parent Education Program (COPE), and the Positive Parenting Program (Triple P). These programs and how they are practiced may differ in whether they are offered in a group or with individual families, but the skills that you learn are very similar across programs and to the skills you learned in this book.

- **Does Medicaid or my insurance pay for these types of parenting programs?** This is a good question, and we highly recommend talking with your insurance company before starting any services. You should also ask any providers of these parenting programs whether they do or don't take insurance. If the provider does take your insurance, the provider can typically bill your insurance if your child's not-okay behavior is occurring in the clinical range. This essentially means that the not-okay behavior is occurring at a level of severity or a frequency that is outside the typical limits for a child their age and that the behavior is causing problems for them at home or school or elsewhere.

One thing to keep in mind is that there have been fairly significant changes in how a variety of professionals, including psychologists, can practice since COVID. For example, psychologists in many, but not all, states can apply and be approved to practice remotely across state lines. One benefit of this is that it allows specialists in one state to provide services to families in another state. Therefore, one option is to look for providers who practice behavioral parent training and ask if they provide remote services. Resources for such services include the Association for Behavioral and Cognitive Therapies (ABCT) "Find a CBT Therapist Directory" on the ABCT website (abct.org).

Another potentially excellent resource for parenting programs is universities if you happen to live near one (or they are providing remote services). Many major universities have social work or clinical psychology training programs, for example, and may see families of young children for behavioral difficulties. Typically, in these settings the parenting programs are delivered by graduate students working on their master's or doctoral degrees, and they are supervised by a licensed professional. Often these clinics provide reduced fees and/or a sliding fee scale for services. As a consequence, they can be a great option in general and especially so for families who may not have health insurance coverage or their behavioral health coverage is less comprehensive.

REFERENCES FOR PROFESSIONALS

The following references may be of interest to professionals who would like additional information on our program. These references include information on the clinical intervention (McMahon and Forehand's *Helping the Noncompliant Child*) upon which this five-week parenting program is based as well as evaluation studies of our clinical program, our parenting class program, and the *Parenting the Strong-Willed Child* book itself:

- Abikoff, H. B., Thompson, M., Laver-Bradbury, C., Long, N., Forehand, R. L., Miller Brotman, L., Klein, R. G., Reiss, P., Huo, L., and Sonuga-Barke, E. (2015). "Parent training for preschool ADHD: A randomized controlled trial of specialized and generic programs." *Journal of Child Psychology and Psychiatry, 56*(6), 618–631.

  This study enrolled families of three- to four-year-old children with ADHD. Findings revealed that Helping the Noncompliant Child (HNC), the intervention upon which this book is based, improved child behavior and parenting outcomes as much as (or more than) the ADHD-specific program.

- Conners, N. A., Edwards, M. C., and Grant, A. S. (2007). "An evaluation of a parenting class curriculum for parents of young children: *Parenting the Strong-Willed Child.*" *Journal of Child and Family Studies, 16,* 321–330.

  This study enrolled families of two- to eight-year-old Head Start children in a group-based curriculum based on *Parenting the Strong-Willed Child.* Families saw significant reductions in child problem behavior and a reduction in parenting stress and improvement in parenting behaviors.

- Forehand, R. L., Merchant, M. J., Long, N., and Garai, E. (2010). "An examination of *Parenting the Strong-Willed Child* as bibliotherapy for parents." *Behavior Modification*, *34*, 57–76.

  This study enrolled families of three- to-six-year-olds, and parents either read *Parenting the Strong-Willed Child* (*PSWC*) or an alternative book targeting child behavior. Results indicated both books, but particularly *PSWC*, were associated with reductions in child problem behavior. *PSWC* parents were satisfied with the book and reported it was useful and easy to use.

- Jones, D. J., Forehand, R., Long, N., and McMahon, R. (2022). "Supervising child behavior management." In E. A. Storch, J. A. Abramowitz, and D. McKay (eds.), *Training and Supervision in Specialized Cognitive Behavior Therapy: Methods, Settings, and Populations*. Washington, DC: American Psychological Association.

  This chapter is intended for those already practicing a behavioral parent training program like HNC who are interested in training others. The chapter focuses on key techniques, including ways to teach therapists to teach parents to use their new skills, ideal training cases, and common mistakes.

- Khavjou, O., Turner, P., Forehand, R., Loiselle, R., and Jones, D. J. "Helping the noncompliant child: An updated assessment of program costs and cost-effectiveness." *Children and Youth Services Review*, 114.

  Too often evidence-based treatments developed in resource-intensive settings are too costly for frontline providers. This manuscript examines the cost of delivering a behavioral parent training program like HNC in a clinical setting and suggests it can be a cost-effective approach. Results reveal that HNC has delivery costs of $293 per family, which includes therapist time and resources (e.g., toys).

- McMahon, R. J. and Forehand, R. L. (2003). *Helping the Noncompliant Child: Family-Based Treatment for Oppositional Behavior* (2nd ed.). New York: Guilford.

   HNC is the evidence-based treatment validated for three- to eight-year-old children with high levels of noncompliance upon which the program in the current book is based. HNC is a therapist-delivered, mastery-based program, meaning families move at their own pace as therapists assess parent level of skill use and impact on child behavior.

- McMahon, R. J. and Forehand, R. (2019). "Helping the noncompliant child." In J. Lebow, A. Chambers, and D. Breunlin (eds.), *Encyclopedia of Couple and Family Therapy*. New York: Springer.

   This chapter presents a brief overview of the Helping the Noncompliant Child program on which the current book is based.

- McMahon, R. J., Long, N., and Forehand, R. (2010). "Parent training for the treatment of oppositional behavior in young children: Helping the noncompliant child." In R. Murrihy and T. Ollendick (eds.), *Handbook of Clinical Assessment and Treatment of Conduct Problems in Youth*. New York: Springer.

   This chapter also presents the Helping the Noncompliant Child program and the outcome data.

- Parent, J., Anton, M., Loiselle, R., Highlander, A., Breslend, N., Forehand, R., Hare, M., Youngstrom, J. A., and Jones, D. J. (2022). "A randomized controlled trial of technology-enhanced behavioral parent training: Sustained parent skill use and child outcomes at follow-up." *Journal of Child Psychology and Psychiatry, 63*, 992–1001.

  This study enrolled 98 parents of two- to seven-year-olds and assigned them randomly to an HNC condition or an HNC technology-enhanced condition. Both treatments increased parenting skills and child compliance, but at follow-up the technology-enhanced condition was more effective.

- Sanders, W., Parent, J., and Forehand, R. (2018). "Parenting to reduce child screen time: A feasibility pilot study." *Journal of Developmental & Behavioral Pediatrics, 39* (1), 46–54.

  This study enrolled parents of five- to twelve-year-old children in a one-session intervention targeting parent management of children's screen time building upon skills in *PSWC* or a wait list control. Results suggest changes in the way parents handle children's use of screens and children's screen time.

- Sullivan, A. D. W., Forehand, R., Acosta, J., Parent, J, Comer, J., Loiselle, R., and Jones, D. J. (2021). "COVID-19 and the acceleration of remote BPT delivery now and in the future." *Cognitive and Behavioral Practice, 28*, 618–629.

  Remote delivery options mean that more families now have access to BPT providers, and services may be both more convenient and cost-effective with less time and transportation for families, but these advances also come with challenges. Considerations for current and future remote practice are addressed in this paper.

PSWC CURRICULUM AVAILABLE

A Parenting Class Curriculum based on *Parenting the Strong-Willed Child* is available. The six 2-hour-session class uses this book as a parent manual. Professionals who are interested in obtaining information about this resource should contact Dr. Nicholas Long at longnicholas@uams.edu or Dr. Deborah J. Jones at djjones@email.unc.edu.

INDEX

Page numbers followed by *f* and *t* refer to figures and tables, respectively.

ABOUT THE AUTHORS

Rex Forehand, PhD, is the Heinz and Rowena Ansbacher Endowed Professor of Psychological Science and University Distinguished Professor at the University of Vermont. He is an internationally recognized expert on parenting, especially as it relates to the development and treatment of child problem behavior. Through his teaching, research, and writing, Dr. Forehand, a licensed clinical psychologist, has made significant contributions to the advancement of treatment and self-help programs for parents. He has published over 400 research articles, book chapters, and books on these topics and trained generations of researchers, clinicians, and policy makers focused on the well-being of children and families. For this and other work, Dr. Forehand has won numerous awards, including the Award for Distinguished Career Contributions to Education and Training in Psychology from the American Psychological Association.

Deborah J. Jones, PhD, is the Zachary Smith Distinguished Term Professor and Associate Chair of the Department of Psychology and Neuroscience at the University of North Carolina at Chapel Hill. She conducts research to advance the understanding and treatment of children and families with a particular interest in increasing the reach and impact of effective parenting strategies. Dr. Jones has published over 100 research articles and book chapters and is the coauthor of a forthcoming book focused on the incorporation of digital tools into children's mental health practice. She is a licensed clinical psychologist who devotes substantial time to training and supervising clinical psychology graduate students to work with parents of young children. She also gives workshops for community agencies, professionals, and parents to provide up-to-date training on effective parenting strategies. Dr. Jones has received numerous awards for her research and training.

Nicholas Long, PhD, is a Professor of Pediatrics in the Department of Pediatrics at the University of Arkansas for Medical Sciences and Arkansas Children's Hospital where he also served as the Director of Pediatric Psychology for 35 years. He is an expert in the areas of parenting, parent education, and family influences on child behavior and adjustment with numerous research articles, book chapters, and books on these topics. Dr. Long has served in leadership roles in numerous state and national organizations, and is the founder of the Center for Effective Parenting at Arkansas Children's Hospital, which aims to facilitate the dissemination and implementation of knowledge and resources on parenting. Additionally, he serves as the Director of the Arkansas Home Visiting Network's Training Institute, which provides supplemental training to home visitors who serve families with young children throughout Arkansas.